Networking Using Novell NetWare® (3.12)

Emilio Ramos
Al Schroeder
Ann Beheler

Richland College

Prentice Hall

Englewoods Cliffs, New Jersey   Columbus, Ohio

Library of Congress Cataloging-in-Publication Data

Ramos, Emilio.
   Networking using Novell NetWare (3.12) / Emilio Ramos, Al Schroeder, Ann Beheler.
     p.   cm.
   Includes index.
   ISBN 0-13-236035-7
   1. NetWare (Computer file) 2. Local area networks (Computer networks) I. Schroeder, Al. II. Beheler, Ann. III. Title.
   TK5105.7.R383   1996
   005.7'1369--dc20   95-38018
                                                                CIP

Editor: Charles E. Stewart, Jr.
Production Editor: Rex Davidson
Production Coordinator: Ben Shriver
Production Manager: Pamela D. Bennett
Marketing Manager: Debbie Yarnell

© 1996 by Prentice-Hall, Inc.
A Simon & Schuster Company
Englewood Cliffs, New Jersey 07632

All rights reserved. No part of this book may be reproduced, in any form or by any means, without permission in writing from the publisher.

Printed in the United States of America

10 9 8 7 6 5 4 3 2 1

ISBN: 0-13-236035-7

Prentice-Hall International (UK) Limited, <u>London</u>
Prentice-Hall of Australia Pty. Limited, <u>Sydney</u>
Prentice-Hall Canada, Inc., <u>Toronto</u>
Prentice-Hall Hispanoamericana, S. A., <u>Mexico</u>
Prentice-Hall of India Private Limited, <u>New Delhi</u>
Prentice-Hall of Japan, Inc., <u>Tokyo</u>
Simon & Schuster Asia Pte. Ltd., <u>Singapore</u>
Editora Prentice-Hall do Brasil, Ltda., <u>Rio de Janeiro</u>

Preface

During the past decade, businesses have experienced unprecedented growth in the use of computer workstations by their employees. Although data communications and networking previously had been an integral part of data processing systems, this new growth area has brought these topics to the forefront in both the business and personal-use sectors.

Courses in networking only recently have become part of the core curriculum at most colleges. This change has caused a shift in course structure for computer students. Some colleges have developed a networking course, while others have modified their data communications course to place a greater emphasis on networking. Whatever the approach, colleges and universities are trying to provide a strong introduction to networking for the computer literate student.

This book was written to serve that need. It features Novell's NetWare version 3.12 to illustrate local area network applications, and it provides hands-on tutorials for the student to implement NetWare 3.12.

NetWare 3.12 was chosen as the software to use because NetWare currently has the largest share of the market. Therefore, it is likely that a student not only would want to study it, but would see it again in business use.

Objectives of This Text

1. To provide an overview of NetWare 3.12, explaining what the system is and what it can do.
2. To explain the process for installing NetWare.
3. To teach how a new network manager would configure a LAN using NetWare's SYSCON utility.
4. To specify the means for organizing and managing a network smoothly and securely.
5. To teach NetWare's programs for customizing both the individual workstation on a LAN and the network as a whole.
6. To outline the different means of printing on a LAN.
7. To explain NetWare's utilities for both the file server and the individual workstation.

Organization of the Text

All chapters are in two parts, which provides flexibility in the learning situation. The first half is an introduction to the specific topics listed above. It provides the essential terminology and concepts for each component of NetWare. The second half of each chapter is a detailed, hands-on tutorial. This provides the student with a how-to look at applying the knowledge gained in the opening sections. End of chapter questions and projects further reinforce concepts and terminology.

A degree of flexibility is inherent in the book's organization, which allows use of either the first or the second half of each chapter, or both parts, as need warrants. Students new to NetWare can profit from studying the whole of each chapter. Those who are adept at using earlier versions of NetWare might only need to study the introductory sections on new capacities of 3.12, or work their way through selected tutorials. The entire book provides an introduction to networking, with hands-on use of the most popular LAN product.

The book assumes a level of computer literacy usually attained in college level Introduction to Computer Science courses or an equivalent continuing education course and a prior foundation in the concepts and terminology of communications and networking. For users who may want to enhance this course of study with materials pertaining to the study of communications and networking, we recommend a companion book, our *Concepts of Data Communications*. For those who in the future may seek a text that combines the teaching of both books, see our *Data Communications and Networking Fundamentals Using Novell NetWare® (3.12)*.

Appendices

Appendix A explains some of the workstation utilities included with Novell NetWare 3.12.

Appendix B explains some of the file server and remote management utilities included with Novell NetWare 3.12.

Appendix C contains several lists of vendors for a variety of network products. You should review this material for familiarity, and use it as needed to identify vendors in any area of communications and networking.

Supplements

For the instructor there is a comprehensive instructor's guide that includes

1. Suggestions on how to organize the course, depending on the desired emphasis and focus
2. Answers to all end of chapter questions

3. Solutions to projects
4. Transparency masters of the art in the book and the chapter outlines
5. Hints for the presentation of material in the classroom
6. Test bank questions for examinations

Acknowledgements

We would like to thank the Prentice Hall staff who participated in this project and provided the opportunity to publish this book. Thank you all for your efforts in helping us complete this project.

Contents

Chapter 1. Introduction to Novell NetWare   1

Objectives 1
Key Terms 1
Introduction 2
Overview of NetWare 2
The User Environment 6
    Network Volumes and Network Drives 6
    DOS Directories 6
    Drive Mappings 8
    Paths and Search Drives 8
    Trustee Rights 10
    Batch Files and Login Scripts 11
A Novell Network Example 12
Summary 15
Questions 16
Project 17
        Creating a Novell NetWare Log Book 17

Chapter 2. NetWare Installation   19

Objectives 19
Key Terms 19
Introduction 20
Installing NetWare 22
    Installation Preparation 24
        NetWare Menus 24
        Client Software 26
        Installing NetWare on the File Server 27
        Logging onto an Existing File Server 27
Hands-on NetWare Installation 29
    Installation Preparation 29
        Making Backup Copies with a Dual Disk Drive Computer:
        Two Disk Drives of the Same Type 29
        Making Backup Copies with a Single Disk Drive Computer 30
    Diskette Installation of the File Server 30
    Creating the Workstation Boot Disk using NetWare DOS Requester 42
        Introduction to the NetWare DOS Requester 42
        Installing the NetWare DOS Requester 42
        Testing the New Boot Process 44
Summary 44
Questions 45
Project 45
        Logging into NetWare 45

Chapter 3. The SYSCON Utility and Login Scripts   47

Objectives 47
Key Terms 47
Introduction 48
SYSCON 48
    Introduction 48
    The SYSCON Options 49
        Accounting 49
        Change Current Server 49
        File Server Information 49
        Group Information 50
        Supervisor Options 50
        User Information 51
    The User Information Options 52
        Account Balance 53
        Account Restrictions 53
        Change Password 53
        Full Name 54
        Groups Belonged To 54
        Intruder Lockout Status 54
        Login Scripts 54
        Managed Users and Groups 55
        Managers 55
        Other Information 56
        Security Equivalences 56
        Station Restrictions 56
        Time Restrictions 57
        Trustee Directory and File Assignments 57
        Volume/Disk Restrictions 58
    Login Scripts 58
        Commands 60
                ATTACH 60
                BREAK 61
                COMSPEC 62
                DISPLAY 63
                (DOS) BREAK 63
                (DOS) SET 63
                DOS VERIFY 63
                DRIVE 64
                EXIT 64
                #Program Name with Command Line Options 64
                FIRE PHASERS 65
                IF Statement 65
                INCLUDE 68
                MACHINE 68
                MAP 68
                PAUSE 70

| PCCOMPATIBLE 70
          REMARK 70
          WRITE 70
Hands-on NetWare 72
    Preparing the Network for Operation 72
    Logging In 73
    Starting the SYSCON Utility 74
    Changing a User Password 75
    Testing the Password 76
    Creating a User Account 77
    The User Information Menu 78
    Checking the Account Balance 79
    The Account Restrictions Menu 79
    Creating a Password 81
    Creating a Login Script 81
    Setting the Security Equivalences 82
    Setting Trustee Directory Assignments 83
    Limiting Disk Space 85
    Testing the New Account 86
Summary 86
Questions 86
Projects 87
          Project 1. Using the SYSCON Utility 87
          Project 2. More Login Scripts 88

Chapter 4. Security, Organization, and Management   89

Objectives 89
Key Terms 89
Introduction 90
Levels of Security 90
    Passwords 90
          Password Length 91
          Force Periodic Password Changes 91
          User Password Changes 92
    Trustee Rights 92
    Directory Inherited Rights Mask 94
    File Attributes 95
    Organization 96
          Types of Users 96
          Groups 97
          Group Hierarchy 97
          Managers 98
          Data Organization 98
          Types of Data 98
          Backing up Data 100
    Network Management 102
          Introduction to FCONSOLE 102

Management Options	103
Broadcast Console Message	103
Change Current File Server	104
Connection Information	104
Down File Server	105
Status	106
Version Information	106
Introduction to MONITOR	106
Hands-on NetWare	108
Levels of Security	108
Password	108
Changing the Password and Minimum Password Length	108
Force Periodic Password Changes	110
Trustee Rights	112
Directory Rights	114
File Attributes	117
Effective Rights	118
Groups	122
Network Control	127
Summary	130
Questions	131
Projects	132
Project 1. FCONSOLE and Trustee Rights	132
Project 2. Practicing the Login Script Commands	132

Chapter 5. Workstation Installation and Customization   135

Objectives	135
Key Terms	135
Introduction	136
Customizing NetWare	136
Network Drivers	136
LSL.COM	137
Network Interface Card Driver	137
IPXODI.COM	137
NetWare DOS Requester	137
Customizing the Workstation Software Through NET.CFG, CONFIG.SYS and AUTOEXEC.BAT	138
DOS Directories	140
Remote Reset	141
Remote Reset Setup	142
The Network Card	142
The Boot Disk	142
Using DOSGEN	147
BOOTCONF.SYS	148
Hands-on NetWare	148
Memory Usage	149
Computers with 640K or Less of RAM	149

Computers with 1 Megabyte or More of Memory	150
Using HIMEM.SYS and Loading VLM.EXE with Flags	151
DOS Versions 5 and 6	151
Remote Reset	153
Testing Remote Reset	156
Summary	157
Questions	157
Projects	158
Project 1. Automating User Logins	158
Project 2. Creating a Remote Boot File	158
Project 3. Modifying a NET.CFG File	159

Chapter 6. Network Printing 161

Objectives	161
Key Terms	161
Introduction	161
Printing in a Novell Network	162
File Server Printing	162
Print Server Printing	162
Remote Printing	163
Print Forms	163
Print Devices	164
Print Queues	166
Print Job Configurations	168
Attaching the Printer	172
Printing with PCONSOLE	174
Printing with NPRINT	175
Printing with CAPTURE	175
Hands-on NetWare	176
Configuring the Print Server and Print Queue	176
Running PSERVER	182
Sending Output to the Print Server	183
Configuring the Print Server for Remote Printing	184
Running PSERVER with a Remote Printer	186
Running RPRINTER	187
Sending Output to the Remote Printer	187
Summary	188
Questions	188
Projects	189
Project 1. Basic Network Printing	189
Project 2. Advanced Network Printing	189
Project 3. Setting up a Print Server with One Locally Attached Printer and Two Remote Printers	190

Chapter 7. Customizing NetWare   191

Objectives 191
Key Terms 191
Introduction 191
Customizing NetWare 192
    Batch Files 193
    Novell Menus 193
        A Simple Menu 193
        Submenus 194
        Menu Commands 195
            Organization Commands 196
            Control Commands 197
        Menu Rules 200
        Batch File Menus 201
Hands-on Creating Menus 203
    The Novell Menu System 203
    Batch Files 205
Summary 207
Questions 208
Project 208
        Creating Directories and Menus 208

Chapter 8. Microsoft Windows 3.1 and Networking   211

Objectives 211
Key Terms 211
Introduction 212
Using Application Software in a Network 212
    Benefits 212
        Sharing Software 213
        Sharing Data 213
        Sharing System Resources 213
        Security and Backups 213
        Easy Maintenance and Upgrades 214
    Choosing Servers 214
    Choosing a Directory for Shared Software 215
    Accessing Shared Programs 216
    Granting NetWare Rights 217
        Group Rights 218
        Program File Attributes 218
    Using Application Programs in a Network Environment 219
    Installing Microsoft Windows 220
        Using the Setup /a Option 220
        Using the Setup /n Option 221
        Using the Setup /h Option 221
    Accessing Windows 228
    Guidelines for Using Windows on a Novell Network 229

Hands-on Installing
Microsoft Windows 230
    Installing Microsoft Windows 3.1 230
    Installing Windows on Users' Disks 231
Summary 232
Questions 233
Projects 233
        Project 1. Installing Microsoft Excel on the File Server 233
        Project 2. Installing Microsoft Word for Windows on the File Server 234

Appendix A. Workstation Utilities   235

Appendix B. File Server Utilities and Remote Management   249

Appendix C   259

    Vendors of Gateways and Related Products 259
    Vendors of EBBS and Related Products 259
    Vendors of Routers, Bridges, and Related Products 260
    Vendors of E-Mail Products 260
    Vendors of Fax Gateways and Related Products 261
    Vendors of Network Management Products 261
    Vendors of Network Operating Systems and Related Products 263
    Commercial Information Services 264
    Vendors of Data Switches, PBXs, and Related Products 265
    Vendors of Network Remote Access Software and Related Products 266
    Vendors of TCP/IP Hardware and Related Products 267
    Vendors of Zero Slot LANs, Media Transfer Hardware and Software, and Related Products ..267

Glossary   269

Index   273

Introduction to Novell NetWare

Objectives

After completing this chapter you will

1. Understand the basic hardware components required to install NetWare.
2. Obtain an overview of the software components of NetWare.
3. Understand Novell's workstation software.
4. Understand the concept of volumes and drive mappings.
5. Understand the concept of trustee and trustee's rights.

Key Terms

Client Computer	Drive Mapping
Login Script	NetWare
Network Interface Card	Search Drive
Server Computer	Trustee
Trustee Rights	User Environment
Volume	

Introduction

Little remains constant in the world of networking. Network operating systems, hardware components, and topologies have changed rapidly over the last several years to keep pace with advancing technology and consumer demand. Novell, Inc. has performed better than most at maintaining a saleable product and a share of the market. Novell's original network product, however, did not do well. The system was a file server and network operating system software, with serial cables to connect to client computers running the CP/M operating system. The product line was expanded somewhat, but the company went bankrupt. Novell's reorganization, however, took place at an opportune point in history. The introduction of the IBM PC gave Novell an entirely new market. Novell's operating system was eventually rewritten to allow the IBM PC to be used as both the file server and the client. Novell has introduced many software and hardware products since then. It now controls the largest single share of the local area networking market with Novell NetWare. "NetWare" refers to all of Novell's network operating system products.

Overview of NetWare

This chapter introduces a network operating system known as Novell NetWare. It will introduce concepts that will be more thoroughly discussed in later chapters. Originally designed for computers running the CP/M operating system, Novell quickly adapted NetWare for use on the IBM PC. This move ensured NetWare's success.

NetWare's major components are

1. Software:

    NetWare Operating System on a shared computer called the file server

    The NetWare client software called the NetWare DOS Requester, a set of memory resident programs which run on the PC that is known as the client, node, or workstation

    DOS 3.3 or later for both the server and the workstation

    Driver software for the LAN card in the server and the LAN card in each workstation

2. Hardware:

    386 or faster PC with at least 6 MB RAM and at least 20 MB hard drive for the file server

> 286 or faster PC for the workstation (hard drive recommended but not required)
>
> Network interface card in all nodes and in the file server which, together with the cable connecting the NICs, provides the network hardware interface

The NetWare Operating System, which is installed on the file server, allows the file server to act as a "traffic cop" which manages access by clients to the files stored on the file server's hard disk.

The NIC physically connects the client (user's) computer to a file server where data can be shared by all the users on the network.

The NetWare client software called the NetWare DOS Requester allows the user to treat the file server as if it were a disk drive attached to his client computer. Ordinary DOS commands can be used on the file server, and several additional functions are available. The user can create drive mappings and search drives to make more effective use of the data and programs on the file server. The data and programs can be protected by assigning the proper trustee rights to the other users on the network.

Novell NetWare was originally designed around hardware using a star topology to communicate with a single file server. The file server simply allowed client computers to store and share files. This structure has influenced all of Novell's products to date. NetWare has become largely hardware independent, allowing many topologies and file servers to be used simultaneously, but communication on the network is still handled almost entirely through a primary file server. Two client computers may be connected directly to each other by a network cable, but for a file to be transferred from one to the other, that file must first be sent to the file server, then to the target client computer. Of course, the network provides many other functions, but they are generally centered around the idea of a client computer connected to a file server.

By far, the most common client on a Novell network is an IBM PC or PC-compatible computer running DOS, although Macintosh and OS/2 clients are also now used. DOS is the software that handles all of the low-level functions of the computer such as reading and writing to the disk drives, loading and executing application programs, and handling input from the keyboard. When running an application program such as a word processor, DOS allocates memory, reads the program from the disk drive and then allows the program to begin. The application program can then use the resources of the computer through what are known as DOS function calls. For instance, there are many different types of printers and dozens of companies manufacturing them. To the application program, this is irrelevant. It will simply make a DOS function call to write data to the printer, and DOS will handle the output to the device.

Since even DOS can't "know" the details of every peripheral device one might attach to a computer, including a network, programs known as drivers are often used to help DOS provide a common environment for application programs to work in. Attaching a Novell network to a computer is a good example of this and essentially involves two components: the network interface card or NIC, and the network driver programs. Novell offers a variety of programs that serve as the drivers depending on the configuration of the workstation.

The NIC is the hardware that is physically connected to the network, much like a telephone is the piece of hardware that is physically connected to the telephone network. It generates the proper electrical signal to communicate on the particular type of network being used. It may use pulses of light or radio waves to send signals across the network.

The network drivers used on a particular workstation must consist of an appropriate combination of the programs needed to perform three functions: provide a hardware dependent driver for the network card, provide the appropriate communications protocol to be used on the network, and provide an interface for the user.

Novell's long-used system of providing the hardware dependent driver and the communications protocol was to use a program called IPX.COM. It was generated at the time NetWare was installed because it is actually built out of two components. One component is the hardware dependent NIC driver and the other is the IPX protocol driver. (IPX stands for Internetwork Packet eXchange.) The resulting IPX.COM program was then unique to the type of NIC it will run on.

More recently, Novell has changed the focus of its efforts to a standard called Open Data-Link Interface. The two functions of the NIC driver and IPX protocol driver have been spread out over three programs.

The first program is called LSL.COM (LSL stands for Link Support Layer). It allows multiple communications protocols, which are loaded later, to be run on the same NIC.

The second program is strictly an ODI-compliant NIC driver program called the Multiple Link Interface Driver (MLID) and is given a name that indicates which brand of NIC it supports. IBM PC Network II cards, for instance, use a program called PCN2L.COM. A network card called the SMC EtherCard PLUS Elite10T/A uses a program called SMCPLUS.COM. These driver programs are packaged with the NIC, and Novell also provides them on their distribution diskettes for major brands of network interface cards.

The third program is the communications protocol driver, IPXODI.COM. As its name indicates, it is an Internetwork Packet Exchange protocol driver that conforms to the Open Data-Link Interface standard and is specific to Novell.

Other communications protocols such as TCPIP may also be loaded so that a given workstation can communicate simultaneously with a TCPIP network and with a Novell IPX network.

Prior to the introduction of NetWare 3.12 and NetWare 4, the third function, that of a user interface, was provided by one of three different versions of essentially the same program: NETX.COM, XMSNETX.EXE or EMSNETX.EXE. The three different versions of this program were needed to take advantage of different memory configurations of the workstation. NETX.COM uses conventional memory, XMSNETX.EXE uses extended memory and EMSNETX.EXE uses expanded memory. The letter "X" appears before the extension (.EXE or .COM) in each of these names to indicate that they can be used with any DOS version. Prior to the release of DOS version 5.0, Novell supplied the rather cumbersome collection of NET2, NET3, NET4, XMSNET2, XMSNET3, XMSNET4, EMSNET2, EMSNET3, and EMSNET4 for use with DOS 2.x, DOS 3.x, and DOS 4.x respectively. Using the ODI approach for IPX, one must merely include the following in one's AUTOEXEC.BAT:

    LSL

    NIC driver such as PCN2L

    IPXODI

    NETX (or XMSNETX or EMSNETX)

Although the NETX version of workstation software will still allow the user to connect to a NetWare 3.12 network, NetWare 3.12 has provided a new version of workstation software called the NetWare DOS Requester. The NetWare DOS Requester version of workstation software is ODI-compliant and still requires the use of LSL, the NIC driver, and IPXODI. However, NETX has been replaced with the workstation VLM (Virtual Loadable Module) manager which coexists with DOS and uses DOS tables. VLMs will be addressed further in Chapters 9 and 12.

Together, the network drivers make up the NetWare client software which provides a complete interface between DOS and NetWare. The NetWare client software provides an interface that allows users to interact with the computer in a transparent or natural manner. This shields users from the complex low-level operations of the computer and the network. Therefore, the NetWare client software protects the user from having to know how to interact directly with the network.

The User Environment

Network Volumes and Network Drives

The highest level in the NetWare directory structure is the NetWare volume. All file servers must have a volume called SYS:, and a file server may have a total of up to 64 volumes. A single NetWare file server can support up to 32 physical disk drives and 32 TB (Terabytes, or trillion bytes) of physical hard disk space. Volumes may span physical disk drives, or they may divide a physical disk drive. In either case, volumes are specified during installation. Volumes are divided into directories.

The NetWare client software allows DOS and the user to treat the file server as a disk drive attached to the client computer. DOS assigns a drive letter to each of the disk drives physically attached to the computer. A and B designate floppy disk drives while C, D, and E usually represent hard disk drives local to the user. On a typical system, with two floppy disk drives and a hard disk drive, DOS would assign A, B, and C to the those disk drives. When the NetWare client software programs are loaded, another drive letter is made available to the user. Typically, F is used to designate the first network drive and is often used to designate the SYS: volume. In this textbook, all references to the F: drive assume that F designates the entire SYS: volume.

Ordinary DOS commands like DIR (which displays a list of the files on the disk) and CHDIR (which moves access to a different area of the disk) can be used on the network drive F. In addition, application programs can make ordinary DOS function calls to carry out their functions on the network drive as if it were a hard disk attached to the computer. The network drive is the hard disk on the file server, the same hard disk accessed by every other user on the network.

Fig. 1-1 shows three computers, a file server and two client computers. The first client has local disk drives A, B, and C. It also has access to drive F, which is actually on the file server. The second client has only one local disk drive, but can also access drive F.

DOS Directories

In DOS you can create directories to organize the data on a disk. A directory contains files grouped together on the disk. Every disk has what is called the root directory even though it is not referred to as "root" in any DOS command. Since a "\" (a backslash) is used to separate directory names, a backslash with no name is considered the root directory.

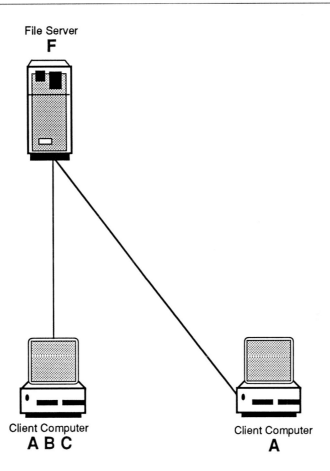

Fig. 1-1. Client computers networked to a server.

Fig. 1-2 shows how a hard disk might be organized. The files in the root directory could be listed by typing the DIR command. The DIR command lists the files in the current directory. In this case DIR C: would list the files COMMAND.COM, LSL.COM, PCN2L.COM, IPXODI.COM, VLM.EXE and a directory called WORD. The files in the directory WORD could be displayed by typing DIR C:\WORD and pressing the ENTER key. WORD.COM and LETTER.DOC would be listed. Another way to view the list of files in the WORD directory would be to use the CHDIR command. CHDIR stands for change directory and can be abbreviated further by using only CD. If you were to type CD C:\WORD, the current directory would be changed to the WORD directory and DIR C: would list the files WORD.COM and LETTER.DOC. In this way the drive letter C moves around the disk drive pointing to different areas. Just as the root directory contains a directory called WORD, the WORD directory could contain another directory and so on.

The same commands can be used on the network drive F. In Fig. 1-1 the first computer could create a directory called F:\HISFILES by using the MKDIR command. MKDIR stands for make directory and can be abbreviated further by using only MD. By typing the command MD F:\HISFILES, the first user

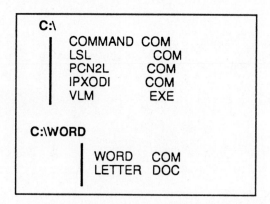

Fig. 1-2. Possible hard disk organization.

can create a place to store files on the file server. The user at the second computer could type MD F:\HERFILES. Now, if either computer user typed DIR F:, both directory names would be listed.

Drive Mappings

With directories containing directories and every user on the network creating directories, the directory structure can become quite complex.

Suppose a user on the network needed quick and easy access to files in both the F:\HISFILES directory and the F:\HERFILES directory. Rather than constantly using the CHDIR command to move drive F to the other area, he could use the NetWare MAP command to create a drive letter for one of the directories. Fig. 1-3 shows the result of the first user typing MAP G:=F:\HERFILES. This creates drive letter G, which points to the HERFILES directory on the same physical drive as F:\HISFILES.

This arrangement does not affect the second user. Drive mappings pertain only to the client computer where the MAP command was issued. Each user still has access to the HERFILES directory through drive letter F. The first user simply has the choice of using drive letter F or drive letter G.

Paths and Search Drives

Drive mappings allow users to access data easily without worrying about the directory names. The DOS PATH statement allows the user to completely ignore the current directory when running programs. NetWare combines these functions in the search drive. Ordinarily, to execute a program, it must reside in the current directory or the full path must be used when referring to the program. The "path" is the complete directory name where the program resides. Referring to Fig. 1-3, the first user may have a program in the HISFILES directory called WORD.COM. If the current directory is F:\HERFILES, he would have to type F:\HISFILES\WORD to execute the

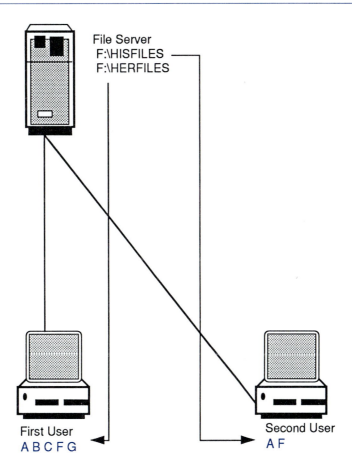

Fig. 1-3. Paths for different network users.

WORD program. DOS provides a means to shorten this in the PATH command. The PATH command tells the computer where to look for a program if it can't be found in the current directory. If the first user types PATH F:\HISFILES he can use all the programs in the HISFILES directory without typing the entire path. He could simply type WORD and the computer would look in the current directory first, then look in the HISFILES directory and find, and then execute, the program. Multiple directories can be included in the PATH command to instruct the computer to search several areas for the program. The command PATH F:\HERFILES;F:\HISFILES would tell the computer to search the current directory first (as it always does), then the F:\HERFILES directory, and lastly the F:\HISFILES directory. A NetWare search drive is a drive mapping that is automatically inserted in the PATH.

In Fig. 1-4, the second user has typed the command MAP S1:=F:\HISFILES. This NetWare command automatically chooses a drive letter starting from the end of the alphabet and maps it to the directory indicated. But the drive letter is more than the pointer used in the other drive letters, it is also a PATH to the directory. The second user can use drive letter Z as she would any other drive letter, but if she is using drive A, for instance, she needs only to type WORD to run the program contained in the F:\HISFILES directory. A user may have up to 16 search drives mapped at a given time.

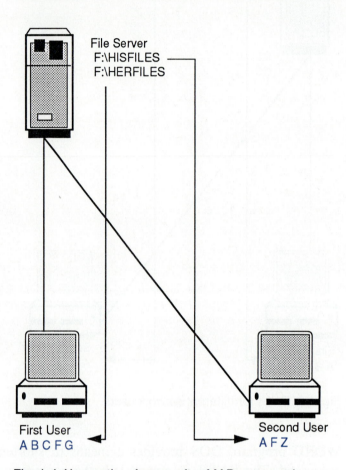

Fig. 1-4. New paths of users after MAP command.

Trustee Rights

NetWare allows users to share data or to restrict access to data. Trustee rights allow access to specific directories on the file server. Without trustee rights to a certain directory, a user cannot access the data in that directory. Trustee rights are composed of several permissions a user may have to a specific directory or file. These permissions include Supervisory, Read, Write, Create, Erase, Modify, File Scan and Access Control. Each of these permissions may be granted or denied to a user. The meanings of these permissions or rights with respect to a directory are listed below:

1. **Supervisory.** The user has all other rights in the directory even if the directory does not allow certain rights.

2. **Read.** The user can open and read files in the directory. The File Scan right is usually also given with the Read right so that the user can see the directory's directory listing.

3. **Write.** The user can write to existing files in the directory.
4. **Create.** The user can create new files in the directory.
5. **Erase.** The user can erase files in the directory.
6. **Modify.** The user can modify the Attribute flags of the files in the directory. The Attribute of a file indicates what access all users have to a file.
7. **File Scan.** The user can see what files and subdirectories are listed in the directory.
8. **Access Control.** The user can grant rights to other users in the directory.

Fig. 1-5 shows the trustee rights each of the users has to the file server using the first letter of the above listed rights. The first user has all rights except Supervisory and Access Control to the F:\HISFILES directory. He can use all of the files there any way he wants, but he cannot grant those rights to any other users. He only has Read and File Scan rights in the F:\HERFILES directory. This means he can only read from the data there, not change it or add to it. The second user has all rights to the F:\HERFILES directory. She could even grant additional rights in that directory to the first user. Her access to the F:\HISFILES directory is restricted to Create and File Scan. This allows her to create new files in the directory but not to read or change the files already there.

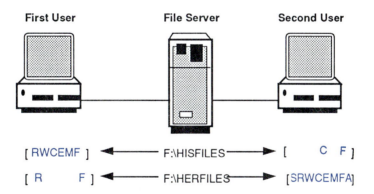

Fig. 1-5. Trustee rights for users.

Batch Files and Login Scripts

Many of the commands described above could become quite tedious if you had to type them every time you used the computer. This is why DOS provides a means for storing these commands in a file known as a batch file. A batch file is a list of commands that can be executed by entering the file name.

For instance, if a user needed to execute the commands listed in Fig. 1-6, those commands could be stored in a file called START.BAT. The ".BAT" portion of the name is called the extension and, in this case, indicates that the file is a batch file. With this file in the current directory the user only needs to type Start. The computer will read the file and execute the commands listed in it.

```
MAP G:=F:\HERFILES
CD F:\HISFILES
WORD
```

Fig. 1-6. Commands for the batch file START.BAT.

NetWare provides a similar function in the form of login scripts. Login scripts are lists of commands that are executed when a user logs into NetWare. Logging in identifies the user to the network so trustee rights can be established. A user might type LOGIN USER1, then a password. NetWare would verify the password is correct, establish the trustee rights for the user, execute the System Login Script, and then execute the login script for that user. Each user may have a different login script, and the login script may execute batch files.

Together, batch files and login scripts free the user from a great deal of typing each time she or he starts working on the computer. Additionally, the user may not need to know many of the DOS and NetWare commands if the login scripts and batch files are already installed.

A Novell Network Example

As outlined before, a local area network links two or more computers and other peripherals together for the purpose of sharing data and equipment. A Novell NetWare-based local area network normally is considered a dedicated file server network. That is, the network has at least one computer whose job is to act as a central data storage system.

Novell networks can consist of one or more file servers, each with dozens of workstations, multiple shared printers, and other devices that can be attached to the file server or workstations.

A small office network or a teaching laboratory can be established easily by creating one for the first time or by using existing networks. The basic components are as follows:

1. A file server (An IBM-compatible computer with a 80836SX or faster processor) with at least 6 megabytes of RAM and a hard disk (preferably with a minimum of 80 megabytes of storage).
2. Network interface cards (NICs) for the server and the workstations.
3. Transmission media (twisted pair, coaxial, or other type according to the type of NICs used).
4. Novell NetWare 3.12.
5. A printer should also be added to the network (preferably more than one).

If a Novell NetWare-based network is not already available, the process for installing one is outlined in Chapter 9. The following list provides a general review of the process.

1. Find a location for the server.
2. Find locations for the workstations.
3. Configure each NIC to contain a unique network address if not already preconfigured from the factory.
4. Install the NIC in each of the workstations and servers that will make up the nodes of the network.
5. Connect each node with the medium chosen.
6. Document all the hardware and the specific hardware configuration settings for all hardware that makes up the network.
7. Install the NetWare network operating system and use the data from item 6 to answer NetWare's requests.
8. Install workstation software.

Fig. 1-7 displays a possible configuration for such a laboratory or work environment. If the network is used to provide instructions on the use of commands and network management, a program called LANSKOOL from Intel, Inc. may be a good addition to the system. This program allows the instructor to project his or her workstation screen on the screen of other users for the purpose of answering questions or for instructional needs.

The other scenario consists of a Novell network that already exists. It is costly to purchase additional workstations, materials, and space if all that is required is a laboratory or room for providing training to users. If a current network is in place with users' workstations available, all that is needed is an additional server that can function as a training server for the users. This server can be connected to the existing wiring and, after NetWare is installed in it, training can be conducted using existing workstations. Fig. 1-8 shows this scenario. The equipment required for this situation is as follows:

1. A file server (An IBM-compatible computer with an 80386SX or faster processor) with at least 4 megabytes of RAM (preferably 6) and a hard disk (preferably with a minimum of 80 megabytes of storage).
2. A network interface card (NIC) for the server.
3. Novell NetWare 3.12
4. A cable to connect the new server to existing network cable.

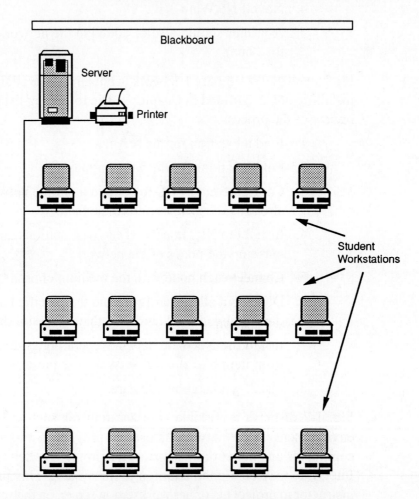

Fig. 1-7. Possible network configuration for training users

The process to install the server is as follows:
1. Find a location for the server. If it is going to be used for training, then probably the classroom is a good place.
2. Install the NIC in the server and, if required, provide a unique address.
3. Connect the server to existing network transmission media.
4. Install NetWare on the server and provide a unique server name.

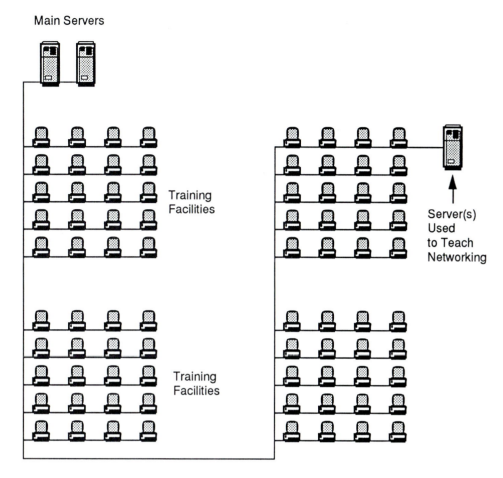

Fig. 1-8. Additional configuration for setting up a network to train users

The process of installing NetWare is provided in the next chapter in this book. After the server goes on line, users who need training will simply attach their workstation to the server. Any commands issued and any modifications to the environment stay in the training server without affecting the rest of the users and file servers. The server can be configured so that users can attach themselves to other servers.

Summary

NetWare provides access to a file server by many client computers through the hardware and software on each computer. The hardware consists of a network interface card, or NIC. Under DOS, using the ODI concept, the NIC is controlled by LSL.COM, a program named to represent the brand of NIC being used, and a program called IPXODI.COM. Another program, NETX or the newer VLM.EXE VLM manager, provides the interface to DOS and to the file server. With these programs loaded, the file server appears to the client computer as a disk drive attached to the client computer. DOS commands can be used to create and access directories on the file server.

The four programs make up the NetWare client software that serves as the interface between the computer operating system and the network operating system. The NetWare client software allows DOS and the user to treat file servers as a disk drive attached to the client computer. This protects the user from having to learn new commands and makes using the network a natural extension of the user's workstation.

With the use of batch files, login scripts, drive mappings, paths, and search drives, a user's environment can be customized without affecting other network users. In addition, security of the network and user files are enhanced by the use of login IDs and passwords and trustee rights. The login ID/password combination controls physical access to the network. Trustee rights determine the specific type of access privileges that each user possesses.

Questions

1. What does DOS do?
2. Under DOS, files may be stored in different areas on the same disk. What are these areas called?
3. What does CHDIR stand for?
4. What NetWare command changes the assignment of drive letters?
5. What does the PATH command tell the computer?
6. A user on a Novell network must have a set of permissions to use a directory on the file server. What are these permissions called?
7. If a user has Read and File Scan rights in a directory, can the user store data there? Why or why not?
8. DOS allows a list of commands to be entered in a file. What is this type of file called?
9. A user executes her login script once only in a session. When?

Project

Objective

Before NetWare can be installed on a system, a listing of hardware, users, and other resources must be recorded. Also, all steps taken during the installation process must be recorded in case something goes wrong and an audit needs to occur.

Additionally, knowing the applications, directories, users, and workstations on the network will help in maintaining the network and in performing future upgrades or expansions that may be required.

Creating a Novell NetWare Log Book

A typical log book contains the information outlined below. One should be created for each server.

Name of the server.

Type of hardware.

Date of installation.

Name of installer.

Operating system:

    Name and version of the operating system in use.

    Installation date of the operating system.

    Name of the operating system installer.

Server:

    Purchase date of the server.

    Server's network address.

    Location of the server.

Volume:

    Volume(s) name(s) in the server.

    Volume disk number.

    Volume(s) size(s).

Users' workstations:

    Users' names.

    Users' locations.

    Users' network addresses.

    Users' workstation types.

Users' workstation RAM.

Users' workstation disk options.

Users' workstation graphics boards and monitors.

Users' workstation hardware options and configuration.

Applications:

Name of the applications in use.

Application's vendor.

Application's purchase date.

Application's version number.

Application's memory requirements.

Application's disk space requirements.

Additional log information.

Using a word processor and the preceding list as a guide, create a NetWare log book and fill in the information requested for the network that you will be installing during the hands-on portion of this class. Make sure that all information is correct because once the network is set up, it is difficult and time consuming to correct major errors or omissions in the setup process.

2

NetWare Installation

Objectives

After completing this chapter you will
1. Understand the use of NetWare utility menus.
2. Understand the STARTUP.NCF and AUTOEXEC.NCF files.
3. Be able to load a valid NetWare DOS Requester set of client software.
4. Understand NetWare Loadable Modules.
5. Be able to configure and install NetWare.

Key Terms

AUTOEXEC.NCF	File Server
Hard Disk	Hard Disk Controller
NetWare Loadable Module	NetWare
Network Interface Card	RAM
STARTUP.NCF	Tape Backup
Workstation	

Introduction

In Chapter 1 some of the fundamental concepts of Novell NetWare were introduced. This chapter will begin to demonstrate the concepts with hands-on exercises in NetWare installation and maintenance. First, one must select the right version of NetWare from Personal NetWare through NetWare version 4.

NetWare version 3.12 represents more than just improvements on the 2.x series. NetWare versions through 2.2 are designed to operate on an IBM-PC compatible with an 80286 or faster central processing unit (CPU). The 80286 CPU is the microprocessor chip that controls the operation of the computer. Beginning with version 3, NetWare has required a more powerful CPU. NetWare version 3 was originally called NetWare 386 because it required a machine based on the Intel 80386 CPU. What once was Novell Netware 386 now runs on other computers such as the 80486 and is now called Netware version 3.1x or 3.12. Even though each version must be written for each type of computer it is to be run on, Novell wanted to show that the network operating system was not limited to an 80386 processor. Many versions are now available from Novell which cover a variety of hardware platforms and user needs.

One significant feature of NetWare 3 and 4 is System Fault Tolerance. This capability ensures data integrity that earlier versions could not. Its five major features are Disk Mirroring, Disk Duplexing, Transaction Tracking, Read-after-Write verify, and Hot Fix.

Disk Mirroring uses two hard disks attached to the same hard disk controller. All the data is written to both hard disks, exactly duplicated. If one of the hard disks should fail, the other contains all the data, and normal operation continues until the LAN administrator or other maintenance person can replace the failed drive.

Another method for ensuring the data on the hard disk remains intact is called Disk Duplexing. It uses two controller cards and two hard disks. Again the data is duplicated on the second hard disk, but it is sent to it separately so that a failure in one controller card disabling one hard drive leaves the other available and working.

Transaction Tracking helps ensure data accuracy by keeping an ongoing record of past changes to the data on the disk. If a user is in the process of making several changes to a database when, for instance, there is a power failure, the incomplete changes can be backed out.

The Read-after-Write verify capability means that data written to the disk is immediately reread and compared to what was supposed to have been written. If it does not match, the system repeats the write/read/verify process until a match occurs. If a match does not occur after a fixed number of tries, the Hot Fix capability is activated.

Hot Fix allows the system to dynamically mark a disk sector bad after a Read-after-Write verify failure. Data intended for the bad spot on the disk is redirected to the Hot Fix area. This allows operation of the file server to continue in spite of a reasonable number of bad spots on the disk.

For IBM-compatible computers, the least expensive and least functional system is Personal NetWare. It is intended for very small networks with limited ability. Novell's latest release is NetWare version 4, a full-featured version of NetWare which is primarily targeted for very large networking environments. NetWare version 3.1x, including versions 3.11 and 3.12, is widely used and very functional for most requirements. It provides a broad range of functions including connectivity to other types of networks. It is also available in versions that provide the same functions with a smaller number of workstations attached. At the writing of this book, Novell had condensed its offerings by selling NetWare versions 3.12, 4, and Personal NetWare.

Novell NetWare 3.12 will be the model for the remainder of this text. Many of the commands available in NetWare 3.12 are also available in version 2.2. Although the most significant difference (for the purposes of this text) is the installation process, a statistical comparison of version 2.2 and 3.12 is shown in Table 2-1.

	Version 2.2	Version 3.12
Logical simultaneous connections on each file server	100	250
Concurrent open files per file server	1,000	100,000
Maximum files concurrently using TTS	200	10,000
Volumes per file server	32	64
Hard disks per volume	1	32
Directory entries per volume	10,240	2,097,152
Maximum addressable RAM memory	15.6 MB	4 GB
Maximum addressable disk storage	2 GB	32 TB
Maximum file size	256 MB	4 GB
Maximum volume size	256 MB	32 TB

Table 2-1. NetWare versions 2.2 and 3.12 compared.

Installing NetWare

Novell has worked very hard to provide the installer with a menu-driven interface that allows easy selection of important options or a relatively simple default installation in which the NetWare installation program determines how NetWare should be installed. Both methods require the installer to have some information and experience.

The installer must have a complete list of the hardware on the file server, including information on the type of hard disk and the type of network card to be used. NetWare's control of the file server depends on its being able to communicate with each peripheral device accurately.

Communication with most devices depends on three pieces of information, the base memory address, the base I/O address, and the interrupt number. The computer's memory is arranged so it can be accessed through use of an address. Memory at the base memory address is often used by the network interface card as a buffer. This buffer stores information the NIC sends to the processor before it is ready to process it. The base I/O address is the address of an I/O port that defines the way the processor communicates with a device. The base memory and base I/O addresses of each peripheral must be known by NetWare and therefore by the installer.

The CPU spends most of its time reading from memory and executing the instructions it finds there. Some devices, however, must interrupt this process so the CPU can perform some special, critical task. A network interface card, for example, must interrupt the CPU so incoming data can be dealt with. Each device needing access is assigned an Interrupt Request Line number. The number and the base memory and base I/O addresses are often selectable on the device so the person installing the equipment can make sure that each device does not use another's address or interrupt number. The Interrupt Request Line number used in each peripheral must also be recorded for use during installation.

Often the equipment on the file server will require special drivers supplied by the manufacturer. A driver, remember, is a program written to control a specific peripheral such as a tapedrive. Novell may not have supplied the driver for a particular unit. If it is intended to be used with NetWare, the manufacturer of the tape drive must supply the driver on diskettes. These drivers must be available at the time of installation. Similar information for each type of workstation on the network will also be needed. The following are items that the network administrator needs to be concerned with before installing NetWare. Use the list below to collect and record this information.

For the file server the information required is as follows:

1. File server. The make and model type of the computer that will be used as a file server. Remember that this machine must be at least a 386 computer with at least 6 MB RAM and a hard drive whose capacity is greater than 20 MB.

2. Hard disk type. Manufacturers and model numbers of all hard disks attached to the file server and the appropriate drive types for each hard drive in the system.

3. Hard disk controller type. Manufacturers and model numbers of the controller cards used with the hard disks, including memory and I/O addresses and Interrupt Request Lines used.

4. Network card type. Manufacturers and model numbers of the network interface cards used, including RAM and ROM addresses and Interrupt Request Lines used.

5. Tape backup type, if tape is to be attached directly to the file server. Manufacturers and model numbers of the tape drive units installed, including memory, I/O addresses, and Interrupt Request Lines used.

6. Types of printers attached to file server. Manufacturers and model numbers of the printers that will be attached to the file server and the ports, LPT or COM, that will be used with each.

For the workstation the information required is as follows:

1. Workstation manufacturer and model. The make and model type of the computer that will be used as a workstation.

2. Amount of random access memory (RAM). Amount of conventional memory. Conventional memory is the memory below 640K. The installer also needs to know the amount of extended or expanded memory. Extended memory and expanded memory are different conventions for using memory above 640K. If the workstation has 1 megabyte of RAM the memory between 640K and 1 megabyte is extended memory and not normally addressable by DOS. Some programs, including NetWare, can use this memory. If the workstation has more than 1 megabyte of RAM it might be extended or expanded. The expanded memory conventions allow programs to switch blocks of data back and forth between the expanded memory region and the conventional memory region below 640K.

3. DOS version. The DOS versions used by each workstation to be attached to the network.

4. IBM or compatible. Some of the installable options in NetWare are specific to IBM computers. This is especially true for IBM PS/2 computers.

5. Interrupt Request setting, I/O address setting, and memory address setting on the network interface card.

The installer should be familiar with DOS. Much of the setup after installation of the file server requires a complete understanding of DOS directories, commands, and batch files.

Installation Preparation

Before installing any program, including a network operating system, backup copies of the distribution diskettes should be made. NetWare is not copy protected, so DOS commands can be used to make copies.

To make the copies, have the number of original disks plus two or three extras. They must be the same type of disks as the NetWare distribution disks. NetWare 3.12 is shipped on 3 1/2-inch high density diskettes or on CDROM. The extra disks may be needed if some of the new disks do not format correctly.

Attach label stickers to the blank disks if needed, and set the write protect tabs on the original disks. When a disk is write protected, the computer cannot write to or change any information on the disk. On 3 1/2-inch disks, the write protect tab is the small sliding tab on the corner of the disk. It should be set in the open position so the hole goes through the disk. The procedures to make the backup copies is the same as for ordinary DOS files. Step by step instructions are provided in the hands-on section of this chapter.

NetWare Menus

All NetWare utility menus are designed around a few relatively simple rules of operation. Understanding how these menus work is essential since many of them change as you use them. In some utilities, completing an option makes another option available. Also, the menus may include different items depending on how the utility was started.

Fig. 2-1 shows an example of the opening menu of the NetWare System Configuration utility SYSCON. Along the top is a box that indicates the name and version of the utility and may also display the date and time. No information in this box can be changed by the user.

Notice that some boxes are drawn with a single line while others are drawn using double lines. Single-line boxes in NetWare menu utilities usually contain information that the user cannot change. The box in the middle of the screen shows the main menu for this utility. It consists of a bright double line with various options inside. To select an item, use the arrow keys to move the highlighted bar to the option desired. Then press the ENTER key.

If there are more items than can fit in the box, a small arrow pointing down will appear in the lower left of the box. Another method for selecting options from a list is to begin typing the name of the option. The highlighted bar will move to the appropriate option as you type.

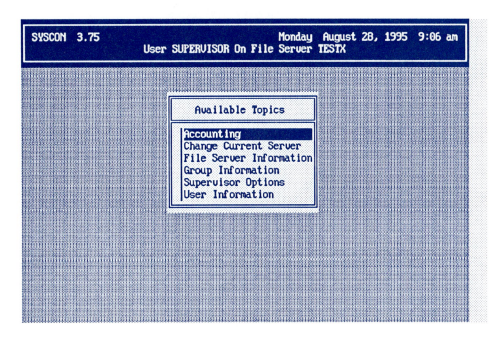

Fig. 2-1. SYSCON main menu.

The NetWare menus often use Novell's names for the keys rather than the commonly accepted name for the key. For example, the SELECT key is the ENTER key on the keyboard. The following list shows the Novell names for certain keys and their functions.

1. Select. The ENTER or RETURN key. The select key is used to choose an item from a list.

2. Help. The F1 key. This key will provide information on the options currently available to the user. Pressing F1 twice usually shows the uses of all the function keys.

3. Modify. The F3 key. Some highlighted options can be changed by pressing the F3 key. If an option can be changed this way, a new box will appear for the user to put the new information in.

4. Mark. The F5 key. Some menu commands can be executed on multiple items. The F5 key marks the items in a list so the next command will affect them all.

5. Accept. Usually the ESCAPE key. This is the most unusual feature of the NetWare menus, because it seems backwards from computer conventions. After making selections in a menu, the

user presses the ESCAPE key to return to the previous menu. Rather than discarding the changes the user made, this choice accepts and saves them.

6. Cancel. The F7 key. This key returns to the previous menu without saving the options selected.
7. Insert. The INSERT key. This key is used to insert a new item in a list. If it is allowed at that point in the menu, the user will be prompted for an item to place in the list.
8. Delete. The DELETE key. This key will delete an item from a list.
9. Exit. ALT/F10. This key combination exits the menu utility without saving any pending information and without prompting the user with "Are you sure?" (Often, however, changes are saved as they are made.)

Client Software

In previous versions of Novell NetWare, an appropriate set of NetWare client software had to be created for each workstation, specific to the type of NIC in the workstation. As discussed earlier, the Netware client software is the software interface to the rest of the network. In versions previous to NetWare 3, NetWare built the main workstation program by combining the IPX shell program code provided on the distribution diskettes with the drivers for the particular network card being used, using a program called SHGEN or WSGEN. This type of network shell is known as a dedicated IPX. NetWare Version 3.12 no longer provides a program called WSGEN, which through NetWare 3.11 could still generate a dedicated IPX. If you desire to create a dedicated IPX, you are referred to the NetWare manuals for information on creating such an IPX, remembering that you must obtain a copy of WSGEN.

In the latest releases of NetWare, however, new NetWare client software is used. It uses the Open Data Link Interface or ODI type of interface and an architecture called the NetWare DOS Requester which employs a modular approach to loading portions of workstation software called Virtual Loadable Modules (VLMs).

The ODI drivers are complete programs for specific network cards that do not need any special linking. Additionally, the IPXODI approach to the NetWare client software allows the same network interface card to support two or more communications protocols at once, for example, NE2000 Ethernet for IPX and IP drivers for TCP/IP.

In either case, ODI or dedicated IPX, the NetWare client programs are usually loaded onto a bootable disk to make access to the network as easy as possible. A bootable disk, also known as a boot disk, is a disk on which the DOS system files have been previously loaded. To create a NetWare boot disk you will need the copies of the NetWare disks, a DOS disk, a blank disk, and any special driver disk that your network interface card may require. The bootable disk may also be configured to be the hard drive of the workstation.

Installing NetWare on the File Server

Installation and loading procedures for NetWare 3.12 are significantly different from those used for the 2.x versions of NetWare, and they are even greatly streamlined over the installation procedures used for installing NetWare 3.11. In the 2.x version, the network operating system had to be configured and then linked prior to installation on the file server. Then, if one or more of the configuration parameters had to be changed, the entire configuration, linking, and installation process had to be repeated.

NetWare versions 3.11 and 3.12 are dynamic and use NetWare Loadable Modules (NLMs) to supply drivers and other software needed to control the network. Drivers can usually be unloaded and reloaded with different configurations without downing the file server.

As with other versions of NetWare, it is still a good idea to choose hardware components which are on Novell's approved list. Also, even though NetWare is fully configurable from NLMs, it is still very important that the installer write down hardware details such as memory addresses, interrupts, and I/O addresses as though configuring a 2.x version of NetWare. Verify that interrupt numbers are not duplicated and that I/O addresses and memory addresses do not overlap within a driver or across drivers.

Like some earlier versions of NetWare, NetWare 3.12 requires some extended memory to operate. It is also a good idea to make sure that you have enough extended memory to support your operation prior to the initial installation process. In general, the amount of memory needed is the greater of 6 MB or the result of multiplying the size of the hard drive in megabytes by .023 and then dividing by block size in kilobytes plus 2 MB for the operating system. For example, assuming a block size of 4KB and a hard disk size of 200 MB, $(200 \times 0.023)/4 + 2 = 3.15$. Therefore, the amount of memory needed is 6 MB. If the volume has added name space (such as support for Macintosh or OS/2), the formula is the same, but instead of multiplying by 0.023, multiply by 0.032.

Logging onto an Existing File Server

Assuming the file server is up and running and the cabling system is complete, a workstation should now be able to login to the server.

To login, a workstation needs to be booted with the NetWare boot disk created earlier, and the workstation's AUTOEXEC.BAT should be modified to include

> LSL
>
> NIC driver (such as NE2000)
>
> IPXODI
>
> NETX or VLM

Note that if the network interface card uses the default interrupt, I/O address, or memory settings, no further action is needed and the VLMs which are loaded by the VLM manager are in the same directory as the VLM manager. Otherwise, one must enter the actual settings into the Link Driver section of a text file called NET.CFG which must be in the same directory as IPXODI.COM.

If the user is successful in communicating with the network via the above four programs, the entry of the DIR F: command will show the LOGIN directory on the file server. The LOGIN directory is where users are placed when they are connected but not logged into the file server.

If the installer is the first user to login to this file server, the only user names available are SUPERVISOR and GUEST. Since GUEST has very few rights, it is the supervisor that creates all other user names allowed to login to the server.

Logging in as the supervisor is achieved by typing LOGIN SUPERVISOR and pressing the ENTER key. A prompt by the LOGIN program to enter a password will appear. Pressing ENTER indicates that the installer does not have a password.

Typing DIR F:\ and pressing the ENTER key shows that even though this is a new file server, it is not an empty one.

NetWare has created four directories called SYSTEM, LOGIN, MAIL, and PUBLIC.

1. The SYSTEM directory contains the NetWare program files that actually run the network.
2. The LOGIN directory contains the LOGIN program and other programs or data files a user might need before logging into the network.
3. The MAIL directory contains a directory for each user with the user's login script in it.
4. The fourth directory created by NetWare is the PUBLIC directory. It contains all the NetWare utilities that users, including the supervisor, use to manage their accounts and files. In the following chapters those utilities will be further explored.

Before leaving any network terminal, a user, especially the supervisor, should logout. Making this a habit is an important component of network security. The LOGOUT program is used to close the user's account on the file server, but it does not completely disconnect the workstation.

To logout, the command LOGOUT is typed at the F> prompt and the ENTER key is pressed. At this stage, workstations can access the LOGIN directory and its contents, but not actually be logged in. The workstation can be turned off without fear of leaving files open on the server.

Typically a network file server is left turned on all the time. This is because the most stressful part of the operation of any computer equipment is turning it on or off. If it is necessary to turn the server off, the DOWN command must be entered at the file server keyboard. It ensures that all files the workstations might have left open are closed and that any files the server was using are closed. The DOWN command also informs workstations and other servers on the network that the server is no longer available. The file server can be safely turned off after it has responded to the DOWN command.

Hands-on NetWare Installation

Installation Preparation

Making Backup Copies with a Dual Disk Drive Computer: Two Disk Drives of the Same Type

If the computer being used to make the backup copies has two disk drives of the same type, specified as A and B, follow the instructions below. If the computer has only one disk drive, skip to the Single Disk Drive instructions.

1. Boot the computer with a DOS disk. The DOS disk should be write protected to help protect against computer viruses.
2. Type **DISKCOPY A: B:** and press the ENTER key.

The DISKCOPY program will instruct you to insert the source disk in drive A: and the target disk in drive B:. The original NetWare disk is the source disk and one of the blank disks is the target.

3. Press the ENTER key when the disks are inserted and the copy process will begin.

When the copy has been successfully made, the DISKCOPY program will ask you if you would like to copy another.

4. Answer Yes by pressing Y and pressing the ENTER key. You will be prompted to insert source and target disks again.

5. Remove the two disks you started with and write the name of the original on the copy. Insert the second source disk and another blank disk. Continue this process with all of the NetWare distribution disks.

Making Backup Copies with a Single Disk Drive Computer

A single disk drive computer will probably have a hard disk installed and will only need to be turned on to be booted with DOS.

1. Type **DISKCOPY A: A:** and press the ENTER key.
2. The computer will ask you to insert the source disk in drive A. Press the ENTER key when ready.

The computer will read the disk and then ask for the target disk to be put in drive A. It then writes to the target disk and may ask for the source disk again. This process continues until the copy is complete. Copying disks with a single disk drive takes a little longer because you may have to change the diskette several times to make one copy. Copy all the NetWare disks, writing the name of each original on its copy.

Diskette Installation of the File Server

Boot the file server with a DOS system diskette to prove that the computer is operating properly as a DOS machine. Optionally, if the installation is to be done from CD-ROM, driver software for the CD-ROM must also be loaded. Note that CD-ROM installation is slightly different from diskette installation and is not presented here. Refer to the NetWare 3.12 Installation Manual for details for CD-ROM installation.

Then, create a bootable DOS or C drive partition on the system disk using FDISK and DOS version 3.3 or higher. (Note that according to Novell, there are potential problems in using DOS versions 3.2 and 4.0.) The partition is needed so that the file server can boot from its hard drive without the requirement of a special boot diskette.

1. Follow the DOS instructions for partitioning the hard drive, and allow 8MB to 10MB for the DOS partition. Make this partition active.
2. Format the DOS partition using FORMAT C:/S so that the system is transferred. This allows the server, once installed, to boot or come up without a diskette in the A: drive.
3. Boot your computer by pressing CONTROL, ALT, and DELETE keys simultaneously to verify that your C: partition is actually bootable.

4. Place the Install diskette in the A: drive of the file server to be created. Change to the A: drive, type INSTALL, and press ENTER. This activates INSTALL.BAT which, among other items, will copy the contents of SYSTEM_1 and SYSTEM_2, including SERVER.EXE, to a directory called SERVER.312 on the DOS partition of the file server.

The rest of the hard disk can be used for NetWare. If you do not create a DOS partition on the hard drive, you must always boot the file server from the special boot diskette. This disk is created by formatting it with the /S format option, copying SERVER.EXE, NUT.NLM, and NWSNUT.NLM from the SYSTEM_1 diskette, and by copying the driver for your hard disk from the System_2 diskette. Also, you should create an AUTOEXEC.BAT file on the diskette with a line which runs SERVER.EXE.

Note that in earlier versions of NetWare, the remainder of the hard drive had to be low-level formatted prior to proceeding with installation. This step is no longer necessary. Do note, though, that if either the FDISK or the formatting step fails, there is a hardware problem that must be corrected prior to proceeding with the installation.

5. Select Install new NetWare v3.12 as shown in Fig. 2-2. Then, select Retain Current Disk Partition and press ENTER. This keeps the DOS partition just created. (See Fig. 2-3.)

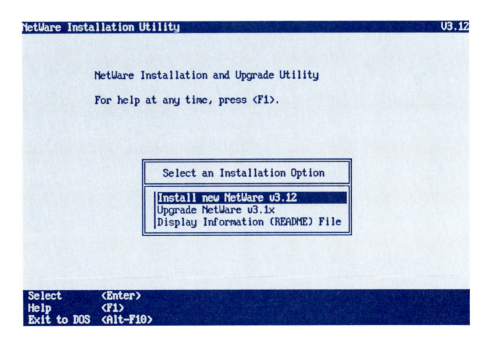

Fig. 2-2. Main installation menu.

6. NetWare then asks for a file server name. Type in a desired name between 2 and 47 characters long with no commas or spaces. (Be aware that many commands reference the file server name; therefore, the name should not be unnecessarily long.) The name

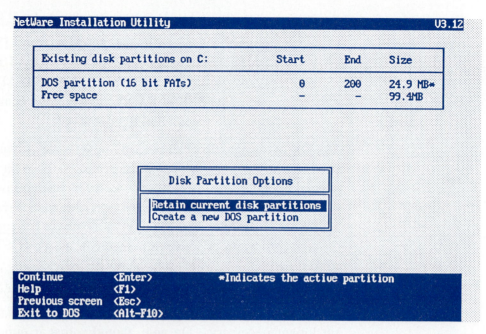

Fig. 2-3. Disk partition options.

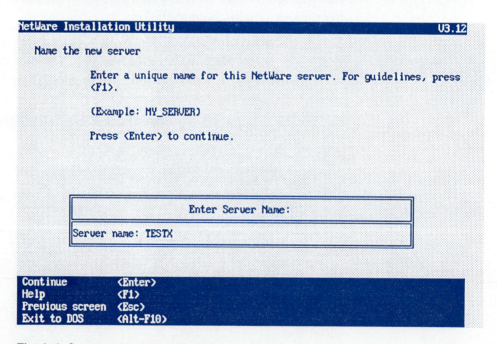

Fig. 2-4. Server name entry screen.

also must be unique among file servers connected together. (See Fig. 2-4.)

7. Then, NetWare asks for a hexadecimal number (one to eight digits and greater than 00000000 and not FFFFFFFF) for the internal network number. This number must be unique among the file servers which are connected to one another. This number is used by the NLMs for communication. The INSTALL utility provides a suggested internal IPX number, but it may be changed by deleting, then inserting, characters. (See Fig. 2-5.)

CHAPTER 2. NETWARE INSTALLATION

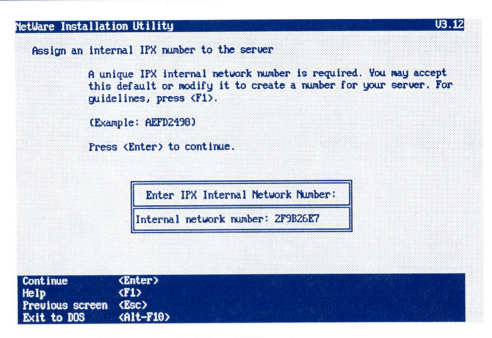

Fig. 2-5. Installation screen for internal IPX number.

8. When requested, insert diskettes labelled SYSTEM_1, SYSTEM_2, and UNICODE, pressing ENTER when each is inserted. This process copies the necessary server boot files to the C: partition of the file server. (See Fig. 2-6.)

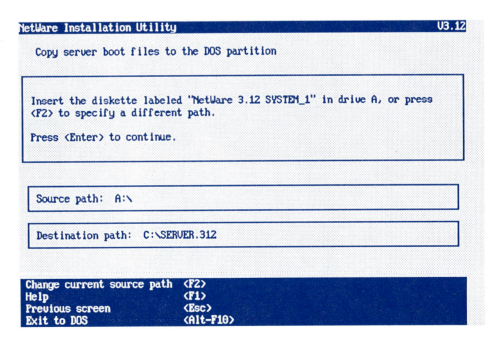

Fig. 2-6. Copying server boot files to the C partition.

9. Assign the country code, code page, and keyboard mappings consistent with the United States as in Fig. 2-7 and press F10.

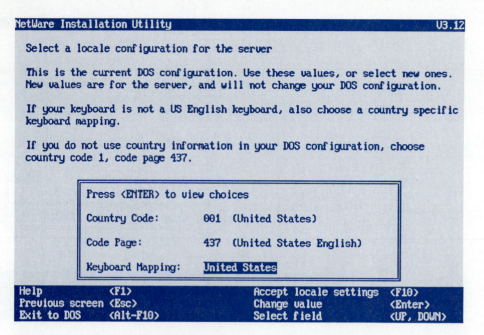

Fig. 2-7. Locale configuration screen.

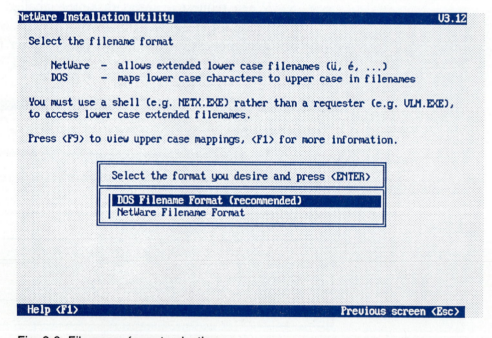

Fig. 2-8. File name format selection.

10. Select DOS Filename Format and press ENTER as in Fig. 2-8.

11. Select No for special startup commands and press ENTER as in Fig. 2-9.

12. The install utility will ask if you want the file server's AUTOEXEC.BAT to automatically load SERVER.EXE. It is recommended that you choose not to have the AUTOEXEC.BAT

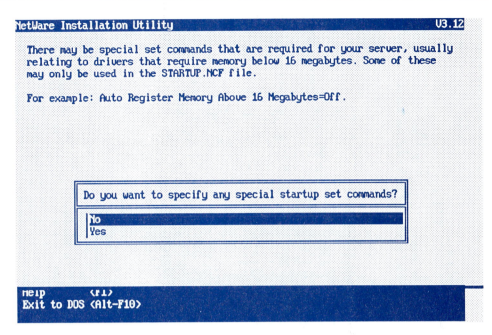

Fig. 2-9. Disabling retention of old STARTUP.NCF.

automatically load SERVER.EXE until you have completed and fully tested the operational NetWare 3.12 server. Then, the AUTOEXEC.BAT can easily be edited to call SERVER.EXE.

13. At this point, SERVER.EXE is automatically loaded and run.

14. You are now ready to load the driver for the hard disk. Novell supplies several standard drivers including ISADISK, DCB, PS2ESDI, PS2MFM, and PS2SCSI. If your hard drive is not among the supplied drivers, your supplier must supply the hard disk driver, and you must load it from diskette. To load a Novell-supplied hard disk driver or one your supplier has provided, type the following and then press ENTER.

    LOAD XXX (where XXX is the name of the driver, including the path name if the driver is to be loaded from diskette or from the C: partition of the file server's hard disk)

15. Now that the file server recognizes itself as a file server, and now that it recognizes its own hard drive, you are ready to load and run the INSTALL program by typing the following and then pressing ENTER.

    LOAD C:\SERVER.312\INSTALL

NetWare will then prompt you through the remaining steps of the installation process.

16. First, the main screen appears (See Fig. 2-10). This screen allows you to specify

    Disk Options

    Volume Options

    System Options

    Product Options

    or to EXIT.

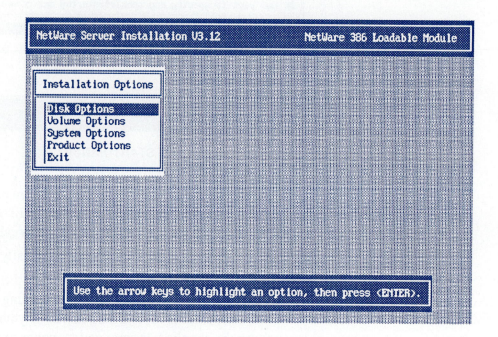

Fig. 2-10. Main INSTALL.NLM screen.

Each of these options can be selected and configured

17. Choose Disk Options by pressing ENTER. With the exception of the Partition Tables option, the options in this submenu are usually needed for diagnostic purposes in the event that the hard disk drive's performance becomes suspicious.

18. Partition Tables must be selected during initial installation to assign the NetWare partition. Select this option by highlighting Partition Tables and pressing the ENTER key.

When you select this option, NetWare will display a Partition Type screen and the Partition Options submenu will be displayed. Prior to creating the NetWare Partition, only the DOS partition and Free Space should appear in the list of drives which are attached to the controller. If no drives or the wrong type of drives appear in this display, stop immediately. If no drives appear, then check connections and retry this option. If the wrong types of drives appear, escape out of this menu back to the : prompt and repeat all file server installation steps. When the correct list of disk drive(s) is displayed, continue.

19. Cursor down to the Create NetWare Partition option and press ENTER. This selection allows you to create a NetWare partition from the remainder of the hard disk drive. (See Fig. 2-11.)

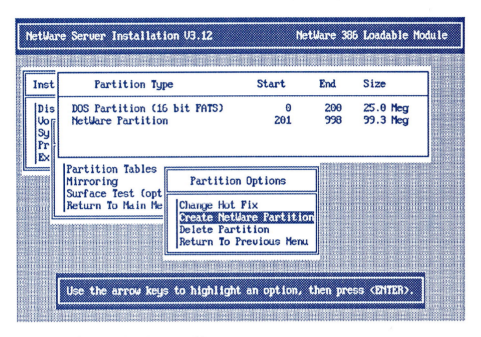

Fig. 2-11. Create NetWare partition screen.

Note that you can change the size of the "Hot Fix" area on the hard drive. While it is not a good idea to reduce the size of the Hot Fix area, it may be advisable to increase the size of the Hot Fix table if the hard disk drive already has many spared sectors upon initial installation. By enlarging the Hot Fix area, you allow more space for redirection in the event a bad block is discovered during processing.

20. Press ESC, then Y and ENTER to create the NetWare partition.
21. Press ESC twice to go back to the Installation Options menu. (Refer to Fig. 2-10)
22. Selecting Volume Options allows you to choose the volume configuration for the file server. Select this option by highlighting it and then pressing the ENTER key. Press INSERT to create the first volume. (See Fig. 2-12).

As mentioned earlier in the text, the first volume of the hard drive must be named SYS:. The default block size is 4K. To use the entire remainder of the hard drive and the default block size, press the ESC key, the Y key, and ENTER to create the SYS: volume.

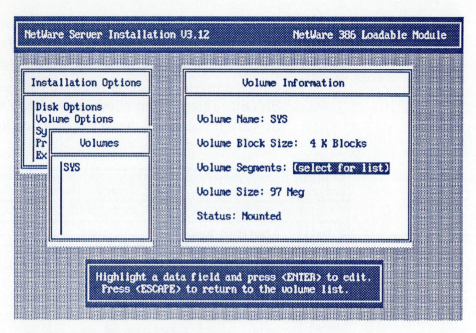

Fig. 2-12. Volume Information screen.

To reset the block size and/or to create additional volumes, first assign the desired number of volume segments to the SYS volume. The number of volume segments can be calculated by taking the size in megabytes of the desired volume and then dividing that number by the block size. For example, to assign 70 MB to the SYS: volume, the volume segment size would be (70 x 1024)/4 = 17,920 blocks. When entries are complete, press the ESC, Y, and ENTER keys to return to the Volume list.

To insert an additional volume, press <Ins> while on the Volume list. NetWare will prompt you for the volume name, block size, and volume segments.

Note that while 4K is the default block size, you can adjust the block size to 8K, 16K, 32K, or 64K. The block size indicates the number of bytes which are read or written at one time to the disk. It is usually a good idea to use the default unless you specifically know that a different block size would function better.

23. Press ESC to return to the Installation Options Menu.

24. The System Options item on the Installation Options Menu allows you to load additional software and drivers so that the file server can function and so that it can automatically boot as a file server. Choose this option by highlighting System Options and then pressing the ENTER key.

25. You must first copy System and Public files from the distribution diskettes to the file server NetWare Partition. To do this, highlight Copy System and Public Files and press ENTER. (See Fig. 2-13.)

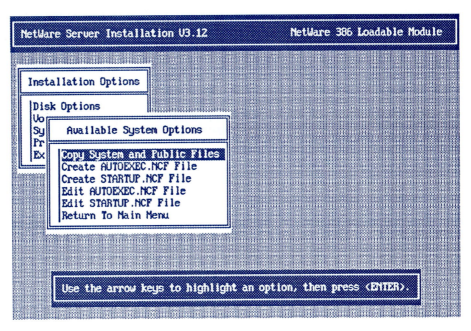

Fig. 2-13. System Options screen.

Since you haven't mounted the volume, you are now prompted to do so. From this point, follow the prompt to copy these diskettes to the file server.

26. After the System and Public files have been copied to the file server, you must create STARTUP.NCF. Highlight this option and press the ENTER key. (See Fig. 2-14.) The option lets you create the file needed to automatically load the disk driver and set the operating environment for the file server. The STARTUP.NCF file is stored on the bootable DOS drive (C: if your server will boot from the hard drive). When selected, this option should display the suggested STARTUP.NCF file based on the disk driver already loaded. To save this STARTUP.NCF file, press the ESC key and then select Yes and press ENTER to save the configuration. To modify the STARTUP.NCF, edit the file and then press the ESC key and select Yes and press ENTER to save the configuration.

27. Press the ESC key to go back to the Installation Options menu.

28. The Product Options selection is used to load such things as the NLM for Macintosh and will not be discussed here.

29. Press the ALT and ESC keys simultaneously to proceed without selecting product options.

At this point, you should be back to the : prompt on the file server monitor, but the Install program is still running. You are now ready to load the LAN drivers, the drivers which will control the operation of the NICs. You must load each driver and then bind it to the IPX protocol.

Networking Fundamentals Using Novell NetWare

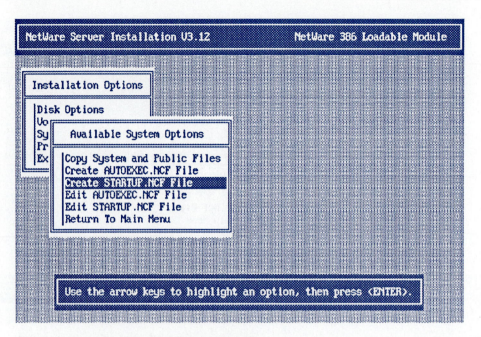

Fig. 2-14. Creating STARTUP.NCF screen.

30. To load a LAN driver, type

    LOAD XXX and press the ENTER key.

Here XXX is the complete path name and file name for the LAN driver. If you are in doubt as to the LAN driver's name, consult the documentation for the network interface card you are using.

NetWare will then prompt you for the memory address, port and interrupt number for the NIC. Again, refer to the documentation for your NIC for this information and for the jumper settings on the NIC itself.

31. Bind the LAN driver to the IPX protocol by typing **BIND IPX to YYY** and pressing the ENTER key.

Here YYY is the name of the LAN driver without the complete path name.

For example, if your network interface cards were NE2000 Ethernet cards, which you wish to use with IPX, you would type:

   LOAD NE2000 and press the ENTER key.

Here, you can accept the default or type in the correct one and press the ENTER key. Then type BIND IPX to NE2000 and press the ENTER key.

The driver must be loaded for each NIC in the file server.

32. You will be prompted to enter a network number. This number is a unique 8-digit hexadecimal number greater than zero and not FFFFFFFF to be assigned to the cable segment to which the network is attached. This is not the internal network address for the file server, and it must not be the same as the internal network

address for this or any other file server which can be seen on the existing cable or through routers on the network. If the cable segment already has been assigned a network number (i.e., if the cabling connects to an operating network), the same network number must be used.

33. Return to the Install utility by pressing the ALT and ESC keys simultaneously.

34. Highlight the System Options and press ENTER. On the system options submenu, highlight Create AUTOEXEC.NCF and press the ENTER key.

The system will then display all of the commands you have entered as part of the installation process and show them as the potential AUTOEXEC.NCF. This file is similar to the AUTOEXEC.BAT file in that it executes when the file server is booted and will automatically load and bind the drivers you have selected individually in the installation process. (See Fig. 2-15.) Make sure the AUTOEXEC.NCF file is correct and edit it to fix anything that is incorrect before saving it by pressing the ESC key and then selecting Yes to save the file.

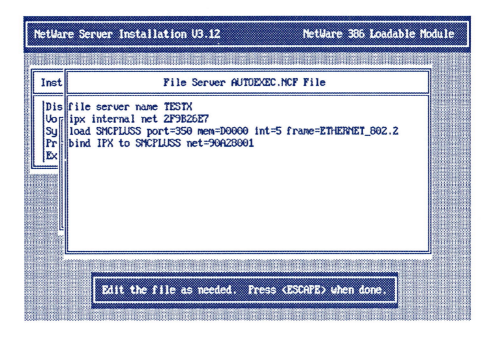

Fig. 2-15. Sample AUTOEXEC.NCF file.

35. Exit Install by pressing the ESC key twice, selecting Yes and pressing ENTER. You should be back to the : prompt.

36. The installation process is now complete. To check to see if your installation process worked, attempt to login to your file server from a workstation as the user SUPERVISOR. If this is successful, you must now only check that you can take the server down

and back up and still be able to login. If this login is not successful, you must begin troubleshooting the installation. Unfortunately, this process is beyond the scope of this class. Probably the best approach is to retrace each step of the installation, verifying its accuracy.

37. Down the file server by typing **DOWN** and press the ENTER key.
38. Wait for the prompt which instructs you to type in EXIT to return to DOS. Type in **EXIT**, and turn off the file server. Turn it back on. Your file server should automatically boot. Change to the SERVER.312 directory and type **SERVER** (or create an AUTOEXEC.BAT to execute SERVER).

Creating the Workstation Boot Disk using NetWare DOS Requester

Introduction to the NetWare DOS Requester

The NetWare DOS Requester is usually installed on the hard drive of the workstation rather than on a floppy diskette. NetWare 3.12 utilizes several Windows-based utilities including its on-line documentation, Dynatext, and the NetWare DOS Requester must modify several Windows configuration files to allow Windows to function properly with these utilities. Additionally, the workstation hard drive must be prepared so that it is a bootable DOS device prior to loading the NetWare DOS Requester.

The NetWare DOS Requester utilizes the LSL (Link Support Layer), the ODI-compliant LAN driver, and IPXODI just as the DOS redirector workstation setup did. However, instead of utilizing NETX to connect the user to the network, it uses a VLM manager, often called the DOS Requester, to load modular workstation routines much like NLMs that are used on the file server itself. Additionally, instead of keeping two sets of system tables as NETX did, the NetWare DOS Requester utilizes the same tables as DOS. This makes the operation of the client more efficient.

Note that the command

LASTDRIVE=Z:

must be placed in the CONFIG.SYS file of the workstation so that VLMs can recognize all 26 drives and thereby make drives available to NetWare.

Installing the NetWare DOS Requester

1. On the machine which will become the NetWare client, install DOS (version 3.3 or later) and WINDOWS. Boot the workstation by pressing the CTRL, ALT, and DEL keys.
2. Insert the diskette labelled WSDOS_1 into the diskette drive, change to the A: drive, and type **INSTALL** and press ENTER.

3. The client installation screen will appear, shown in Fig. 2-16.

4. Accept the default C:\NWCLIENT for the directory in which the NetWare client software is to be installed by pressing ENTER.

5. Answer "Yes" to allow for changes to the CONFIG.SYS and AUTOEXEC.BAT files for automatic loading of the workstation software and press ENTER. Note that the previous CONFIG.SYS and AUTOEXEC.BAT files will be stored in files called CONFIG.BNW and AUTOEXEC.BNW respectively so that reclamation of these files will be possible if the client install does not go smoothly.

6. Accept the default, Yes, to allow for Windows Support by pressing ENTER.

7. Enter the name of the directory in which WINDOWS is installed, usually C:\WINDOWS on the hard drive and press ENTER.

8. Press ENTER to choose the name of the appropriate LAN driver for the network board which is installed in the workstation. (Note: You may need to have the driver diskette which was included with the LAN card when it was purchased or an updated driver diskette as part of this process.)

9. If the "Insert the Driver Disk" message appears, put the WS-DRV_2 diskette or the diskette indicated into the floppy diskette drive.

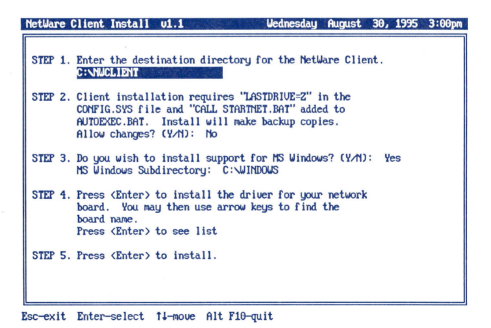

Fig. 2-16. Network Client Installation screen.

10. Press ENTER to begin copying files to the workstation hard drive, changing diskettes as prompted.

The installation, when complete, will have inserted the LASTDRIVE=Z: command into the CONFIG.SYS file, and it will have inserted a call to a file called STARTNET.BAT in the NWCLIENT directory. STARTNET.BAT will then set the language for NetWare and load LSL, the LAN driver, IPXODI, and will execute VLM to load the VLMs. Remember that configuration information for the workstation is stored in NET.CFG which may need to be edited for specific equipment configuration information.

Testing the New Boot Process

1. With the workstation cable to the network firmly installed, press the CTRL, ALT, and DELETE keys simultaneously to boot your workstation. Wait for LSL, the NIC driver, IPXODI, and VLM to run.
3. Type **F:** and press the ENTER key.
4. Type **LOGIN XXXXX\SUPERVISOR** where XXXXX is the name of the file server and press the ENTER key.
5. Type the SUPERVISOR's password, if one has been assigned.

Note that the boot files copied to the hard disk can be copied to a diskette if desired. If desired, copy the CONFIG.SYS, AUTOEXEC.BAT, and the entire NWCLIENT directory to the diskette for backup purposes.

Summary

NetWare must be installed for both the workstation and the file server. Using NetWare Version 3.12, the NetWare DOS Requester client software can be activated by executing a series of programs via the AUTOEXEC.BAT file on the workstation.

The file server is prepared with the installation process. Through use of the INSTALL.BAT file and the INSTALL NetWare Loadable Module, the file server is configured and configuration files called STARTUP.NCF and AUTOEXEC.NCF are created. This allows the file server to automatically boot with the configuration selected during the INSTALL process.

The workstation is prepared by installing the NetWare client software, which creates the NWCLIENT directory containing the files STARTNET.BAT and NET.CFG.

With the file server completely installed and running, a user can login by running the AUTOEXEC.BAT on the workstation which automatically runs the NetWare DOS Requester client software to link the workstation to the network.

Questions

1. In a NetWare utility menu, can the user change data in a box made with a double line?
2. In most NetWare menus, what key is pressed to accept the selections and return to the previous menu?
3. Does a NetWare workstation boot disk need DOS on it in addition to the NetWare DOS Requester programs?
4. How is the Open Data-Link version of IPX different from earlier versions of IPX?
5. Is 00000001 a valid network address?
6. Is FILESERVER a valid server name?
7. What are the four directories created on the file server during the installation process?
8. What is a NetWare Loadable Module?
9. What must be done to change a network interface card driver on a NetWare 3 file server which has already been installed?
10. How much memory is needed for a file server with a single 255 MB volume?

Project

Objective

The following project is designed to familiarize you with the process of booting a workstation, logging into the network, and using the help facility available in NetWare.

Logging into NetWare

1. Boot a workstation that has the NetWare client software installed.
2. The AUTOEXEC.BAT should cause you to be attached to a file server.
3. Type **DIR F:** and notice the number of bytes free listed at the bottom of the screen.
4. Login as the SUPERVISOR. Press SHIFT/PRINT SCREEN to record the results.
5. Type **DIR F:** and notice the number of bytes free listed at the bottom of the screen. Why is this figure larger than the one shown earlier?

3

The SYSCON Utility and Login Scripts

Objectives

After completing this chapter you will

1. Understand the importance of the System Configuration utility, SYSCON.
2. Understand the functions of each of the main menu selections in SYSCON.
3. Understand the purpose of a login script.
4. Understand login script commands.
5. Understand how to use login script variables.
6. Be able to login and logout of a file server.
7. Be able to create a user with appropriate login script using SYSCON.

Key Terms

Account Balance   File Server
Groups   Login Script
Passwords   Rights
SYSCON   Trustees

Introduction

In the last chapter, Novell NetWare was installed on the file server and the workstation was booted with the network workstation software. That arrangement allowed the user supervisor to login to the file server and view the files listed there. Now the file server must be set up to allow other users to login and easily manage their files and directories.

The NetWare System Configuration utility SYSCON is used to accomplish this. With it the supervisor can create user accounts and groups of user accounts. Each account or group can have different access rights, legal login times, and other attributes. Many of the controls used to set up the user's environment are executed when the user logs in through the use of a login script. It can set the user's drive mappings, check various conditions at the time the user logs in, and write messages to the screen.

SYSCON

Introduction

SYSCON allows the network supervisors to create, change, and delete users and groups of users in addition to enabling many other functions. It is by far the most important utility Novell provides with NetWare since it is used to set up the most fundamental aspects of the network. As with many NetWare utilities, some menu options only appear for the supervisor. Users can choose other limited menu options themselves to view and change their own accounts.

Fig. 3-1 shows SYSCON's main menu, which is labeled Available Topics. These topics comprise the essentials of managing the network as a whole. Starting from the top of the menu, SYSCON's primary functions are

1. Accounting
2. Change Current Server
3. File Server Information
4. Group Information
5. Supervisor Options
6. User Information

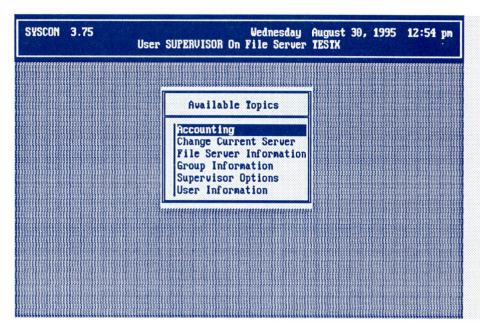

Fig. 3-1. SYSCON's main menu.

The SYSCON Options

Accounting

NetWare is capable of tracking how much each user uses the network. The supervisor can set up each account to be charged a certain rate for various functions of the network. This process is referred to as accounting because it is often used by companies who want to charge each department for its use of the network.

Change Current Server

With the SYSCON program, the supervisor can manage up to eight file servers. He or she can perform all of the functions provided by SYSCON on each of the file servers attached to the network but not simultaneously. Through NetWare version 3.12, the supervisor must select the file server to be used, then create users or make other changes to each individual file server. Some other networks, most notably Banyan VINES, allow the supervisor to create users and groups that can login to any server attached to the network. NetWare version 4 also provides for a user to be set up as a network user, not just a user on a particular file server.

File Server Information

This option displays a list of information about the file server currently selected. Fig. 3-2 shows a typical File Server Information box. Note that it is a single line box, which means that the information in it cannot be changed.

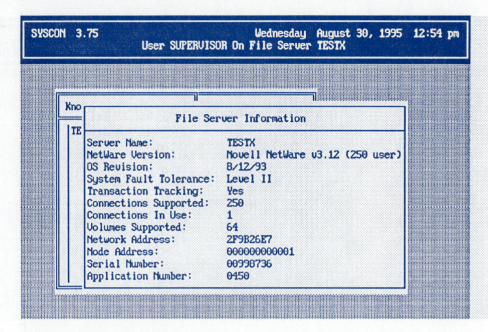

Fig. 3-2. File Server Information box.

Group Information

This selection displays a list of groups of users on this server. Each group name in the list can be selected to display a list of options available. The options are very similar to those available for individual users. Using carefully arranged groups, the supervisor can avoid many details when creating individual accounts and can make changes to the characteristics of many users by making changes to the groups to which they belong. Fig. 3-3 shows the list of groups on the left and the options available after a group has been selected on the right. Notice that create and delete a group are not listed as options. As in most of the NetWare utilities, creating a new item is accomplished by pressing the INSERT key and deleting an item is accomplished by highlighting it and pressing the DELETE key.

Supervisor Options

Not all the information for setting up a user account needs to be entered for each user or even each group. The supervisor has several options that can be used to establish defaults that will be in effect for each new user created. For instance, if the supervisor wanted login time restrictions for all of the new users, he or she could set those defaults from the Supervisor Options menu shown in Fig. 3-4. The defaults set in this menu do not affect existing users. Only users created after the default values have been saved are affected. Even then, characteristics of all users created using the default parameters can be manually reconfigured by the supervisor.

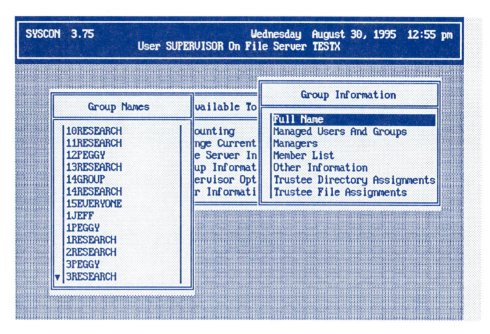

Fig. 3-3. Group Information for a file server.

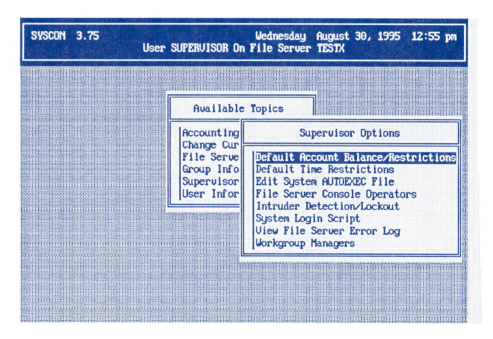

Fig. 3-4. Supervisor Options menu.

User Information

As in Group Information, the User Information option displays a list of existing user names. The supervisor can press INSERT to create a new user, press DELETE to delete a listed user, or highlight a user name and press the ENTER key to select it. Selecting a user name brings up the User Information menu, as shown in Fig. 3-5. This menu provides the most important options for running the network. From here the supervisor controls the most fundamental options a user has.

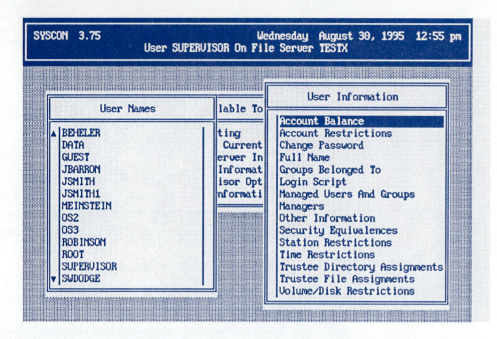

Fig. 3-5. The User Information menu.

The User Information Options

The User Information menu allows the supervisor to set up individual accounts and assign different attributes to each. The options available in this menu are:

1. Account Balance (appears only if Accounting is enabled)
2. Account Restrictions
3. Change Password
4. Full Name
5. Groups Belonged To
6. Intruder Lockout Status (appears only if enabled)
7. Login Script
8. Managed Users and Groups
9. Managers
10. Other Information
11. Security Equivalences
12. Station Restrictions
13. Time Restrictions

14. Trustee Directory Assignments
15. Trustee File Assignments
16. Volume/Disk Restrictions

Account Balance

This option allows supervisors to initialize and monitor a user's account balance. This option does not appear if Accounting has not been enabled on a given file server.

Account Restrictions

There are many separate options that can be set from the Account Restrictions menu as seen in Fig. 3-6. All of these options except Account Disabled can be set under the Supervisor Options as Default Account Balance/Restrictions (see Fig. 3-4). These options include the ability to limit the time periods during which a user can login, limit the number of simultaneous sessions under the same user ID, and limit the use of a password. The user can be forced to use a password or allowed to login without one. With a password he or she may or may not be allowed to change it, or may be forced to change it at specified intervals.

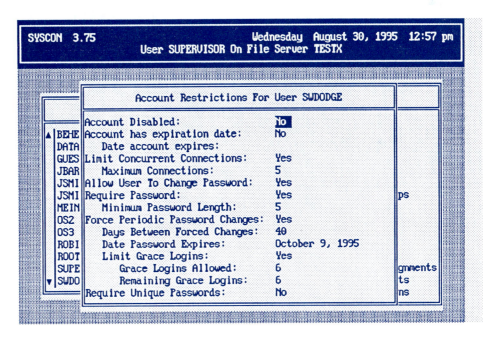

Fig. 3-6. The Account Restrictions menu.

Change Password

An important part of network security is the ability to frequently change the user's password. The user can change it (if this was allowed in the Account Restrictions menu) or the supervisor can change it using this option. Note that neither the user nor the supervisor can view an existing password, but can only change it.

Full Name

For accounting purposes a Full Name can be assigned to each user name. While a user name may be something like JSMITH the full name might be JOHN MAXIMILIAN SMITH.

Groups Belonged To

Each user may belong to several groups or to no groups at all. When selected, this option displays a list of all the groups a user belongs to on the right, as seen in Fig. 3-7.

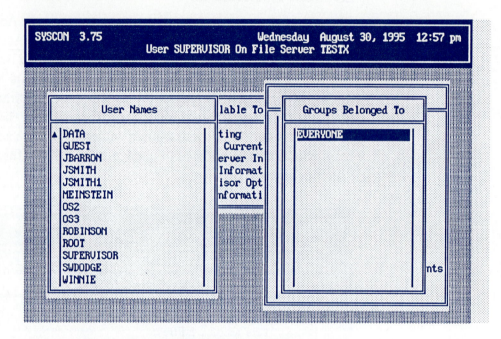

Fig. 3-7. Screen displaying a particular user's group.

Intruder Lockout Status

This option shows whether or not an account has been locked out due to Intruder Detection. The supervisor can reenable a locked account using this selection. Intruder Lockout Status appears only if Intruder Detection/Lockout, one of the Supervisor Options (Fig. 3-4), has been enabled

Login Scripts

NetWare allows each user name to have a login script which establishes much of the user's environment each time he or she logs in. SYSCON provides the supervisor with a simple editor for creating and modifying the login script. The login script in Fig. 3-8 performs several mapping operations such as mapping the \SOFTWARE\DATA directory to appear as the root directory of drive I. A message is displayed to the user, and finally the EXIT command sends a command to DOS to display a directory listing. All of these commands are executed each time the user DATA logs in. NetWare does not require each user to have a login script since the supervisor can set a System Login Script in the Supervisor Options menu. However, it is usually important that each user be given a login script for security reasons.

Earlier versions of NetWare were distributed with a mail package of questionable value. The existence of this mail package has influenced the directory structure of NetWare to this day. A weakness in NetWare is in its handling of login scripts and user mail. Specifically, they are both stored in the same directory, a subdirectory under the MAIL directory. Since every other user on the network must have create access to the mail directory in order to leave mail, those other users could conceivably create a login script and copy it to any user who did not already have a login script.

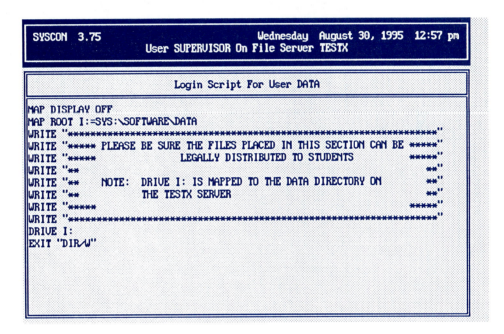

Fig. 3-8. A sample login script.

Managed Users and Groups

Fig. 3-9 shows a box that lists the users and groups which are managed by this user. It displays those users and groups to which the user can grant and revoke rights. The users and groups which are designated as Direct are specifically assigned to this user to manage. Those users and groups marked as Indirect arc managed by a group to which this user belongs.

Managers

This option specifies the managers of the user.

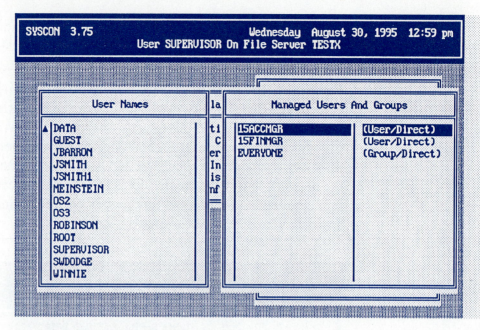

Fig. 3-9. Managed Users and Groups.

Other Information

This option displays information such as the date the user last logged in, disk space usage information, and the user ID number (the object ID for the user). The object ID identifies the users to the NetWare bindery and also identifies the subdirectory under the SYS:MAIL directory where the user's login script is stored.

Security Equivalences

After assigning all the directory rights and groups for one user, the supervisor may wish to duplicate those rights for another user. To do this, the supervisor can select Security Equivalences after creating the new user. From there the supervisor simply selects the name of an existing user or group from a list. This feature is commonly used to make users' security equivalent to the supervisor. It should be noted, however, that security equivalences should not be overused because they present difficulties when maintaining accounts. It is better to create a group, assign trustee rights to the group, and then make users members of the group.

Station Restrictions

Each network interface card on the network has a unique number consisting of the network number and the node number. Together they are known as the network address. The supervisor can restrict a user to logging in only at specific network addresses, which effectively means only at specific computers. This restriction should be used sparingly because it limits a user's ability to work on another station when his or her own machine is unavailable.

Time Restrictions

In addition to restricting a user to specific computers, the supervisor can also restrict a user to certain times of the day on certain days of the week. Fig. 3-10 shows the chart used by the supervisor to assign these times. Each asterisk represents a half hour interval. Here, user SWDODGE is given access to the network every day from 3:30 a.m. until 12:00 midnight.

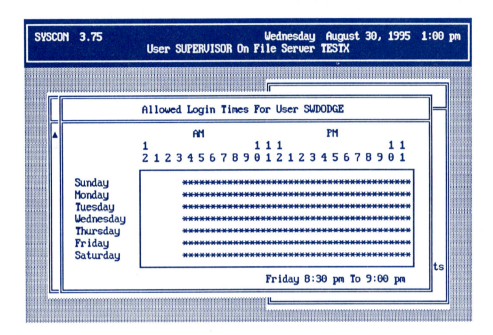

Fig. 3-10. Chart used to assign time restrictions.

Trustee Directory and File Assignments

When a user is given any access to a directory on the file server he or she is known as a trustee of that directory. The supervisor must assign the user as a trustee to each directory he or she will need to access. The supervisor must also assign which rights the user will have in each directory. This is the most direct way of making a user a trustee of a directory, but there are two other ways. First, the user could be a member of a group that is a trustee. Second, the user could be made a Security Equivalent to a user with access to a certain directory. Either way, a user must be given access to a directory to have any rights there. From a documentation point of view, it is better to give a user explicit rights to a directory rather than rely on security equivalences to obtain those rights.

Fig. 3-11 shows user DATA's trustee assignments. It does not show trustee assignments that DATA may have from being a member of a group or from being a Security Equivalent to another user. From the screen in Fig. 3-11 the supervisor has three options. First, by selecting a directory listed and pressing ENTER the supervisor can modify the rights user DATA has to one of those directories. Second, the supervisor can press DELETE on a directory to completely remove the user as a trustee. Third, the INSERT key can be used to add a new directory to the list. The ESCAPE key accepts any changes made, and SYSCON returns to the User Information menu.

Trustee File Assignments give rights to specific files rather than to all files in a directory. Explicit rights to a file override any earlier limitations in Trustee Directory assignments.

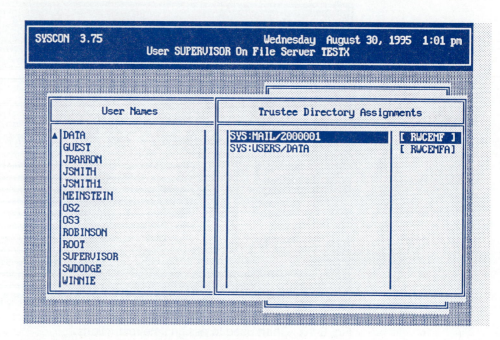

Fig. 3-11. Trustee assignments for user DATA.

Volume/Disk Restrictions

This option enables supervisors to limit the disk space a user may use on each volume of the file server. It also displays the amount of space a user has used on each volume. (See Fig. 3-12.)

Login Scripts

As mentioned earlier, every time a user logs in, NetWare executes the system login script, and then a user login script if one exists for that user. Its function is to issue all the commands needed to set up the user's environment. The environment, in this case, refers primarily to the drive mappings created for the user, but there are many other commands available in login scripts for customizing the login.

The login script is essentially a program that the supervisor writes using a strict set of rules and commands available. A user might type LOGIN JSMITH at the F> prompt after loading the appropriate network drivers. The

Chapter 3. The SYSCON Utility and Login Scripts

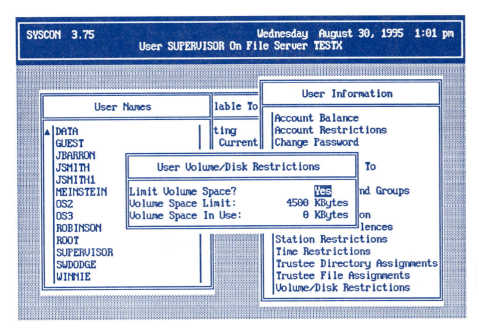

Fig. 3-12. Volume/Disk Restrictions.

LOGIN program checks the user name given and executes the system login script set up by the supervisor using SYSCON (see Fig. 3-4), and then executes the user's login script. Many of the commands that can be used in a login script can also be used from the command line. In other words, if the appropriate PATHs have been established, a user can issue several of the commands by typing the name of the command at the F> prompt. The ATTACH command is a good example. The ATTACH command can be used in a login script, and a program called ATTACH.EXE resides in the F:\PUBLIC directory. ATTACH.EXE performs exactly the same function as the ATTACH command in a login script.

The following is a list of login script commands and their uses. Items listed in parentheses are options that may be used. Notice the /user name option in the ATTACH command listed first. Since this option is shown inside the parentheses for the file server name option it can be used only if the file server name option is used and cannot be used by itself. Similarly, the ;password option is shown inside the parentheses for the /user name option, which indicates the ;password option cannot be used unless the /user name option in used. The "|" symbol between two options means one or the other may be used, but not both. Some commands require a parameter. In these cases the parameters are not shown in parentheses. In addition, some commands have several other forms. In such cases, the optional form or forms of the command are displayed following the default syntax.

1. ATTACH (file server name (/user name (;password)))
2. BREAK ON | OFF

3. COMSPEC = drive:(\)file name
   COMSPEC = *n:(\)file name
   COMSPEC = Sn:(\)file name
4. DISPLAY file name
   FDISPLAY file name
5. DOS BREAK ON | OFF
6. (DOS) SET name="value"
7. DOS VERIFY ON | OFF
8. DRIVE drive letter:
   DRIVE *drive number:
9. EXIT ("file name")
10. #program name with command line options
11. FIRE PHASERS number TIMES
12. IF condition (AND condition) THEN command
    IF condition (AND condition) THEN BEGIN
    commands
    END
13. INCLUDE file name
14. MACHINE = "name"
    MACHINE NAME = "name"
15. MAP
16. PAUSE
    WAIT
17. PCCOMPATIBLE
    COMPATIBLE
18. REMARK remark statement
    REM, *, or ; are all remark statements
19. WRITE "comment to be displayed"

Commands
ATTACH

Ordinarily a user logs in to a single file server using the LOGIN command. The ATTACH command in a login script attaches the user to another file server that may be on the same network. This command can also be executed from the command line. Suppose user JSMITH has an account with the same password on two file servers on the network called FS_ONE and FS_TWO.

JSMITH's workstation is normally connected to FS_ONE but he usually needs access to FS_TWO also. An ATTACH command could be placed in the login script of his account on FS_ONE that reads

    ATTACH FS_TWO

The LOGIN program will execute the ATTACH command and login JSMITH to FS_TWO using the same user name and password that was used on FS_ONE. The system and user login scripts on FS_TWO are not executed when access to FS_TWO is via the ATTACH command.

Another possibility is that JSMITH might log into any one of many workstations that may be connected to either file server, and he needs access to both servers. If he logs in at a workstation that is already connected to FS_ONE he would need to use the ATTACH command to log into FS_TWO. Likewise, if the workstation is already connected to FS_TWO, he would ATTACH to FS_ONE. In this case an ATTACH command would exist in the login scripts for both of the accounts. Each would ATTACH to the other file server. On FS_ONE the login script would read

    ATTACH FS_TWO

And on FS_TWO the login script command would be

    ATTACH FS_ONE

The other options of the ATTACH command are used only if the user name or password is different on the other file server. If user JSMITH's supervisor changed her mind about how much access he should have to FS_TWO, she could remove his account there and insist that he use another account for such purposes called STAFF with a password of PICNIC. JSMITH's login script on FS_ONE would now read

    ATTACH FS_TWO/STAFF;PICNIC

The login script for the STAFF account would not need an ATTACH command.

Note that although the syntax of the ATTACH command allows for a password to be explicitly coded in the login script, it is not usually a good idea to do so because it limits the ability to change the password regularly without changing the login script.

BREAK

The BREAK command controls how the keyboard responds during execution of the login script. If the command BREAK ON is used, the login script can be halted by holding down the CONTROL key and pressing BREAK. The BREAK key may also be labeled SCROLL LOCK. If the command is in the form BREAK OFF, the execution of the login script cannot be stopped with CONTROL-BREAK. Note that this command affects only the execution of the login script.

COMSPEC

The COMSPEC command can be very important to the proper operation of the workstation. DOS always keeps a pointer (called the COMSPEC environment variable) to the file containing the command processor program. The command processor provided with every version of DOS is a program called COMMAND.COM. DOS must be told where this file is located because it must often be reloaded into memory after the execution of a program. Ordinarily when a computer is booted the COMSPEC variable is set to point to the COMMAND.COM that was used to boot the computer. If the computer was booted from floppy disk drive A:, the COMSPEC variable would probably read

COMSPEC=A:\COMMAND.COM.

But if the boot disk was then removed, COMMAND.COM would no longer reside where the COMSPEC variable points to. If this computer were on a network, the COMSPEC variable could be set to point to a copy of COMMAND.COM on a network drive where it cannot be removed.

The COMSPEC login script command allows the variable to be set automatically when the user logs in. In its simplest form, the command COMSPEC = drive:(\)filename sets the COMSPEC variable to a value such as

COMSPEC = F:COMMAND.COM

where F: has already been mapped to a directory containing a copy of COMMAND.COM. The drive option can indicate any drive letter that exists at the time the COMSPEC command is executed.

The two other forms of the command allow the COMSPEC variable to be set to a value that is indicated at the time the login script is executed. An "*n:" indicates a drive number that might be used in the login script. The command might read

COMSPEC = *2:COMMAND.COM

The result is to set the COMSPEC variable to point to a copy of COMMAND.COM in a directory on the second network drive, already mapped to whatever the drive letter may be.

The "Sn:" in the third form of the command indicates a search drive number. Under NetWare, a special type of drive mapping called a search drive can be made to allow the computer to automatically search a directory for a program that is not in the current directory. When mapping such a search drive, the user maps a search drive number such as S1: or S2:. NetWare designates the associated drive letter by starting at the end of the alphabet, so S1: becomes drive letter Z: and S2: becomes Y: unless those letters are already in use. By using a command such as

COMSPEC = S1:COMMAND.COM

the supervisor can ensure that the COMSPEC variable points to the first search drive already assigned, without knowing what drive letter it is using.

In any of the three forms of this command, the drive letter used should point to the directory containing the COMMAND.COM program, because the command accepts only twelve characters after the drive specification. With this restriction a command such as

>COMSPEC = S1:\DOS\COMMAND.COM

would not be legal. The path \DOS\COMMAND.COM is too long.

DISPLAY

Using the DISPLAY command, a message can be displayed on the screen each time a user logs in. The message is contained in a file represented by the file name option in the command. The file name can include a complete directory path such as

>DISPLAY F:\PUBLIC\MESSAGE.TXT

DISPLAY is used when the file contains only the ASCII characters that are to be displayed. FDISPLAY is used when the file contains control characters placed there by a word processing program that are not intended to be displayed. FDISPLAY will filter out these characters before printing the message on the screen.

(DOS) BREAK

DOS also has a BREAK command. This login script command sets the DOS environment variable to BREAK ON or BREAK OFF.

(DOS) SET

The SET command is used to set any DOS environment variable to any value. These values can be checked later by other login script commands, batch file commands, or other programs. This command is identical in function to the DOS command SET. The only differences are the optional word DOS and the use of quotation marks around the value in the login script command. Some examples are

>DOS SET USER="JANE"

>SET ROOM="D229"

>SET PROMPT="PG"

Several login script variables can be used to place special values in an environment variable. These variables will be discussed later.

DOS VERIFY

The DOS VERIFY flag can be set so that each time a file is copied DOS will read the newly created copy and compare it with the original to ensure it is correct. The login script command DOS VERIFY can be used to turn this feature on or off.

DRIVE

The drive command is used to set the default drive. Normally the default drive is the first network drive, usually drive F. With the DRIVE drive letter: command it can be set to any valid local or network drive letter. The DRIVE *drive number: form of the command is used to set the default drive to a number indicating the order in which the drive was mapped. For instance, the command

>DRIVE *1:

would set the default drive to the first network drive letter, which might be F.

The command

>DRIVE C:

could be used to set the default drive to be the local hard disk drive C:

EXIT

The EXIT command is used to terminate a login script and to start another program. It is often necessary to start another program, usually a menu program, at the conclusion of the login script. When the LOGIN.EXE program finishes processing the login script, it can pass control on to any executable program named in the parameter "file name". For example, if user JSMITH needed a menu program called MENU.EXE executed each time he logged in, the last line in his login script might be

>EXIT "F:MENU"

The item in quotes can actually be any DOS command as long as it is fourteen characters or less in length. Therefore, in addition to any executable program, any batch file or DOS internal command can be used. For example, suppose a user simply needed a directory listing each time he logged in. The last line in the login script would be

>EXIT "DIR /W"

The login script for user DATA in Fig. 3-8 uses the EXIT command in this way. Since the option in quotes is sent directly to DOS, drive numbers cannot be used. Also, programs that terminate and stay resident should not be used.

#Program Name with Command Line Options

The "#" symbol is known as the External Program Execution command. This command tells the LOGIN program to temporarily suspend its operations to load and run the program named. When the program is finished, control is returned to the LOGIN program and the login script resumes execution at the next line. The program called by the External Program Execution command must have either an .EXE or .COM extension, but it can be called from any directory with any command line options it needs. The login script command

>#F:\APPS\LOTUS\LOTUS COLOR.SET

loads and executes a program called LOTUS from the F:\APPS\LOTUS directory and passes the command line parameter COLOR.SET to it. As with the EXIT command, terminate and stay resident programs are excluded.

The example above, however, would be a very unusual case since after the user exited the LOTUS program, control would return to the LOGIN program and the rest of the login script would be executed.

FIRE PHASERS

The FIRE PHASERS command is used to catch the user's attention by generating a science fiction-like sound. The "number" parameter tells the login script how many times to make the sound. The command

>   FIRE PHASERS 3 TIMES

would cause the alarm to sound three times. This command should be used judiciously, especially if it is placed in the System Login Script which is executed by all users. Execution of this command must totally complete prior to the login script's continuing.

IF Statement

This command structure allows the login script to test conditions and execute different commands based on the result. The command executed as a result of the comparison can be any valid login script command. In the diagram of the IF THEN structure, the "condition" represents a true or false comparison of two items. The comparison will always be in the form

>   ITEM OPERATOR ITEM

where the operator tests the relationship between the two items. In the first form of the command, a single command is executed as the result of any number of comparisons, if they are all true. In the second form of the command, the key word BEGIN is used to start a list of commands to be executed. The key word END is used to indicate the end of the list of commands. Between the BEGIN and END may be any number of commands that will be executed only if all the conditions are true. It is important to note that the IF THEN statement must be allowed to wrap naturally when it extends beyond one line of the screen. Also, the IF THEN with the BEGIN and END option must be allowed to wrap naturally until the BEGIN has been entered. Then, each additional command should wrap naturally with the ENTER key being pressed at the end of each command.

The IF THEN command will accept many different operators in the testing of the two items, as shown below:

To represent equal	To represent not equal
IS	IS NOT
=	!=
==	<>
EQUALS	#
	DOES NOT EQUAL
	NOT EQUAL TO

Four more relationships can be tested using the following operators. Either the symbols on the right or the words on the left may be used in the IF THEN command.

IS GREATER THAN	>
IS LESS THAN	<
IS GREATER THAN OR EQUAL TO	>=
IS LESS THAN OR EQUAL TO	<=

Several pairs of items can be compared using the AND operator. Also, the AND operator may be replaced with a comma. Comparisons such as these are possible:

IF DAY_OF_WEEK IS "Monday" AND HOUR >= "09"

THEN SET NOW="*"

This command tests whether a variable DAY_OF_WEEK is equal to Monday and checks whether a variable HOUR is greater than or equal to 9. If both conditions are true a DOS environment variable NOW is given a value of "*".

IF DAY > THAN "15", DAY_OF_WEEK IS NOT "Sunday"

THEN BEGIN

FIRE PHASERS 2 TIMES

DOS SET REMIND="Pay the bills today!"

END

This command checks to see if the day of the month is greater than 15 and makes sure the day of the week is not Sunday. If those conditions are met, the alarm will sound two times and a DOS environment variable is set to the string "Pay the bills today!"

The variables DAY, DAY_OF_WEEK, and HOUR are login script variables that are set before execution of the login script. Many more such variables are available for use in the IF THEN command as well as other commands. The following is a complete list of the login script identifier variables available. (Note that all are character variables and, as such, must be compared to constant values in double quotes.)

Variable	Possible Values
AM_PM	(am or pm)
DAY	(01 - 31)
DAY_OF_WEEK	(Sunday - Saturday)
ERROR_LEVEL	(0 - 255)
FULL_NAME	(The user's full name recorded in SYSCON)
GREETING_TIME	(Morning, Afternoon, Evening)
HOUR	(1 - 12)
HOUR24	(00 - 24)
LOGIN_NAME	(The user's login name)
MACHINE	(The name of the workstation type of computer)
MEMBER OF	(The MEMBER OF variable is a special case in that it is not used with a comparison operator. It is used to check if the user is a member of a given group.)
MINUTE	(00 - 59)
MONTH	(01 - 12)
MONTH_NAME	(January - December)
NDAY_OF_WEEK	(1 - 7 where Sunday is 1 and Saturday is 7)
NEW_MAIL	(YES or NO indicating whether new mail is waiting for the user)
OS	(The operating system running on the users' workstation)
OS_VERSION	(The version number of a DOS workstation)
P_STATION	(The physical node number of the workstation)
SECOND	(00 - 59)

SHELL_TYPE	(A code number indicating the type of network shell running on the user's workstation)
SHORT_YEAR	(The last two digits of the year)
SMACHINE	(A shortened name for the workstation type)
STATION	(The connection number assigned to the workstation)
YEAR	(The year)

INCLUDE

This login script command tells the login script to pull in a second file as a part of the currently executing login script. When the commands are finished executing in the second login script, control is returned to the calling login script. Each script file can call other script files to a maximum of ten login scripts.

Nesting login scripts in this way can be very helpful if many different users need a section of their login script to be the same, but heavy nesting is not recommended because it makes documenting a user's actual login script unneccesarily difficult.

MACHINE

The MACHINE command sets the MACHINE variable to a name intended to represent the type of workstation computer being used. The two forms of the command are equivalent.

MAP

The MAP command is used to display or set the drive mappings of the workstation. It assigns drive letters to directories on the file server or drives on the local workstation or displays those assignments. There are fourteen separate forms of this command, each requiring a complete description. This command is another in which the login script variables can be used. Directory names used in the MAP command can contain login script variables preceded by a "%".

Suppose that F: is mapped to volume SYS:\ and that a directory has been created for each user with the user's name being the name of the directory. For user JSMITH the directory would be F:\JSMITH. A directory for each user is usually referred to as a user's home directory. Each user might need a drive letter assigned to his or her home directory in the login script. To do this a MAP command could be placed in each user's login script that includes the login script variable LOGIN_NAME.

> MAP H:=F:\%LOGIN_NAME

When LOGIN.EXE executes this command it will replace the %LOGIN_NAME with the individual user's name and, in the case of user JSMITH, the result would be

    MAP H:=F:\JSMITH

giving the user a new drive letter H: that points to the F:\JSMITH directory.

In its simplest form, the MAP command alone displays all drive letter assignments, including the drive letters assigned to local disk drives. The command

    MAP drive:

displays the directory or local drive that the drive letter listed points to.

    MAP drive:=directory

sets the drive letter listed to point to the directory listed. The directory may contain the volume name.

    MAP drive:=directory ; drive:=directory ; ...

shows that multiple drive letter assignments may be made following a single MAP command. Each assignment is separated by a semicolon.

    MAP directory

changes the current drive letter to point to the directory listed. The directory may contain a volume name.

    MAP drive:=

assigns the drive letter listed to point to the current directory.

    MAP drive:=drive:

assigns the drive letter on the left to point to the directory pointed to by the drive letter on the right.

    MAP INSERT search drive:=directory

creates a new search drive pointing to the directory listed.

    MAP DEL drive:

deletes the drive letter assignment.

    MAP REM drive:

removes the drive letter assignment, exactly the same as the MAP DEL command.

    MAP DISPLAY OFF

instructs LOGIN.EXE not to display the drive mappings made when the user logs in. Ordinarily the drive mappings are displayed.

MAP DISPLAY ON

explicitly tells the LOGIN.EXE program to display the drive mappings when the user logs in.

MAP ERRORS OFF

instructs LOGIN.EXE not to display any error messages that may be generated as a result of an incorrect MAP command in the login script. Ordinarily all errors would be displayed.

MAP ERRORS ON

explicitly tells the LOGIN.EXE program to display all error messages concerning MAP commands in the login script.

PAUSE

The login script command PAUSE works exactly the same as the DOS batch file command of the same name. It halts execution of the login script and displays the message "Strike a key when ready...". After the user presses a key the login script is resumed at the next command. The word WAIT may be used for the same function.

PCCOMPATIBLE

This command is only necessary when the workstation has been set to identify itself incorrectly as not being an IBM PC-compatible computer. It allows other commands in the login script to treat the workstation as compatible, even though the login script variables MACHINE and SMACHINE may indicate a different type of computer. The two forms of the command, PCCOMPATIBLE and COMPATIBLE are, of course, completely compatible.

REMARK

Often the supervisor will wish to place remarks or comments in the text of the login script that are not intended to be executed. These might include explanations of a particularly complex IF THEN structure, the need for various drive mappings, or a message for future supervisors. Any one of the four forms of the REMARK command will prevent LOGIN.EXE from attempting to execute the remark statement following it. They are REMARK, REM, * (asterisk), and ; (semicolon).

WRITE

The WRITE command is roughly equivalent to the PRINT command in the BASIC programming language or the ECHO command in a batch file. It displays the text following it on the user's screen at the time it is executed. The easiest way to use the WRITE command is to simply put a message in quotes.

WRITE "Welcome to file server FS_ONE."

The WRITE command above would tell the user which file server he or she just logged in to. But WRITE commands can be much more flexible. The text to be displayed can use the same login script variables that the IF THEN command can use. As in the MAP command the variable is preceded by a "%" to tell the LOGIN.EXE program to convert it to the value it represents. In the command

WRITE "Welcome %LOGIN_NAME to file server FS_ONE."

the %LOGIN_NAME would be converted to the user name. In the case of user JSMITH, the message displayed would read;

Welcome JSMITH to file server FS_ONE.

The login script variables can also be used outside the quotes without the preceding "%". The command

WRITE "Welcome ";LOGIN_NAME;", to file server FS_ONE."

is exactly equivalent to the write command above. Notice that a semicolon is used to separate the components of the text when a variable is used outside the quotes and without the "%". Also note that identifier variables must be in upper case in most instances, so it is a good idea to use upper case all the time.

In addition to the login script variables, there are four special symbols that may be used within the quotes to control the format of the text printed on the screen. They appear in Table 3-1.

Symbol	Description
\r	Carriage return. Causes the cursor to return to column one on the same line of the screen.
\n	New line. Causes the cursor to go to the first column of the next line.
\"	Embedded quotation mark. Must be used to display a quotation.
\7	ASCII character seven. Causes a beep sound to be generated.

Table 3-1. Format symbols.

The WRITE command below shows the effects of some of these symbols.

WRITE "HAPPY\n   \"BIRTHDAY\"\n   ";LOGIN_NAME

For user JSMITH, the output on the screen would look like this:

HAPPY

"BIRTHDAY"

JSMITH

The login script commands listed above give the supervisor a very powerful language to meet the user's needs. With them a user's environment can be constructed to allow him or her to use the network freely or to take the user directly into an application. The possibilities are endless.

In the next section of this chapter, SYSCON will be used to create users, assign them trustee rights, and create login scripts.

Hands-on NetWare

In the previous chapter, Novell NetWare was completely installed on a file server. However, the installation of the NetWare software was only a small part of creating a usable network. The structure of the directories, the creation of user accounts, the setting up of network printers, and many other tasks will require much more work and thought. A network's supervisor is the one who must consider how the network will be used and determine how best to serve each user, while maintaining overall system continuity and security.

When NetWare is installed, a user account is automatically created called SUPERVISOR. It has complete trustee rights over the entire server and permission to use all menus in each of the NetWare utilities. Originally the account has no password, so the first thing that should be done on any newly installed Novell network is to give the user SUPERVISOR a password. To do this, the file server must be running, and a workstation must be booted with the proper network drivers. In this section you will prepare the server and workstation for operation, login to the network, start the SYSCON utility, and give the account SUPERVISOR a password of FIRST. All commands shown here are written in upper case characters for clarity. However, they can be entered as either upper or lower case.

Preparing the Network for Operation

1. Prepare the server for operation by simply turning it on. A message saying that the LAN is initializing and the volumes are being mounted should appear.
2. Boot the workstation. If the computer is off, simply turn it on. If the computer is on, press the CTRL, ALT, and DELETE keys simultaneously.

If you are using the IPXODI version, your AUTOEXEC.BAT should already be modified to load the shell. Otherwise, you must do steps 3 through 6.

3. Type **LSL** and press ENTER

4. Type the name of your NIC driver and press ENTER

5. The network drivers must now be loaded into memory. Type **IPXODI** and press the ENTER key. A message should appear confirming that the IPXODI program has successfully loaded.

6. Type the VLM which will load the appropriate workstation VLMs.

If the workstation booted successfully and the network drivers were loaded successfully, the screen should appear similar to the one in Fig. 3-13. The DOS version, the version and type of IPXODI, and the version of the VLM program may all be different. The "C>" prompt shows the default drive is still the local drive C:. To perform any network operations it is necessary to access the network drive, typically F.

```
Novell Turbo RxNet & RxNet/2 MLID   v1.35 (921221)
(C) Copyright 1991 - 1992 Novell, Inc.  All Rights Reserved.

Int 4, Port 350, Mem E0000, Node Address 43 L
Max Frame 4202 bytes, Line Speed 2500 Kbps
Board 1, Frame NOVELL_RX-NET, LSB Mode

C:\NWCLIENT>lh C:\NWCLIENT\IPXODI

NetWare IPX/SPX Protocol  v2.12 (931007)
(C) Copyright 1990-1993 Novell, Inc.  All Rights Reserved.

Bound to logical board 1 (TRXNET) : Protocol ID FA

C:\NWCLIENT>lh C:\NWCLIENT\VLM
VLM.EXE    - NetWare virtual loadable module manager  v1.10 (931209)
(C) Copyright 1993 Novell, Inc.  All Rights Reserved.
Patent pending.

The VLM.EXE file is pre-initializing the VLMs.............
The VLM.EXE file is using extended memory (XMS).
You are attached to server TESTX

C:\NWCLIENT>
C:\NWCLIENT>
```

Fig. 3-13. Screen displaying a successful load of network drivers.

Logging In

Once the network drivers have been loaded, the workstation is attached to the file server, but no one is logged in. Logging in tells the file server who the user is and how much access that user has.

1. Type **F:** and press the ENTER key. At this point no user is logged in, so the workstation has only limited access to the server.

2. Type **DIR** and press the ENTER key. The files available to all workstations, whether a user is logged in or not, should be displayed on the screen or scroll by depending on how many files are stored in the system. They are stored in a directory already created by NetWare called F:\LOGIN.

3. Type **LOGIN SUPERVISOR** and press the ENTER key.

If the system asks for a password, type the password for SUPERVISOR and press ENTER.

Starting the SYSCON Utility

The SYSCON utility is a program on the file server stored in a directory called F:\PUBLIC. It is used for much of the setup and maintenance a supervisor must do.

1. Type **CD\PUBLIC** and press the ENTER key.

2. Type **DIR** and press the ENTER key. This step is included to familiarize you with the environment of the file server. A directory listing of all the files the NetWare installation program has placed in the PUBLIC directory should scroll by. The list is quite long and represents all the NetWare utilities a general user might need. The SYSCON utility is here because a user can view or modify many of his or her own attributes.

3. Type **SYSCON** and press the ENTER key. SYSCON's main menu should appear, similar to the screen in Fig. 3-14.

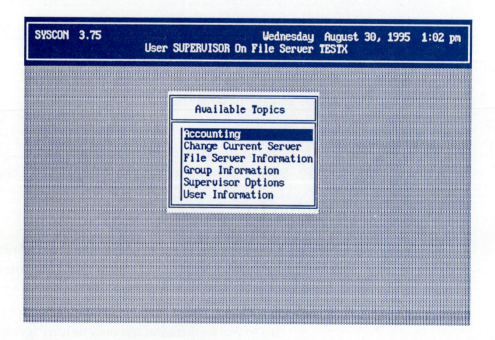

Fig. 3-14. The SYSCON main menu.

CHAPTER 3. THE SYSCON UTILITY AND LOGIN SCRIPTS

Changing a User Password

Each user account on a NetWare file server can be given a password. The password is intended to be kept secret so that only a certain person or set of people can access the account. The user's name is intended to be public so everyone on the network can interact with the user through electronic mail or other network services. The supervisor's account is a special case in two respects. It is absolutely important that unauthorized people do not use the supervisor account, and it is absolutely critical that the supervisor does. If a user forgets his password the supervisor can change it to a new one. But, if the supervisor forgets his or her own password and has not created a supervisor-equivalent user, NetWare must be reinstalled. A good idea is to write down the supervisor password and place it in a sealed envelope. Then, place the envelope in a secure place such as a locked cabinet or vault.

Remember that, in a NetWare utility, an item can be highlighted by moving the cursor or by typing the name of the item to be selected. A list of users on a large network can be quite long, so the easiest way to find the supervisor account is to type SUPERVISOR. The cursor will move to the first occurrence of the letters typed. For instance, when "S" is typed the alphabetically first user name that begins with "S" will be highlighted. If the only other name that began with "S" was SUE, it would stay highlighted until the "P" in the word supervisor was typed.

1. Move the cursor down to User Information and press the ENTER key. The list of user accounts should appear.
2. Press the ENTER key when the user name SUPERVISOR has been highlighted and the User Information box will be displayed on the right side of the screen.

Notice that there are now three menu boxes on the screen. Only one menu is active at any one time, and SYSCON tells the user which one by highlighting the border of the active box.

3. Move the cursor down to the option Change Password and then press the ENTER key. Another box will appear at the bottom of the screen as shown in Fig. 3-15.

   The Change Password option will not display the old password; it only prompts for a new one. In fact, there is no method for finding out what a current password is. Even as a password is typed, it is not displayed on the screen. When ENTER is pressed after typing a password, the password box flickers away for an instant and returns. The password must be typed a second time for verification. If the two entries do not match, the user must start over.

4. In either upper or lower case letters, type the word **FIRST** and press the ENTER key.

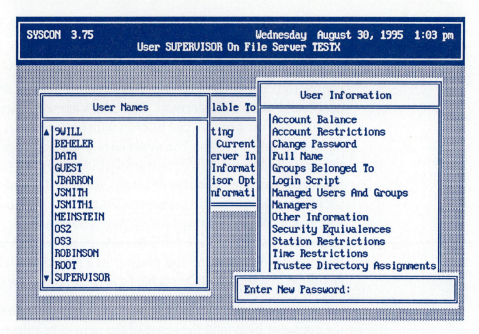

Fig. 3-15. Screen displaying dialog box to change the password.

5. Type **FIRST** again to verify and press the ENTER key. When this operation has been completed, the cursor will return to the User Information menu.

Testing the Password

Presumably, the password has been set to the word FIRST, but, as with any complex system, nothing can be believed until it has been tested. In some situations the supervisor will create all user passwords and not allow any changes. In others, the supervisor only creates an initial password. After the user has logged in, he or she may be allowed to change it. In either case, a good supervisor will test everything possible. To test a password, the user must log out of the network, then log back in.

1. Press the ESC key several times until you see the SYSCON final menu box, as shown in Fig. 3-16.
2. Select Yes to exit SYSCON by pressing Y and the ENTER key.
3. At the F> prompt type **LOGOUT** and press the ENTER key. A message should appear saying what time user SUPERVISOR logged out, from which station, and from which server.
4. At this point the workstation is still attached to the file server. Type **DIR** and the listing of the F:\LOGIN directory should be displayed on the screen or scroll by as it did earlier in the Logging In section.
5. Type **LOGIN SUPERVISOR** and press the ENTER key.
6. Type **FIRST** at the password prompt and press the ENTER key.

CHAPTER 3. THE SYSCON UTILITY AND LOGIN SCRIPTS

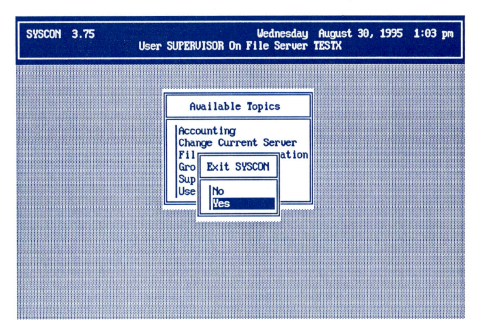

Fig. 3-16. Exit option from the SYSCON utility.

The word FIRST will not appear on the screen as it is typed. If you were able to login successfully, the password was correctly entered in SYSCON twice and in the LOGIN program once. As a general rule, after changing a password, if you cannot login using the password, try variations of misspellings of the word.

    7. To complete the exercise, type **LOGOUT** again and press the ENTER key.

After installing NetWare and giving the account SUPERVISOR a suitable password, the system supervisor should use the actual SUPERVISOR account as little as possible. For maximum security, new user accounts should be created that allow the supervisor to perform the tasks required of him or her at lower security levels. The supervisor account is simply too important and powerful to use frequently. In the next section a new user will be created. This user will be able to perform all supervisor tasks needed for the rest of the exercises in this book.

Creating a User Account

Only the supervisor, a supervisor equivalent, or a workgroup manager can create accounts. The last section ended by giving the supervisor account the password FIRST. That account and password must be used again to create supervisor equivalent accounts to be used for the exercises after this chapter. The file server and the workstation must be running, and the network drivers should be loaded on the workstation for the following steps.

To enter SYSCON
1. Type **F:** and press the ENTER key.
2. Type **LOGIN SUPERVISOR** and press the ENTER key.
3. Type **FIRST** at the password prompt and press the ENTER key. The word FIRST will not appear on the screen as it is typed.
4. Type **CD\PUBLIC** and press the ENTER key.
5. Type **SYSCON** and press the ENTER key.
6. Highlight Accounting and press the ENTER key.
7. If an Install Accounting? message appears, press Y and press the ENTER key.
8. Press the ESC key.

The User Information Menu

Creating a new user in SYSCON involves using the User Information Menu. This menu is not reached directly; it appears only after a user name has been selected. If the user name does not yet exist, it must be inserted into the list of user names. When the User Information option is selected from the SYSCON main menu, the list of names appears first. After a name has been selected or inserted, the User Information menu allows the supervisor to establish the users' attributes such as trustee rights, group status, and login scripts.

1. Move the cursor to the User Information line and press the ENTER key. The list of users should appear on the left of the screen.
2. Press the INSERT key. A box asking for a new user name should appear in the center of the screen.
3. To establish a unique user name for each student on the network, type in your first initial and last name, then press the ENTER key. A message could appear informing you that name already exists. If it does, try a different form of your name.
4. Press the ENTER key. A box appears giving a suggested name for a directory to be created for the user's home directory.
5. Press ESC to reject.
6. Press ENTER on the highlighted new user name.

When a user name has been successfully entered, the user's name should be in the list of users on the left and the User Information menu should be on the right. In the following sections, most of the options in the User Information menu will be used.

Checking the Account Balance

Depending on how other options may have been set, this user may be charged for connect time. By setting charge rates and account balances the supervisor can limit the time a user is connected to the network or how many of the network services a user can access without checking with the supervisor. When creating a new user, it is important to ensure that the account balance allows the user to login.

1. Highlight the Account Balance line in the User Information menu and press the ENTER key. A small box similar to the one in Fig. 3-17 should appear.
2. Move the cursor to the line that reads Allow Unlimited Credit.
3. Press the Y and ENTER keys.
4. Press the ESC key to accept the changes and return to the User Information menu.

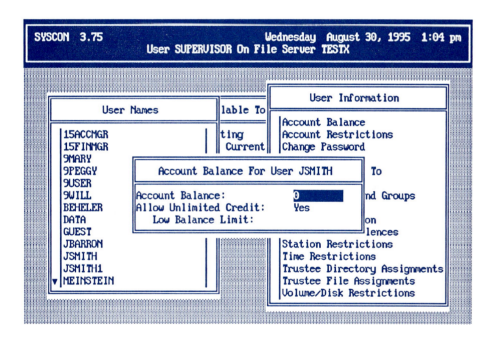

Fig. 3-17. Account balance dialog box.

The Account Restrictions Menu

This screen allows you to change many of the fundamental attributes of the account. The cursor can be moved up or down the list of account restrictions. When an item is highlighted, a new value can be simply typed in. The ESCAPE key is used to accept the changes after all modifications have been made. Follow the instructions below to ensure that all of the values are correct. Move the highlighted area to the appropriate field by pressing the up or down cursor keys.

Before proceeding make sure the Accounting feature is turned on for this server.

1. From the SYSCON Available Topics menu, highlight Accounting.
2. Press ENTER.
3. Press Y to answer Yes to Install Accounting (this will show up if Accounting is off).
4. Press the ESC key to exit the Accounting menu options.

Now you are ready to proceed with the Account Restrictions menu.

1. Move the cursor to the Account Restrictions line of the User Information menu and press the ENTER key. A large box should appear with the title Account Restrictions For User USERNAME. (Here, USERNAME is a generic term that represents the name of the user that you are working with.)
2. The field at the end of the Account Disabled line should now be highlighted and should say No.
3. Account Has Expiration Date should say No. Without an expiration date, the cursor will skip to the Limit Concurrent Connections field when the down cursor key is pressed. Move the cursor to this option.
4. Press the Y and ENTER keys. The cursor should move to the Maximum Connections field.
5. Press the 1 and ENTER keys. With a one in this field only one workstation can be logged in under this user name.
6. With the cursor on the Allow User To Change Password field, press the Y and ENTER keys.
7. With the cursor on the Require Password field, press the Y and ENTER keys.
8. With the cursor on the Minimum Password Length field, press the 4 key and press the ENTER key.
9. With the cursor on the Force Periodic Password Changes field, press the N and ENTER keys.
10. With the cursor on the Require Unique Passwords field, press the N and ENTER keys.
11. Press the ESC key to return to the SYSCON User Information menu.

Creating a Password

This account will need to be password protected just as the supervisor account is. Ordinarily a password should be unusual and not associated with the user in any way.

1. Highlight the Change Password option on the User Information menu and press the ENTER key.
2. Type the word **NEWPASS** in the box provided and press the ENTER key. The word will not show on the screen as it is typed.
3. For verification the password must be entered again. Type the word **NEWPASS** and press the ENTER key.

Creating a Login Script

To facilitate this user's access to the network, a login script can be created which maps search drives to frequently used directories. The directories that would be helpful are F:\PUBLIC, F:\SYSTEM and F:\LOGIN. Other information may be put in a login script that displays a message when the user logs in.

The following steps create a login script that maps the proper search drives and displays an interesting message.

1. Select the Login Script option from the User Information menu by highlighting Login Script and pressing the ENTER key.

Since this user does not have a login script, SYSCON offers to make a copy of another login script. A Copy Login Script From box appears to allow you to type in the name of another user with a login script.

2. Press the ENTER key to indicate that no other login script is to be used. A blank screen similar to the one in Fig. 3-18 should appear.

At this point, any login script can be typed in. Like most word processors, the cursor keys move only where characters or spaces have been typed. The login script can be any length because the screen inside the box will scroll as it is filled up. Also, the INSERT and DELETE keys function much as they would in any full screen editor.

3. Type **MAP S1:=SYS:\PUBLIC** and press the ENTER key.
4. Type **MAP S2:=SYS:\SYSTEM** and press the ENTER key.
5. Type **MAP S3:=SYS:\LOGIN** and press the ENTER key.
6. Type **IF DAY_OF_WEEK IS "Monday" WRITE "Monday Again!"** (all on one line) and press the ENTER key.

7. Type **WRITE "Another %DAY_OF_WEEK %GREETING_TIME."** (all on one line) and press the ENTER key.
8. Press the ESC key. A box will appear asking you if you want to save the changes.
9. Press the Y and ENTER keys. The User Information menu should reappear.

The SYS: in the above login script commands specifies a volume on the file server. Volumes are major divisions of the file server's hard disk.

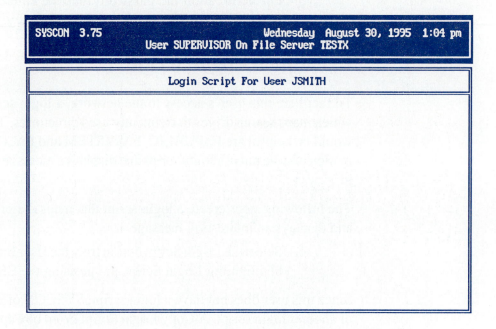

Fig. 3-18. Data entry screen for creating login scripts.

Setting the Security Equivalences

On any NetWare network, there should be at least one account that has a security equivalence to user SUPERVISOR. That other account should be used most of the time that supervisor maintenance is required. In this exercise the user account will be given supervisor security equivalence.

1. Highlight the Security Equivalences option in the User Information menu and press the ENTER key. A list of current security equivalences for this user will appear on the right side of the screen as it does in Fig. 3-19.
2. Press the INSERT key.
3. Type the word **SUPERVISOR**. As the word SUPERVISOR is typed the highlighted bar will move along a list of users and groups of users until user SUPERVISOR is marked.

4. Press the ENTER key on the user SUPERVISOR. SUPERVISOR will be added to the list of security equivalences.

5. Press the ESC key to accept the changes and return to the User Information menu.

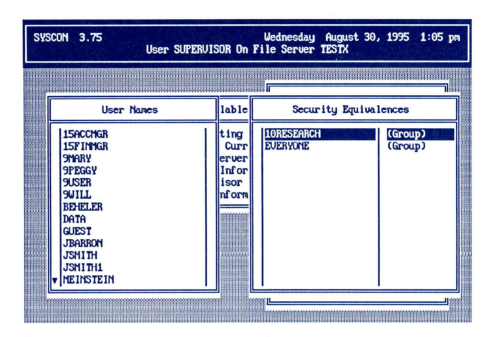

Fig. 3-19. Screen displaying security equivalences for a user.

Setting Trustee Directory Assignments

Directory access rights are called Trustee Directory Assignments in NetWare. Each user with privileges in a certain directory is said to be a trustee of that directory. In this example the user being created is equivalent to user SUPERVISOR and so is automatically given trustee rights in all directories. However, most users will not be given such rights. The following steps demonstrate the process of modifying the trustee privileges of a user.

1. Highlight the Trustee Directory Assignments option of the User Information menu and press the ENTER key. The current Trustee Assignments for this user will be displayed on the right of the screen.

2. To add a trustee assignment to this list, press the INSERT key twice.

A long box labeled Directory In Which Trustee Should Be Added will appear near the top of the screen when you press INSERT the first time. The complete directory name could be typed in at this point, but SYSCON allows you to select from the available directories also if you press INSERT again.

3. Press the ENTER key on the file server name.

4. With volume SYS highlighted, press the ENTER key. A list of directories should appear.
5. Move the cursor to the SYSTEM directory and press the ENTER key.
6. Press the ESC key to accept the directory as it is shown in the long box along the top of the screen and press the ENTER key.

A new directory should now be in the list of trustee assignments. But when an assignment is made, the default values for access rights are only Read and File Scan as denoted by the [R   F] after the directory name.

7. Highlight the SYS:SYSTEM directory in the Trustee Assignments box and press the ENTER key. The Trustee Rights Granted box will appear on the left of the screen.
8. Press the INSERT key and a Trustee Rights Not Granted box will appear on the right.

Fig. 3-20 shows the two boxes. Each right that needs to be granted to this user can be selected individually or a number of them can be marked and granted all at once. Most of the time a block of rights will need to be given to a user, so that is what will be done in this case.

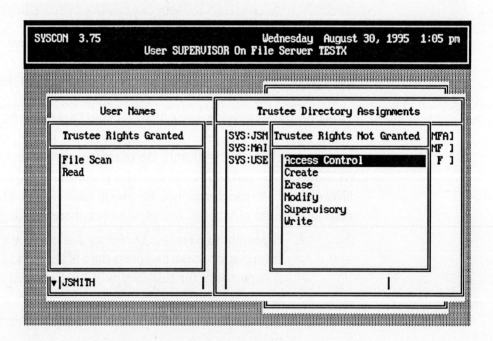

Fig. 3-20. Dialog box to assign rights to trustees.

9. Press the F5 function key. This marks the rights to be added to the user.
10. Press the DOWN ARROW key to move the highlighted bar to the next trustee right not granted.

11. Press F5 again.
12. Continue marking the trustee rights not granted until they are all marked.
13. Press the ENTER key. The rights not granted should move to the rights granted box.
14. Press the ESC key twice and the User Information menu should reappear.

Limiting Disk Space

1. Highlight the Volume/Disk Restrictions option on the User Information menu and press ENTER.
2. Press ENTER on SYS.
3. With the cursor on the Limit Volume Space field, press the Y and ENTER keys.
4. With the cursor on the Volume Space Limit (in KB) field, type the number 1024 and press the ENTER key.
5. The User Volume/Disk Restrictions menu should now look similar to the one shown in Fig. 3-21. Press the ESC key to accept these changes and return to the User Information menu.

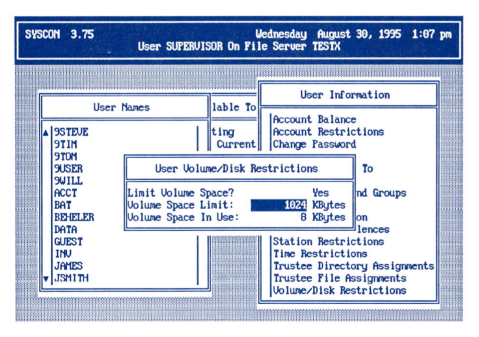

Fig. 3-21. Account restriction dialog box.

Testing the New Account

This user should now be set up to be able to perform any task the supervisor might need to do. But again, the job is not finished until it has been tested. To do this the current user, SUPERVISOR, must logout and the new user must login.

1. Press the ESC key three times until the Exit SYSCON? box appears.
2. Press the Y and ENTER keys.
3. Type **LOGOUT** and press the ENTER key.
4. Type **LOGIN** and the name you gave to the user just created on the same line and press the ENTER key.
5. Type the password given to the user just created, and press the ENTER key.

For now it will be assumed that if the user can login, the account has been set up correctly.

6. Type **LOGOUT** and press the ENTER key.

Summary

The most important aspect of managing a network involves the creation of user accounts. These accounts control how and when the user will be able to use the network. With the System Configuration utility, SYSCON, the supervisor can create accounts that allow users to do the work they need to do and provide them with login scripts that set up helpful environments. The login script commands and variables available allow the supervisor to create very complex programs that can take different actions based on who the user is, the time of day, and other factors.

When creating a user, the supervisor can specify user equivalences. The new user can be given security equivalence to any user or group already on the server, including the supervisor.

Questions

1. How can a supervisor record how much time a user spends on the network?
2. How can a supervisor save time when creating individual user accounts and also be able to easily make changes to collections of users?

3. In a network with many file servers running NetWare version 3.12, can the supervisor update the user accounts on all the file servers simultaneously?

4. Under which of SYSCON's main menu options can the supervisor set default values for all users created in the future?

5. How can the supervisor affect the user's environment each time the user logs in?

6. What can the supervisor do if a user forgets his password?

7. What should the supervisor do to ensure the security of the SUPERVISOR account?

8. Explain the function of the following lines in a login script:

    IF DAY IS EQUAL TO "29" AND MONTH = "02" THEN BEGIN
    WRITE "Today is special!"
    END.

Projects

Objective

The following projects will provide additional practice on how to create a user and login scripts. Login scripts provide a mechanism by which the system manager can customize the network and thereby make using the system easier for users.

Project 1. Using the SYSCON Utility

1. Use the SYSCON utility to create a new user. Use your initials as the name of the user.

2. Give the new user Read and File Scan rights to the SYS:\LOGIN, SYS:\SYSTEM, and SYS:\PUBLIC directories. Leave the default trustee rights for the Mail directory.

3. Create a login script for the user that maps the drive letters F:, G:, and H: to SYS:\LOGIN, SYS:\SYSTEM, and SYS:\PUBLIC respectively.

4. Add statements to the login script that print the message "Today is the first day of the rest of your life" only if the user logs in on today's date.

5. Using SHIFT/PRINT SCREEN, print the login script just created.

6. Login as the new user. Use the SHIFT/PRINT SCREEN keys to record the results of the login script.
7. While still logged in as the new user, start the SYSCON utility and attempt to create another user.
8. Exit the SYSCON utility and login under the supervisor equivalent account.
9. Start the SYSCON utility and delete the new user created in step 1.
10. Exit the SYSCON utility.

Project 2. More Login Scripts

1. Using the SYSCON utility create two new users, US1 and US2.
2. Give them the same rights as GUEST and assign US1 to a new group named DATABASE. US2 should not be a member of the DATABASE group.

The rest of the exercise would normally be created from the SYSCON utility under the Supervisor Options/System Login Script options. However, since this is a student exercise and since the System login script would affect all users, you must create the same login script for both US1 and US2. DO NOT MODIFY THE SYSTEM LOGIN SCRIPT!

3. Turn off the map display.
4. Type the basic login script commands. (MAP a search drive to the PUBLIC directory, and set up COMSPEC.)
5. Type all mappings to the basic applications installed on your file server.
6. Make sure that everyone's first network drive is mapped to his or her home directory.
7. Type a greeting to be displayed when a user logs in.
8. Type the commands necessary to display the type and version of the operating system.
9. Type the commands necessary to display the current date and time of day.
10. Type the commands needed to display "USER IS A MEMBER OF DATABASE".
11. Type the commands necessary to remind all users of a meeting that begins at 12:00 noon every day of the week.
12. Turn the map display on and display the mappings at the end of the script.
13. Login as both new users (one at a time) and test the scripts. Print the results of each login using SHIFT/ PRINT SCREEN.
14. Print both login scripts.

4

Security, Organization, and Management

Objectives

After completing this chapter you will

1. Understand the need for organization in the network.
2. Know the advantages of organizing users into groups.
3. Recognize the available trustee rights.
4. Understand the available file attributes.
5. Understand the main menu functions of the FCONSOLE program.
6. Be familiar with the four levels of security.
7. Know how to assign restrictions to a user's account.
8. Know how to create groups.
9. Know how to use FCONSOLE and MONITOR to observe network activity.

Key Terms

Data Organization	Directory Rights
FCONSOLE	File Attributes
Groups	Group Hierarchy
Levels of Security	Passwords
Trustee Rights	

Introduction

A network may have many functions. It may have electronic mail, shared printers, or shared modems. But all of these functions are usually secondary to providing users with shared disk space for programs and data. In addition to the shared space, most users will need to be able to store data in a private area.

Creating a structure in which users can access the shared data they need and protect their private data is the supervisor's most challenging task. Usually programs and data must be placed in different areas with different access rights. Different users will have many different needs, and normally several groups of users will have similar needs. Under NetWare, the supervisor can grant trustee rights to these groups and still be able to customize the accounts of each user. The principle of allowing some users access to data while restricting other users is known as network security. NetWare establishes security at four levels, through passwords, trustee directory and file rights, directory rights, and file attributes. This multilevel approach allows the supervisor to customize the security requirements to fit any need.

Careful management of the users and their data must involve backing up the data. Backing up the data on the file server is important to preserve both the application software and the NetWare files. In addition to managing file software, the supervisor must maintain control over the network as a whole. Part of this can be done using the File Server Console program FCONSOLE.EXE.

Levels of Security

There are four main levels of security:
1. Passwords
2. Trustee Directory and File rights
3. Directory rights
4. File attributes

Passwords

Each NetWare account can be given a password. The password is a string of characters that the user types in when he or she logs in. The LOGIN.EXE program compares the login name and password to those stored by NetWare.

If they match, the user is allowed access to the account. The login name is intended to be known by everyone while the password is kept secret by the user.

The supervisor can give the user a password or allow the user to choose one the first time he or she logs in. After it has been entered, neither the user nor the supervisor can view it. If it is forgotten, the only way to access the account is for the supervisor to change the password. In the System Configuration program, SYSCON.EXE, the supervisor can set defaults concerning passwords for all new accounts. Fig. 4-1 shows the Supervisor Options menu in SYSCON. By selecting Default Account Balance/Restrictions, the supervisor can access the menu shown in Fig. 4-2. This menu is almost identical to the Account Restrictions menu that can be accessed for each user. It shows the restrictions that can be placed on the user's password.

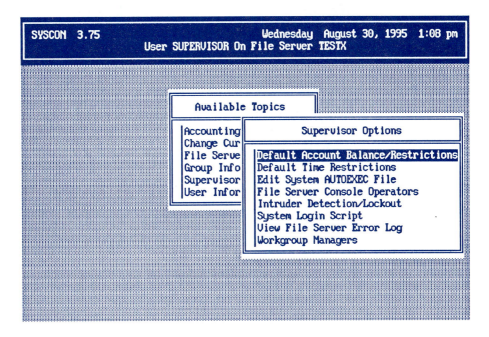

Fig. 4-1. Supervisor Options menu in SYSCON.

Password Length

The account can be required to have a password or not required to. If it does have a password, a minimum length can be set. The default minimum password length is 5 characters; the maximum is 128 characters.

Force Periodic Password Changes

A password is effective only if it is secret. If the same password is used for a very long time, the opportunity for an unauthorized person to discover it may be increased. This is why the account can be set to periodically force the user to change the password. If this feature is set, after the specified number of days has passed, LOGIN.EXE will automatically prompt the user for a new password when he or she logs in. The account can be set to allow a certain number of grace logins that prompt the user for a new password but do not require one. If the Require Unique Passwords option is set to YES the user must enter a different password each time. NetWare remembers the last eight passwords so one could begin repeating passwords after the eighth password is used. While using the same password for too long may allow someone to discover it, forcing the user to change it too frequently may also force the user to write it down too often or to use obvious words.

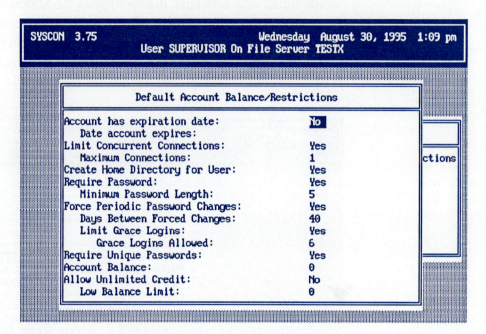

Fig. 4-2. Default Account Balance and Restrictions dialog box.

User Password Changes

One account restriction that cannot be set in the Default Account Restrictions/Balances menu is Allow User to Change Password. This can only be set in the User Information menu for each individual user. If the option Allow User to Change Password is set to No, the supervisor must enter a password for each user and accept responsibility for changing it.

Trustee Rights

Each user must be given trustee rights through his or her individual account or through a group to have any access to the server at all. In NetWare version 3.12, both Trustee Directory and Trustee File assignments are possible. When a user is given some access to a directory, he or she is said to be a trustee of that directory. Fig. 4-3 shows the trustee rights for user DATA in a directory called SYS:GATE\GW. The column on the right of the Trustee Directory

Assignments shows all of the rights given to the user in each directory. The Trustee Rights Granted box on the left is really a menu allowing the supervisor to insert new rights or delete existing ones.

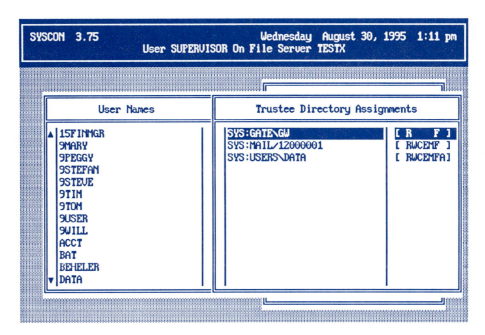

Fig. 4-3. Trustee rights for user DATA.

The rights that can be given are:

1. Read.

    Directory Right: The user can open and read files in the directory. The File Scan right is also needed to view the directory listing for the given directory.

    File Right: The user can see the information in a closed file to use it or to execute it even if the directory does not allow the Read permission.

2. Write.

    Directory Right: The user can change the contents of existing files in the directory.

    File Right: The user can change the contents of the given file even if the directory does not allow the Write permission.

3. Create.

    Directory Right: The user can create files and subdirectories in the directory.

    File Right: The user can salvage a file if it has been deleted.

4. Erase.

    Directory Right: The user can erase files and subdirectories of the directory.

File Right: The user can delete a file even if the directory does not allow the Delete permission.

5. Modify.

   Directory Right: The user can modify the Attributes and names of the files and subdirectories in the directory. The Attribute of a file indicates what access anyone has to the file.

   File Right: The user can modify the attributes and the name of the file.

6. File Scan.

   Directory Right: The user can see what files and subdirectories are listed in the directory.

   File Right: The user can see the file in the directory listing.

7. Access Control.

   Directory Right: The user can grant rights he or she has to the directory to other users.

   File Right: The user can grant any right he or she has to the file to other users.

8. Supervisory.

   Directory Right: The user has supervisory, and hence, all rights to the directory.

   File Right: The user has all rights to the file.

Directory Inherited Rights Mask

Normally, if a user has specific trustee rights to a given directory, the user inherits these rights for all subdirectories of the original directory. When a directory is created, it has the same rights as the full set of trustee rights. These directory rights, called the inherited rights mask, are attached to the directory. The inherited rights mask for a directory may be altered using utilities such as Filer to limit any user's inherited rights to that directory, except for the supervisory right. The Supervisor right cannot be eliminated from the inherited rights mask.

Suppose a user is given Read, File Scan, Create, and Erase rights to a directory called PROGRAMS. This means that the user will also inherit the same rights for all subdirectories of the directory PROGRAMS unless the inherited rights mask for a subdirectory limits these rights. Suppose that the subdirectory called COBOL under the PROGRAMS directory has the limited inherited rights mask of Read, File Scan, and Modify. This would mean that the user's effective rights for the directory \PROGRAMS\COBOL would be only Read and File Scan because these rights are the only rights the user had to the parent directory (PROGRAMS) that are also present in the inherited rights mask of the subdirectory (PROGRAMS\COBOL).

Note also that when a user is given explicit trustee rights to a directory, these rights override any limitation indicated by the inherited rights mask for the directory. The inherited rights mask has an effect only on those rights which would normally be inherited in a directory.

File Attributes

Information stored on the file server is stored in files. These files can have several different attributes that may further inhibit the user's access or track the use of the file. Attributes limit what a user can do with a file in much the same way that directory rights limit what can be done with the files in a directory. For instance, a file can have a Read Only attribute, which means the user cannot write to it or delete it. The file is said to be "flagged" Read Only. If the user has the Modify File Name/Flags right, he or she can remove the Read Only flag from the file using either the DOS Attrib command or the NetWare Flag command. This allows the supervisor or the user to safeguard certain files against accidental changes or deletions, while still being able to make those changes if necessary. If the user does not have the Modify File Name/Flags right, he or she cannot remove the Read Only attribute. This would give the supervisor the ability to protect individual files in a directory. The file attributes available in NetWare are as follows:

1. Read Only. The file and its file name cannot be changed or deleted.
2. Shareable. The file can be read by several users simultaneously.
3. Hidden. The file name is hidden from directory searches so it is not listed in the DOS DIR command. Unlike the DOS file attribute Hidden, a program file flagged Hidden cannot be executed.
4. System. The file is one of the operating system files. It cannot be deleted or changed by the user.
5. Transactional. This attribute is a safety feature that is usually applied to a database file. NetWare ensures that changes to the file are either completed or not made at all in case of an interruption during the process.
6. Purge. This attribute indicates that the file will be purged from the file system after it has been deleted. It will not be possible to undelete this file later.
7. Archive Needed. Identifies files modified after last backup. It is assigned automatically.
8. Read Audit. The user will be charged for reading this file. This feature is not yet implemented under NetWare.

9. Write Audit. The user will be charged for writing to this file. This feature is not yet implemented under NetWare.
10. Execute Only. The file, which must have an .EXE or .COM extension, can be executed only. The program cannot be copied. This attribute cannot be removed once set.
11. Rename Inhibit. The file cannot be renamed.
12. Delete Inhibit. The file cannot be deleted.
13. Copy Inhibit. For Mac users, the file cannot be copied.

Three utility programs can be used to set file attributes, the DOS program ATTRIB.EXE and the NetWare utilities FLAG.EXE and FILER.EXE. Fig. 4-4 shows how the FILER.EXE program displays attribute information for a file. This particular file has only the Read Only, Shareable, Delete Inhibit, and Rename Inhibit attributes.

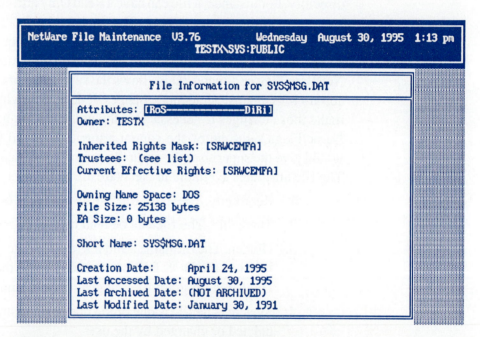

Fig. 4-4. File information about SYS$MSG.DAT.

Organization

Types of Users

When NetWare was installed, it automatically created a user account called SUPERVISOR. The person who assumes the role of supervisor is responsible for the smooth operation of the entire network. It is the supervisor's job to ensure easy and productive access to the network. A user must be given an account with access to the necessary directories and files. Most users will need drive mappings to particular directories. A typist in an office, for example, may need only read access to the directory containing a word processing program and write access to a document directory. A casual user or a user whose uses of the network are not very well defined may also need a menu system and may not be given permission to alter his or her account. A more sophisticated user may want to control as much of his or her account as possible. In addition, this user may want to be able to configure the software he or she is using. A typist probably would not need to be able to change the configuration of the word processing program, but the office manager might.

If it is a large office there may be many people needing the same access rights and menus. One solution is to have all the typists log in under the same user name. An account called TYPIST could be set up which allows several users to be logged in at the same time. This one account could have everything a typist might want, and all the typists would share the same directory space, software, and data. This situation could work well as long as the typists could agree on how their directory space was to be handled. Having everyone login using the same login name can be inconvenient, however. Individual typists may need a more customized environment to work with. Electronic mail and other messages could not be sent to individuals.

Groups

With various users needing different attributes to their accounts, individual accounts would have to be created. But since many users may need the same access rights, it is possible to create groups of users that can be given the same rights. A group could be created called TYPIST rather than an individual account. The group would be given the rights, and then each member of the group TYPIST in the office would be made a user in that group. Each typist in the office could have his or her own login name, login scripts, passwords, and other attributes. Each member of the group TYPIST, for example, may have programs he or she wants in addition to the word processing software provided by the company. If the supervisor sets up the accounts properly, the users could have private areas on the file server to store their programs. Some of the members of the group TYPIST may wish to share some of their private directory space with only certain other individuals, not everyone in the group TYPIST. Users can make these modifications themselves assuming the supervisor has set up their accounts correctly and they know how.

Group Hierarchy

NetWare does not explicitly provide for groups of groups, but the same thing can be accomplished logically. Suppose there were several office managers overseeing the network users. They would need access to everything the members of the group TYPIST have plus additional space for confidential employee information. A group called MANAGER could be created that has only the additional rights needed. A manager would then belong to both groups, MANAGER and TYPIST. A member of the board might need even more information available. That position might need access to pending contracts, for instance. A group called BOARD would give those members access to very critical data only, but since a member of the board might not need to see the work in progress by the members of the group TYPIST, he or she might be a member of the group BOARD and MANAGER and not TYPIST. In this way a hierarchy of users can be established so changes can be made to each group according to the functions they require.

Managers

The supervisor does not have to set up all the user accounts and manage all the groups. NetWare version 3.12 provides for two additional classifications of managers called Workgroup Managers and User Account Managers. Both the Workgroup Manager and the User Account Manager can give rights to any directory he or she has rights to. The Workgroup Manager can also create new users and give them any subset of the rights the Workgroup Manager has.

For example, if a user, who was designated by the supervisor as a Workgroup Manager, had rights to a directory called ACCOUNTS, he or she could create new users who have access to that directory or a subdirectory of it and assign any access rights the Work Group Manager possesses. For instance, a manager of the directory ACCOUNTS could create a user with rights to only the ACCOUNTS\RECEIVE directory and another user with rights to only the ACCOUNTS\PAYABLE directory.

Data Organization

The way data is organized on the file server hard disk can greatly influence the efficiency of the network. Since the supervisor is responsible for providing the users with a convenient working environment, he or she must arrange the items stored on the server in a way that will make it easy for the user to access them. This implies that it must be easy for the supervisor to assign the proper rights in order to maintain security. The items on the server would need to be arranged by function, as much as possible, with data, application software, operating system software, NetWare public utilities, and NetWare system software in separate areas.

Types of Data

All of the above items may be referred to as data. However, in this context, data is the information created and stored by the user. Application software is the set of programs used to create the data. The operating system consists of DOS and its program utilities such as FORMAT.COM and CHKDSK.COM. NetWare has several public utilities that are intended to be used by any user who knows how, since they cannot harm the accounts of anyone else. Other utilities, software, and data used only by NetWare itself or the supervisor is known as system software.

Suppose a company had the same types of users as above with members of the groups TYPIST, MANAGER, and BOARD. Since each user has his or her own account, the supervisor might be tempted to arrange the directories something like the way shown in Fig. 4-5.

```
F:\JACK
        |
        __F:\JACK\APPS
        |       |
        |       __F:\JACK\APPS\WORD
        |       |
        |       __F:\JACK\APPS\DATABASE
        |
        __F:\JACK\DATA
                |
                __F:\JACK\DATA\LETTERS
                |
                __F:\JACK\DATA\BILLS

F:\JILL
        |
        __F:\JILL\APPS
        |       |
        |       __F:\JILL\APPS\WORD
        |       |
        |       __F:\JILL\APPS\DATABASE
        |
        __F:\JILL\DATA
                |
                __F:\JILL\DATA\EMPLOYEE
                |
                __F:\JILL\DATA\BIDS
```

Fig. 4-5. Directory arrangement.

In Fig. 4-5 user JACK is a member of the group TYPIST who needs access to a word processing program and a database program. JACK stores only low security letters and bills in his data directory. JILL on the other hand, is a manager and needs to use the same type of software but must store very sensitive data such as employee evaluations and contract bids. JACK could be made a trustee with full rights in the F:\JACK\DATA directory and only read rights in the F:\JACK\APPS directory. JILL would then need similar rights in the directories under F:\JILL, but she would also need full access to JACK's data directory. Since there are usually more members of the group TYPIST than managers supervising them, JILL would need full rights to all the members of the group TYPIST.

The network supervisor would have to list the data directories of each of the members of the group TYPIST under JILL's trustee assignments. Also, the software that each of these users needs is being duplicated, wasting space and installation time. A more efficient approach would be to put all the software under one directory and all the data under another.

Fig. 4-6 shows a better directory structure. Under this structure the group called MANAGER would have read and write access to the entire F:\DATA directory and read access to the F:\APPS directory. The group TYPIST would have read and write access to only the F:\DATA\TYPIST directory, and it would also have read access to the F:\APPS directory.

With these groups created, there could be as many members of the group TYPIST and as many managers as necessary. JACK may not have any explicit trustee rights but instead belongs to the group TYPIST. JILL also might have no trustee assignments listed in her account but her membership in the MANAGER group would give her all the rights she needs.

Backing up Data

Often the supervisor must manage all the types of data for the users. Critical data should periodically be stored on a diskette or, more likely, on tape to ensure its safety. Backing up the data, as it is called, serves two main functions. First, it allows the user to retrieve information that may have been changed or deleted in the normal course of operations. Second, it saves information that could be lost if a disaster were to strike the file server. A hardware failure could destroy all the information on the file server. If the data were backed up in a timely manner, it could be restored using the backup diskettes or tapes. Arranging the data so that it can be easily assigned to different users also makes the job of backing up the information easier.

Not only the user's data should be backed up. All types of information should be saved to make the recovery as fast as possible. The time schedule to make these backups will depend on the type of data. Generally, the more often the data changes, the more frequently the backup procedure will need to take place.

```
      __F:\SYSTEM
   |
      __F:\PUBLIC
   |
      __F:\APPS
   |     |
   |        __F:\APPS\WORD
   |     |
   |        __F:\APPS\DATABASE
   |
   __F:\DATA
   __F:\DATA\MANAGER
   |     |
   |        __F:\DATA\MANAGER\EMPLOYEE
   |     |
   |        __F:\DATA\MANAGER\BIDS
   |
      __F:\DATA\TYPIST
            |
               __F:\DATA\TYPIST\LETTERS
            |
               __F:\DATA\TYPIST\BILLS
```

Fig. 4-6. A more efficient directory arrangement.

In Fig. 4-6, F:\PUBLIC and F:\SYSTEM are directories containing NetWare files. These directories should be backed up at a rate consistent with the changes that are made to the setup of NetWare itself. Such changes would include adding new users and changes to existing user accounts. The files under the F:\APPS will probably not change very often. Also, these programs are probably already stored on the original diskettes as well as on backup diskettes. Unless frequent configuration changes are made to these programs, they will probably be backed up the least often. The files under the F:\DATA directory are the most critical. All the other information could probably be reconstructed if necessary. That might not be the case for important contracts, billing information, or databases that change on an ongoing basis.

Critical data should be backed up frequently and on a rotating schedule. A rotating schedule uses different backup media on different intervals. For instance, a set of tapes could be labeled Monday through Friday. A backup would be made each weekday using the tape labeled for that day. Then, two additional tapes could be used alternately on Saturday. Two or more tapes could be used alternately at the end of each month.

A schedule like this is necessary to be reasonably sure of having a good set of backup tapes at any given moment since the backup hardware and media can also fail, producing unreadable copies. Also, and this is the more frequent problem, a user may ask for a file to be restored that was erased days or weeks ago. With a rotating schedule such as this, the supervisor has a good chance of finding the file the user wanted.

The exact schedule used in a particular installation would of course depend on many factors, including the nature of the business and the amount of data. There may even be data on the server that were placed there for the purpose of being backed up. Many users may wish to copy data from their local hard disk or floppies to the file server for safe keeping. On the server, it becomes the network supervisor's responsibility to back it up. In actual practice there would also be a backup made at regular intervals that would be archived. That is, the tape would not be used to make another backup, but rather it would be placed in long-term storage.

Network Management

Introduction to FCONSOLE

Network control might be considered a fifth level of security. A Novell Network is a very complex system. Almost all of the functions of the system are controlled through the file server. With a program called FCONSOLE, which stands for File Server Console, much of the network activity can be controlled or at least observed. Many of the functions of the FCONSOLE program are available at the file server itself, but in a less attractive format. Also many more functions are available at the file server.

By observing the processes on the server, as well as the activities of the users, a supervisor can sometimes avoid problems or catch them as they start. With FCONSOLE, critical values that may not have been set correctly in installation can be detected. Users can be monitored and disconnected if they cause trouble. Users can also be warned of problems that require their immediate attention.

The SYSCON utility can be used to establish other network control features. User accounts can be set to be restricted to certain workstations or certain times of the day. These restrictions and FCONSOLE's monitoring abilities give the supervisor a great deal of power in determining how, when, and where the network will be used.

Management Options

Fig. 4-7 shows FCONSOLE's main menu. FCONSOLE is to network management what SYSCON is to network security. The different management options that can be performed with FCONSOLE are explained in the following paragraphs. In NetWare version 3.12, some of the options available in earlier versions of FCONSOLE are not available. Four of the options (File/Lock Activity, LAN Driver Information, Purge All Salvageable Files, and Statistics) are no longer on the FCONSOLE menu. Equivalent functions are available using V3.12 MONITOR utility, which is run from the server console.

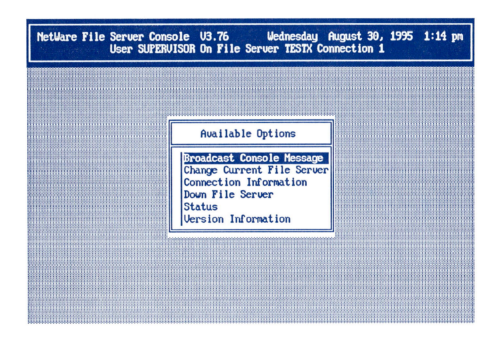

Fig. 4-7. FCONSOLE's main menu.

Broadcast Console Message

The supervisor can send a short message to every workstation attached to the server. The message sent appears on the bottom line of the workstation screen. Any workstation program that may have been running at the time is halted until the user presses the keys CTRL-ENTER. Only very critical messages should be broadcast in this way since it is very interruptive to everyone on the network.

Change Current File Server

The Change Current File Server option displays a list of servers to which the workstation is attached. In Fig. 4-8 the file server is named TESTX. When a new file server is selected, all the other options pertain to the selected server only.

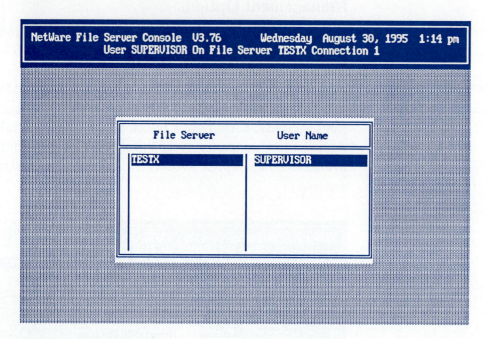

Fig. 4-8. List of servers to which the workstation is attached.

Connection Information

One of FCONSOLE's most important functions is to provide information on the users actually logged in at the moment. When Connection Information is selected a list of users currently logged in appears on the left, as it does in Fig. 4-9. In this case, user SUPERVISOR is the only person logged in. The second column in the Current Connections box shows the connection number. Each station attached to a file server is assigned a connection number. The first workstation to attach is given the value 1, the second 2, and so on. The file server uses these numbers to identify the station.

The connection number is temporally assigned to a workstation, not a user. Many users may log on and off the same workstation during the day. Assuming the workstation was never disconnected from the file server, all the users would use the same connection number.

When one of the users is selected, the Connection Information menu appears on the right as in Fig. 4-10. These options allow the supervisor to send a message to the user, disconnect the user, or examine various aspects of the user's usage of the file server.

CHAPTER 4. SECURITY, ORGANIZATION, AND MANAGEMENT

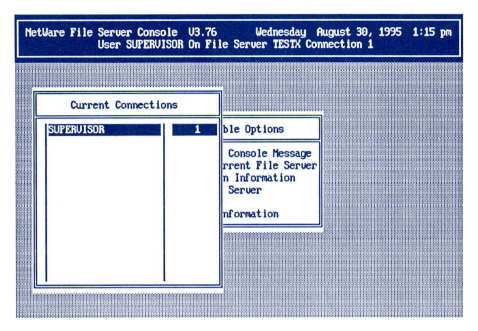

Fig. 4-9. List of current connections to the server.

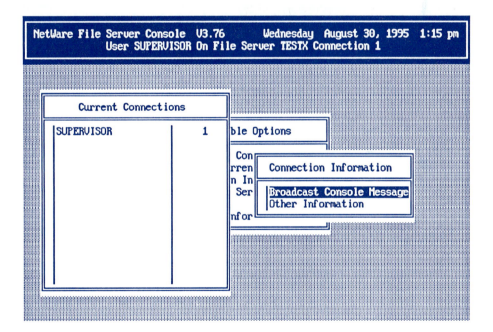

Fig. 4-10. Screen displaying Connection Information.

Down File Server

As noted in Chapter 9, the file server must be properly shut down in order to close any open files. This option shuts down the server after prompting for verification.

Status

The Status option on FCONSOLE's main menu has only four components, as seen in Fig. 4-11: Date, Time, Allow New Users To Login, and Transaction Tracking. These can be changed by highlighting the item and typing in a new value. The date and time will, of course, need occasional adjustment. Allow New Users To Login might be set to No near the end of a day or a few minutes before the server must be brought down for some other reason. Transaction Tracking simply displays the status of this feature.

Version Information

This option displays the exact version the file server is running.

FCONSOLE permits the supervisor to examine some of what the file server is doing at a given moment. In the Hands-on section, FCONSOLE and other utilities will be used to demonstrate some of the processes needed to run a secured and well-organized network.

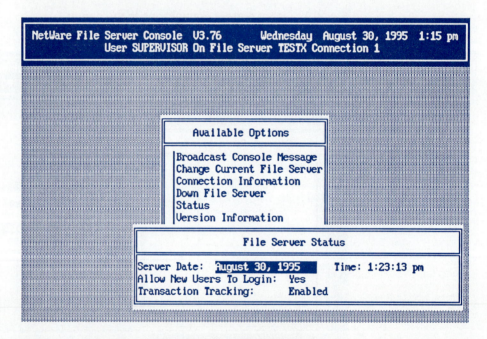

Fig. 4-11. File Server Status option in FCONSOLE.

Introduction to MONITOR

MONITOR, like FCONSOLE, provides management information about a NetWare file server. Unlike FCONSOLE, a DOS executable program which is executed from a workstation logged into the network, MONITOR is an NLM which must be loaded from the file server's console. In addition to the functions provided by FCONSOLE, MONITOR provides detailed information about such things as the server's memory usage, its LAN statistics, and its disk statistics. MONITOR is a far more comprehensive utility than

FCONSOLE. If the server has been physically protected by placing it in a locked room, a person needing to run MONITOR must gain access to the server room or must be able to remotely manage the console of the 3.12 server.

To run MONITOR at the server console's colon prompt type LOAD MONITOR. Two screens from MONITOR are shown in Fig. 4-12 and 4-13.

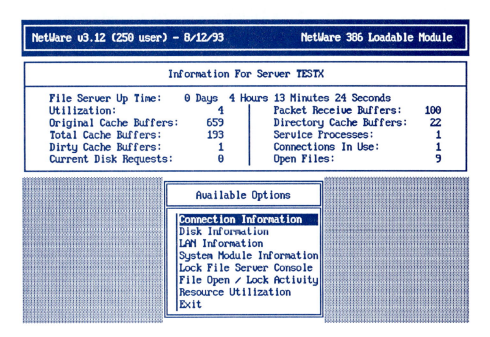

Fig. 4-12. Main Monitor screen.

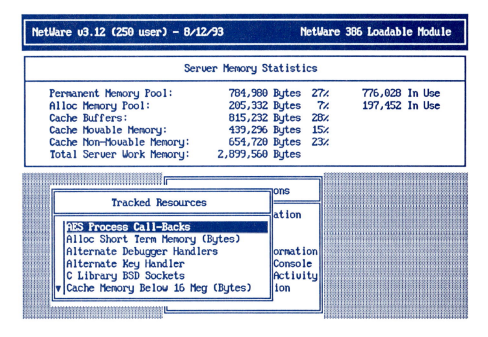

Fig. 4-13. Resource Utilization screen.

Hands-on NetWare

In order to complete the hands-on section of this chapter, the file server and a workstation should be ready to use.

1. The file server must be on.
2. A workstation must be booted and the appropriate network drivers must be loaded.
3. Network Drive F: should be the default drive at the workstation.
4. The user account created in the previous chapter must still be available.

In the example below, **TYPE THE NAME OF YOUR ACCOUNT WHERE JSMITH IS USED.** For instance, if the instructions read "Type LOGIN JSMITH", you should type LOGIN followed by the name of the account you created earlier.

Each numbered set of instructions can be completed at different times, as long as they are finished in order. For instance, the exercise on Minimum Password Length must be completed before the exercise on Force Periodic Password Changes.

Levels of Security

As discussed earlier, NetWare provides the supervisor with four levels of security. With these four levels, a blanket can be woven around the data providing just the right amount of access for each user. The following instructions will demonstrate the properties of each of the four levels.

Password

Passwords are the "first line" of defense against intentional attempts to break network security. Two restrictions that can be placed on the password are Minimum Password Length and Force Periodic Password Changes.

Changing the Password and Minimum Password Length

If a user is allowed to change the password, he or she may be tempted to use very short words to make memorizing it easier. Unfortunately, it also becomes easier to guess. For this reason a minimum length can be set on the password. A program called SETPASS (see Fig. 4-14) is available in the F:\PUBLIC directory that allows the user to quickly change his or her password.

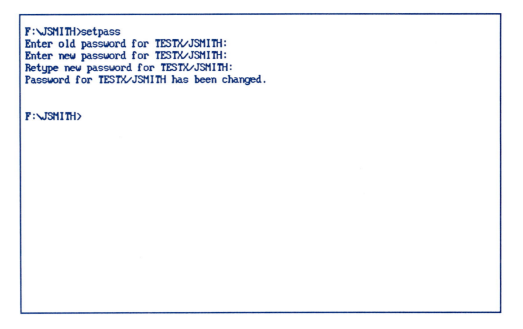

Fig. 4-14. Screen display of output generated by SETPASS.

1. Type **F:** and press the ENTER key
2. Type **LOGIN** and your user name. Then press the ENTER key. The password prompt should appear.
3. Type the original password and press the ENTER key.
4. Type **SETPASS** and press the ENTER key.
5. A prompt should appear asking for your old password. This ensures that no one could change your password while you were momentarily away from your workstation.
6. Type existing password and press the ENTER key. The password will not appear on the screen.
7. Type a new password at least 5 characters in length and press the ENTER key.
8. For verification, type the new password again and press the ENTER key.
9. If you are connected to more than one file server, a message asking you if the password should be synchronized on all attached servers should appear. If the account exists on other file servers that are now attached, the SETPASS program can change those passwords as well.
10. Type **LOGOUT** and press the ENTER key to end this session.

Force Periodic Password Changes

Forcing a user to periodically change his or her password is considered an important component of password security. However, changing the password too often makes it difficult to remember. The following steps illustrate the process of setting Force Periodic Password Changes and what happens when the password expires.

1. Type **F:** and press the ENTER key
2. Type **LOGIN** and your user name. Then press the ENTER key. The password prompt should appear.
3. Type your password and press the ENTER key.
4. Type **SYSCON** and press the ENTER key.
5. Use the ARROW keys to highlight User Information and press the ENTER key.
6. Type the name of your user account. When your account name is highlighted, press the ENTER key.
7. Press the DOWN ARROW key to highlight Account Restrictions and press the ENTER key.
8. Move the cursor with the ARROW keys until the value for Force Periodic Password Changes is highlighted.
9. Press the Y and the ENTER key. The Account Restrictions dialog box should appear similar to the one shown in Fig. 4-15. A 40-day interval is the default until the next required change.
10. Highlight the date on the Date Password Expires line using the ARROW keys.

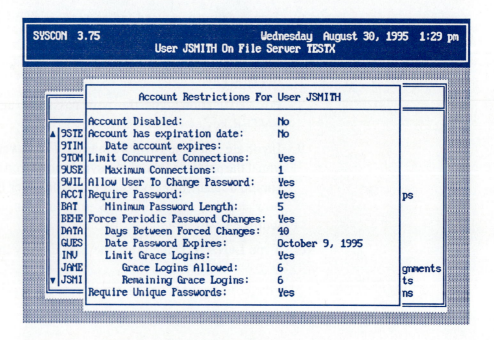

Fig. 4-15. Account Restrictions dialog box.

11. Look at the date shown in the upper right corner of the screen. It should be the current date. Type in the day before the day shown as the current date on your screen. In Fig. 4-16 the current date is August 30, 1995. For the purpose of this exercise, user JSMITH typed in August 29, 1995 to indicate that the password has expired.

12. Press the ESC key four times until the EXIT box appears.

13. Press the Y key and then press the ENTER key.

14. Type **LOGOUT** and press the ENTER key. The file server should respond with a message indicating the login time and the logout time.

15. Type **LOGIN** and your user name. Then press the ENTER key. The password prompt should appear.

16. Type your password and press the ENTER key. Since the password expired yesterday, a message will appear asking you if you would like to change it.

17. Press the Y and the ENTER key.

18. Type a new password. The new password will not appear as it is typed. Press the ENTER key.

19. Type the new password again and press the ENTER key to verify the change.

20. Type **LOGOUT** and press the ENTER key to end this session.

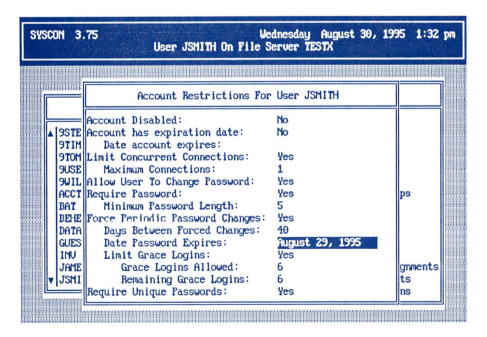

Fig. 4-16. Change password expiration date.

Trustee Rights

The second level of security, trustee rights, requires the most work on the part of the supervisor. SYSCON is used to identify each directory in which the user or group has trustee rights. In the following steps you will use your account to give yourself trustee rights in a new directory. This exercise would never be done quite this way in the real world since the supervisor (or a user with supervisor equivalence) does not need to give himself or herself trustee rights. The supervisor would only need to give other users or groups trustee rights.

1. Type **LOGIN** and your user name. Then press the ENTER key. The password prompt should appear.

2. Type your password and press the ENTER key.

3. Type **SYSCON** and press the ENTER key.

4. Use the ARROW keys to highlight User Information and press the ENTER key.

5. Select your user name from the list by typing the name and pressing the ENTER key when it is highlighted.

6. Use the ARROW keys to highlight the Trustee Directory Assignments option at the bottom of the User Information menu and press the ENTER key.

7. The Trustee Directory Assignments box should appear, similar to the one in Fig. 4-17. Press the INSERT key.

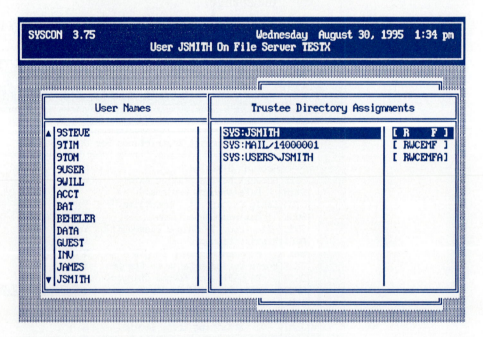

Fig. 4-17. Trustee Directory Assignments dialog box.

Chapter 4. Security, Organization, and Management

8. A long box labeled Directory In Which Trustee Should Be Added should appear along the top of the screen. The complete directory name can be typed in at this point but SYSCON offers a method for selecting the directory from a list.

9. Press the INSERT key again and the file servers available will be listed.

10. If there is more than one file server listed, use the arrow keys to highlight the one you are using. Fig. 4-18 shows user JSMITH's file server as File Server TESTX.

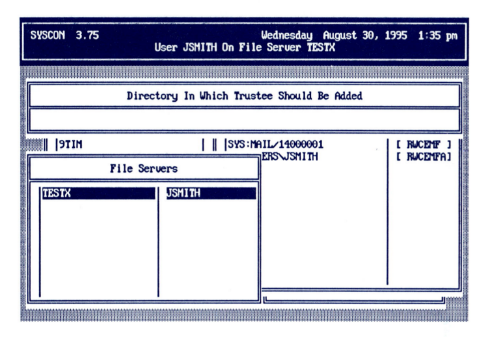

Fig. 4-18. User JSMITH's file server.

11. Press the ENTER key with the proper file server name highlighted.

12. The list of volumes is displayed. Press the ENTER key after highlighting the SYS: volume.

13. The list of directories on the selected volume is displayed. Do not select one of these directories.

14. Press the ESC key. The cursor should return to the long Directory In Which Trustee Should Be Added box.

15. Type the name of your user account and press the ENTER key.

16. Fig. 4-19 shows how SYSCON responds to a new directory. Press the Y and the ENTER key. The new directory is now listed in the Trustee Assignments box with rights Read and File Scan.

17. Highlight the new directory with the ARROW keys and press the ENTER key.

Networking Fundamentals Using Novell NetWare

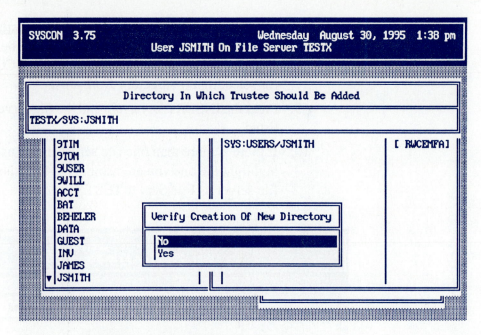

Fig. 4-19. SYSCON's response to a new directory.

18. With the Trustee Rights Granted Box on the left of the screen press the INSERT key.

19. Press the F5 function key and then the DOWN ARROW key. Continue this until all of the rights listed in the Trustee Rights Not Granted box are marked, except for Supervisory.

20. Press the ENTER key. All of the rights should move to the trustee rights granted box. Press the ESC key again to accept these changes.

21. All of the rights except supervisory should now be listed for the directory with your name as they are for user JSMITH in Fig. 4-20.

22. The user now has complete access to the directory. A directory such as this may be referred to as the user's home directory. It is clearly identified as belonging to this particular user and the user has full rights in it. Press the ESC key four times until the Exit box appears. Then press the ENTER key.

23. Type **LOGOUT** and press the ENTER key to end this session.

Directory Rights

The supervisor can set each user's access rights to particular values in particular directories. The user automatically has the same rights in any subdirectory. For instance, user JSMITH in the preceding example was given complete rights to the JSMITH directory. If any directories are created below the JSMITH directory, user JSMITH will have complete rights to those as well.

Chapter 4. Security, Organization, and Management

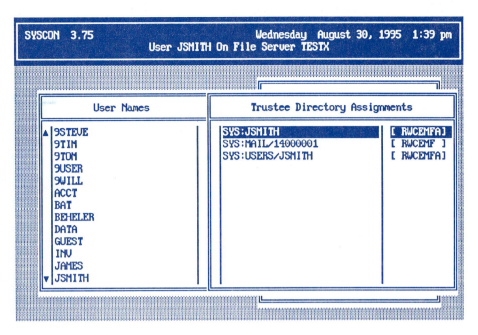

Fig. 4-20. Rights for user JSMITH.

Often, in a large directory structure, one or two directories may need to be restricted so that users have rights to these directories only when they are explicitly given via granting Trustee Directory Rights. Inherited Rights can be restricted by creating an inherited rights mask which restricts all users except those with supervisory authority. The following directions illustrate how the NetWare utility program FILER is used to make the directory rights changes.

1. Type **LOGIN** and your user name. Then press the ENTER key. The password prompt should appear.

2. Type your password and press the ENTER key.

3. Type **CD** and your user name. For user JSMITH the command would be CD\JSMITH. Then press the ENTER key.

4. Type **FILER** and press the ENTER key. Fig. 4-21 shows FILER's main menu.

5. Press the ENTER key with the Current Directory Information option highlighted. Fig. 4-22 shows the Current Directory Information for the JSMITH directory.

6. Highlight the Inherited Rights Mask field and press the ENTER key.

7. Highlight Modify Directory/File and press the DELETE key.

8. A box will appear as in Fig. 4-23 asking for confirmation to revoke the right. Press the Y and the ENTER key.

9. Press the ESC key three times until the Exit Filer box appears.

115

10. Press the Y and ENTER key.
11. Type **LOGOUT** and press the ENTER key to end this session.

At this point, any user other than supervisor-equivalent users are not allowed to inherit the Modify Directory/File right unless that right in this directory is listed in their trustee assignments list.

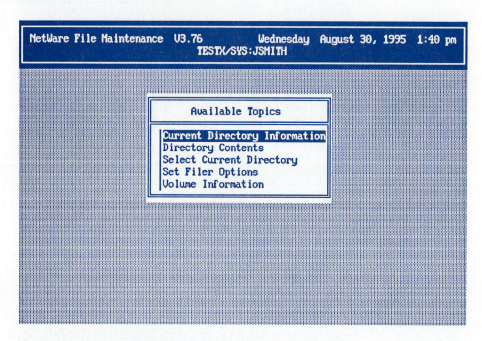

Fig. 4-21. FILER main menu.

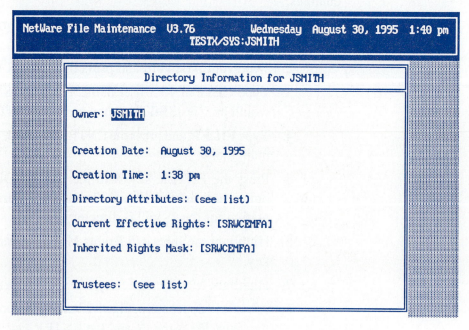

Fig. 4-22. Current directory information for directory SYS:JSMITH.

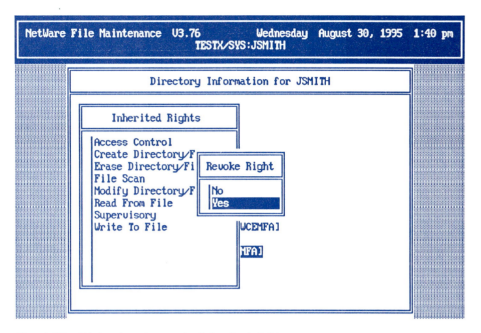

Fig. 4-23. Dialog box to revoke inherited rights.

File Attributes

File attributes could be said to be the last line of defense in security since often they are used to prevent accidental erasure or changes to files. With a file flagged as Read Only, no user, including the supervisor, can change or delete the file. If the user has the Modify File Names/Flags right in the directory, the Read Only attribute can be set to Read Write, which then allows changes. The following short exercise demonstrates this point.

1. Type **LOGIN** and your user name. Then press the ENTER key. The password prompt should appear.

2. Type your password and press the ENTER key.

3. Type **CD** and your user name. For user JSMITH the command would be CD\JSMITH. Then press the ENTER key.

4. Type **COPY CON THIS** and press the ENTER key. This DOS command instructs the computer to copy a file from the console to a file called THIS. In other words the next thing you type will go into the file THIS.

5. Type **THIS IS A TEST** and press the ENTER key.

6. Hold down the CONTROL key and press the Z key. This character combination marks the end of the file.

7. Press the ENTER key. The message 1 File(s) copied should appear.

Networking Fundamentals Using Novell NetWare

8. Type **FLAG THIS RO** and press the ENTER key. The utility program FLAG is used solely to change file attributes. The FILER program can also be used to change file attributes. This command tells the FLAG program to set the Read Only flag on the file called THIS.

9. Fig. 4-24 shows the result. Type **DEL THIS** and press the ENTER key to delete the file called THIS. The message Access denied should be displayed. The file was not deleted because of the Read Only attribute assigned to it.

10. Type **LOGOUT** and press the ENTER key to end this session.

```
F:\JSMITH>COPY CON:   THIS
THIS IS A TEST
^Z
        1 file(s) copied

F:\JSMITH>FLAG THIS RO
     THIS                       [ Ro - A - - - - - - - DI RI ]

F:\JSMITH>
```

Fig. 4-24. Screen displaying rights assigned by the FLAG utility.

Effective Rights

The combination of trustee rights and directory rights is called a user's effective rights. The effective rights are those rights that are granted specifically in the user trustee assignments and/or inherited by a combination of rights inherited from the parent directory which are not limited by the inherited rights mask. To show this, a non-supervisor-equivalent user account is needed. The following steps create such a user.

1. Type **LOGIN** and your user name. Then press the ENTER key. The password prompt should appear.

2. Type your password and press the ENTER key.

3. Type **SYSCON** and press the ENTER key.

4. Press the DOWN ARROW key to highlight the User Information option and press the ENTER key.

CHAPTER 4. SECURITY, ORGANIZATION, AND MANAGEMENT

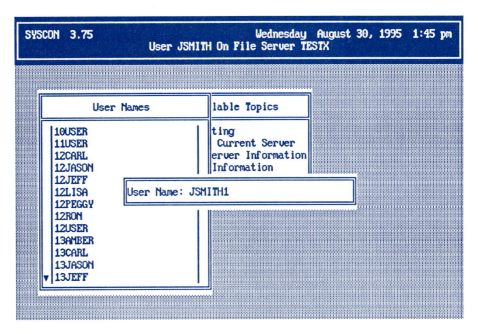

Fig. 4-25. Dialog box to insert a new user name.

5. Press the INSERT key and a box requesting a new user name will appear as it does in Fig. 4-25.

6. Type your user name followed by a **1** on the same line. User JSMITH typed JSMITH1 for a new user name. Press the ENTER key after typing the name.

7. Press the ENTER , Y, and ENTER keys again to accept the creation of the Home Directory.

8. Press the ENTER key again to select the name from the list.

9. Select Account Restrictions from the User Information menu by moving the highlighted bar to that option and pressing the ENTER key.

10. Move the cursor down to the Require Password option with the ARROW KEYS.

11. Press the N key and ENTER key.

12. Press the ESC key to return to the User Information menu.

13. Press the DOWN ARROW key to highlight Login Script and press the ENTER key. A message box will appear as it does in Fig. 4-26.

14. This box allows the supervisor to copy a login script from any other user to the user just created. To copy your login script, simply use the BACKSPACE key to remove the 1 at the end of the name displayed and press the ENTER key.

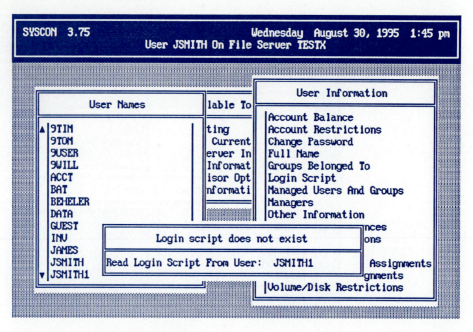

Fig. 4-26. Login script creation.

15. The Login Script editor should now appear. With the cursor in the upper left corner of the box, press the ENTER key once.

16. Move the cursor back up to the top line and type **MAP F:=SYS:**. This line maps the drive letter F to the root directory of the volume SYS.

17. The line MAP S1:=SYS:\PUBLIC should already be there. If not, press ENTER and type it in.

18. The line MAP S2:=SYS:\SYSTEM should already be there. If not, press ENTER and type it in.

19. If the next line is MAP S3:=SYS:\LOGIN change it to read **MAP INS S2:=SYS:\LOGIN** and press ENTER. This command will insert the new mapping for S2: and move the previous mapping for S2: to S3:.

20. Press the ESC key. The Save Changes box should appear.

21. Press the Y and the ENTER key.

22. Next the new user must be given trustee rights. Select Trustee Directory Assignments from the User Information menu by pressing the DOWN ARROW key to highlight the proper line and pressing the ENTER key.

If the directory SYS:USERNAME (where USERNAME is the name of the user you are setting up) is listed in the Trustee Directory Assignments box with rights [RWCEMFA], then skip to step 30.

23. Press the INSERT key.

24. Type **SYS:** followed by your user name. For User JSMITH1 you would type SYS:\JSMITH1. Press the ENTER key when the line has been typed in. Press Y and ENTER to verify creation of the new directory.

25. With the new directory in the Trustee Directory Assignments box highlighted, press the ENTER key.

26. With the Trustee Rights Granted Box on the left of the screen, press the INSERT key.

27. Press the F5 key, then the DOWN ARROW key. Continue this until all of the rights listed in the Trustee Rights Not Granted box are marked except for the supervisory right.

28. Press the ENTER key. All of the rights except supervisory should move to the trustee rights granted box.

29. Press the ESC key.

30. Press the INSERT key.

31. Type **SYS:PUBLIC** and press the ENTER key.

32. Press the INSERT key.

33. Type **SYS:SYSTEM** and press the ENTER key.

34. Press the ESC key four times. When the Exit box appears, press the ENTER key.

35. Create a subdirectory of the JSMITH1 directory called LIMITED by typing **MD\JSMITH1\LIMITED**.

36. Using FILER, change the inherited rights mask for JSMITH1\LIMITED directory to Read, File Scan, and Supervisory only. (Refer to the steps on Directory Rights as necessary.)

37. Type **LOGOUT** and press the ENTER key to end this session.

The user JSMITH1 was given all rights except supervisory to the JSMITH1 directory. Normally, he would inherit all these rights in every subdirectory of the JSMITH1 directory. However, the fact that you have created a limited inherited rights mask will alter the effective rights JSMITH1 will have in the directory JSMITH\LIMITED.

The following steps test the effective rights of the new user.

1. Type **LOGIN** followed by your user name and a 1. User JSMITH would type LOGIN JSMITH1. Then press the ENTER key.

2. Type **CD** followed by your user name. User JSMITH1 would type CD \JSMITH1. Then press the ENTER key.

3. Type the command **RIGHTS** and press the ENTER key. All rights except supervisory should be displayed because they were explicitly given to the user JSMITH1.

4. Type **CD\JSMITH1\LIMITED** and press the ENTER key.

5. Type the command **RIGHTS** and press the ENTER key. The effective rights are limited by the inherited rights mask you assigned to this directory.

6. Type **MD \JSMITH1\NEW** and press the ENTER key.

7. Type **CD \JSMITH1\NEW** and press the ENTER key.

8. Type the command **RIGHTS** and press the enter key. The effective rights in this subdirectory of JSMITH1 are the same as the effective rights in JSMITH1 because a limited inherited rights mask has not been created (see Fig. 4-27).

9. Type **LOGOUT** and press the ENTER key to end this session.

```
F:\JSMITH1\NEW>RIGHTS
TESTX\SYS:JSMITH1\NEW
Your Effective Rights for this directory are [ RWCEMFA]
  * May Read from File.                      (R)
  * May Write to File.                       (W)
    May Create Subdirectories and Files.     (C)
    May Erase Directory.                     (E)
    May Modify Directory.                    (M)
    May Scan for Files.                      (F)
    May Change Access Control.               (A)

* Has no effect on directory.

    Entries in Directory May Inherit [ RWCEMFA] rights.
```

Fig. 4-27. Display of Effective Rights.

Groups

The new account created in the previous section was not given supervisor equivalence. Therefore, the only rights available were those granted in the Trustee Assignments list. Since it can become tedious to maintain many users' accounts when new directories are added, NetWare provides the ability to assign users to a group, and then simply grant the group trustee rights. The following example illustrates the use of groups when assigning trustee rights.

1. Type **LOGIN** and your user name. Then press the ENTER key. The password prompt should appear. Use the original account, not the username1 account.

2. Type your password and press the ENTER key.

CHAPTER 4. SECURITY, ORGANIZATION, AND MANAGEMENT

3. Type **SYSCON** and press the ENTER key.
4. Use the DOWN ARROW key to move to the Group Information Option and press the ENTER key.
5. Press the INSERT key and a box asking for a new group name will appear.
6. Type the name of the account you are now using. User names and group names can be the same. Press the ENTER key after typing in the name.
7. With the new group name highlighted, press the ENTER key. The Group Information menu should appear.
8. Use the DOWN ARROW key to highlight Member List and press the ENTER key.
9. Press the INSERT key and a Not Group Members list will appear.
10. Type the name of your user account followed by a **1**. In the example the user name is JSMITH1. Press the ENTER key when the name is highlighted.
11. The name should move to the Group Members box as it does in Fig. 4-28. Press the ESC key to return to the Group Information menu.

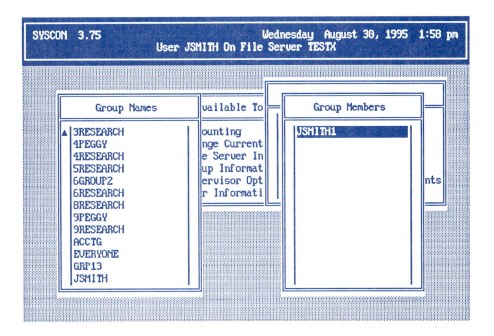

Fig. 4-28. Screen displaying JSMITH1 moved to the Group Members dialog box.

12. Use the DOWN ARROW key to highlight Trustee Directory Assignments and press the ENTER key. Then press the INSERT key.

13. Type **SYS:** followed by your user name and a **1**. This is the home directory created earlier. User JSMITH1 would type SYS:JSMITH1. Press the ENTER key when the line has been typed.

14. With the new directory in the Trustee Directory Assignments box highlighted, press the ENTER key.

15. With the Trustee Rights Granted box on the left of the screen, press the INSERT key.

16. Press the F5 function key and then the DOWN ARROW key. Continue this until all of the rights listed in the Trustee Rights Not Granted box except supervisory are marked.

17. Press the ENTER key. All of the marked rights should move to the Trustee Rights Granted box. Press the ESC key again to accept these changes.

18. Press the ESC key three times to return to SYSCON's main menu called Available Topics.

19. Use the DOWN ARROW key to highlight User Information and press the ENTER key.

20. Type the name of your user account, followed by a **1**. In the example the user name is JSMITH1. Press the ENTER key when the name is highlighted.

21. Use the ARROW keys to highlight the Trustee Directory Assignments option and press the ENTER key.

22. Notice one of the directories is a number listed under the MAIL directory. This numbered directory is automatically created for each user and group and contains the login script for the user. The number may contain letters because it is a hexadecimal number. Write down the number for use later in this exercise.

23. Highlight your account's home directory. In the example, user JSMITH1 would highlight SYS:\JSMITH1. Press the DELETE key with the proper directory highlighted.

24. A box asking you if you wish to remove the trustee from the directory will appear as it does in Fig. 4-29. Press the Y key and then press the ENTER key.

25. Press the ESC key to return to the User Information menu.

26. Use the ARROW keys to highlight Login Script and press the ENTER key.

CHAPTER 4. SECURITY, ORGANIZATION, AND MANAGEMENT

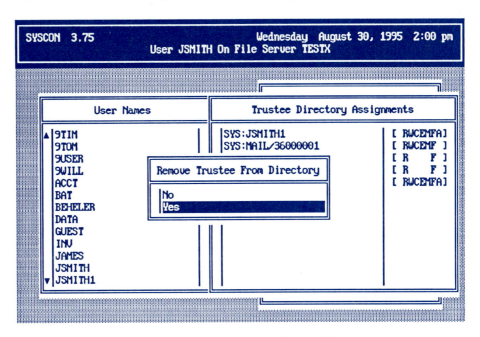

Fig. 4-29. Dialog box used to remove trustee from a directory.

27. Move the cursor to the end of the last line in the login script and press the ENTER key to create a new line.

28. Type in the new line as it appears in Fig. 4-30, except use the name of the group you created earlier in place of JSMITH. Your group name should also be in quotes.

29. Press the ESC key and then press Y and press the ENTER key to save these changes.

30. Press the ESC key three times until the Exit box appears, then press the ENTER key.

31. Before testing the new login script, it may be of some interest to see where it is located. Type **CD\MAIL** followed by the number you wrote down earlier in this exercise. For user JSMITH1 in Fig. 4-29, the command would be CD \MAIL\36000001. Press the ENTER key at the end of the command.

32. Type **DIR** and press the ENTER key. The login script and a backup of the old login script should appear as files in the directory.

33. Type the command **TYPE LOGIN** and press the ENTER key. This DOS command displays the contents of the file called LOGIN and should appear similar to the one shown in Fig. 4-31.

34. Type **CD** and press the ENTER key.

35. Type **LOGIN** followed by your account name and a **1**. In the example the command would be LOGIN JSMITH1. Press the ENTER key at the end of the line.

125

```
 SYSCON  3.75                    Wednesday  August 30, 1995  2:03 pm
                         User JSMITH On File Server TESTX

                         Login Script For User JSMITH1
 MAP F:=SYS:\
 MAP S1:=SYS:\PUBLIC
 MAP S2:=SYS:\SYSTEM
 MAP INS S2:=SYS:\LOGIN
 IF MEMBER OF "JSMITH" THEN WRITE "IN GROUP JSMITH"
```

Fig. 4-30. Login script for user JSMITH1.

```
F:\PUBLIC>CD \MAIL\36000001

F:\MAIL\36000001>DIR

 Volume in drive F is SYS
 Directory of F:\MAIL\36000001

 .            <DIR>
 ..           <DIR>
 LOGINBAK              0  08-30-95   1:45p
 LOGIN    OS2          0  08-30-95   1:45p
 LOGIN               130  08-30-95   2:03p
         5 file(s)          130 bytes
                        1,040,384 bytes free

F:\MAIL\36000001>TYPE LOGIN
MAP F:=SYS:\
MAP S1:=SYS:\PUBLIC
MAP S2:=SYS:\SYSTEM
MAP INS S2:=SYS:\LOGIN
IF MEMBER OF "JSMITH" THEN WRITE "IN GROUP JSMITH"
F:\MAIL\36000001>
```

Fig. 4-31. Contents of file LOGIN.

When the new user logs in, the login script will identify the account as a member of the group and print the message:

   IN GROUP JSMITH

On your screen JSMITH1 will of course be replaced with the name of your account. JSMITH1 is now a member of the group called JSMITH. It is in the group trustee assignments list where the user is assigned trustee rights to the

\JSMITH directory. Many more members could be added to the group without assigning individual trustee rights to that directory.

36. Type **LOGOUT** and press the ENTER key to end this session.

Network Control

The FCONSOLE utility is helpful in observing the functioning of the network as well as establishing control over the use of the network. It provides information on the file server and on the use of the file server. The following instructions illustrate some of the uses of the FCONSOLE utility.

1. Type **LOGIN** and your user name, then press the ENTER key. The password prompt should appear. Use the original account, not the username1 account.

2. Type your password and press the ENTER key. Then, type **CD \PUBLIC** and press the ENTER key.

3. Type **FCONSOLE** and press the ENTER key. The FCONSOLE main menu should appear, similar to the one in Fig. 4-32.

4. Move the highlighted bar down with the ARROW keys to highlight the Connection Information option and press the ENTER key.

5. Type the name of your user account. The highlighted bar will move to your name. Press the ENTER key.

6. Highlight the Broadcast Console Message option and press the ENTER key.

7. Type **THIS IS A GREAT DAY** into the broadcast box and press ENTER. This message should be displayed across the bottom of your screeen. Press the CTRL/ENTER keys to return to the Connection Information menu.

8. Use the ARROW keys to highlight the Other Information option and press the ENTER key.

9. The box displayed, similar to the one in Fig. 4-33, shows when and where this user logged in. Write down the number labeled Network Address. Remember to include the ":". The first eight digits of this number indicate the network being used. This is the same network number entered when NetWare was installed. The last twelve digits identify the actual network card in the workstation being used. Ordinarily a supervisor would create a complete map of the network showing the location of every node number.

10. Press the ESC key four times, and when the Exit box appears, press the ENTER key.

11. Type **SYSCON** and press the ENTER key.

12. Use the ARROW keys to highlight User Information and press the ENTER key.

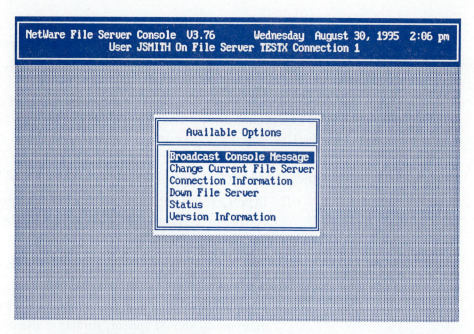

Fig. 4-32. FCONSOLE main menu.

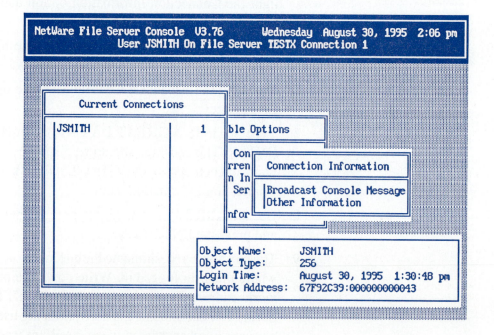

Fig. 4-33. Time and location of user login.

13. Type the name of your account and a **1**. In the example the name is JSMITH1. Press the ENTER key with the correct name highlighted.

14. Use the DOWN ARROW key to highlight the Station Restrictions option and press the ENTER key.

15. Press INSERT. A box labeled Network Address will appear as it does in Fig. 4-34. This box allows the supervisor to restrict the user to any workstation on the network indicated by the network number.

16. Type in the first eight digits of the number you wrote down earlier and press the ENTER key.

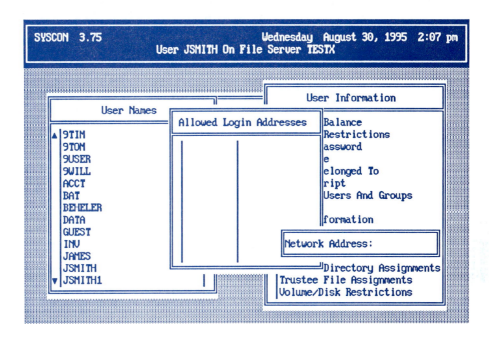

Fig. 4-34. Dialog box used to restrict a user to a specific workstation(s).

17. Type **N** in response to the question regarding allowing the user to log in from any node, and press the ENTER key to indicate that further restrictions apply.

18. A Node Address box will appear below the Network Address box. Type in the last twelve digits of the Network Address you wrote down earlier. Do not include the ":"; it only separates the two components of the number. Press the ENTER key at the end of the number. Notice that Novell is not consistent with what it calls the Network Address. In FCONSOLE the Network Address was the entire 20-digit number and in SYSCON the Network Address is only the network number portion. Both numbers are represented in hexadecimal format, which is why they contain numbers and letters.

19. The Allowed Login Address box should now show the number you just typed in and no others. Fig. 4-35 shows the only address where user JSMITH1 is allowed to login to be network number 90A28001, node number 0000C03C1B2D.

20. Press the ESC key four times. When the Exit box appears, press Y and press the ENTER key.

21. The Network Address this user is restricted to is the address of the workstation you are now using. Type **LOGOUT** and press the ESC key.

22. Trade workstations with a student next to you or simply move to a vacant workstation. At the new workstation type **LOGIN** followed by your user name and a **1**. User JSMITH would type in LOGIN JSMITH1.

The file server will not allow you to log in with that account at the new workstation because it has a different node number. With this feature, the supervisor can restrict certain user accounts to certain workstations. For maximum security, those workstations could even be diskless.

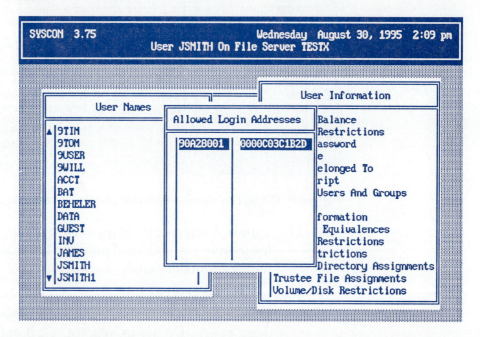

Fig. 4-35. Dialog box displaying the address where user JSMITH1 is allowed.

Summary

Network security is broken down into four levels; passwords, trustee rights, directory rights, and file attributes. The supervisor can put certain restrictions on the password that are intended to force the user to maintain a secure password. The only rights a user has in a given directory are those granted by the supervisor. These rights will be listed in the user's trustee assignments, or the user must belong to a group with the proper rights. The rights granted can be masked by directory rights. The inherited rights for all users except the supervisor are restricted by the inherited rights mask placed on a directory. File attributes are primarily used to prevent accidental damage to files; therefore the attributes apply to the supervisor as well as the other users. With the proper rights in a directory, the file attributes can be changed. The combination of all the rights and restrictions a user has in a given directory is known as the effective rights. Users usually fall into categories that require different rights and restrictions. NetWare provides the ability to put these users into groups that can be given the same rights as the users. The groups can then be structured to allow the supervisor to easily make changes to many user accounts by changing only the group account.

Information on the server must be organized as well. Programs and operating system software should be placed in one region and data created by the users in another. This structure has several advantages. The software and data can be more easily shared. The trustee assignments can be more easily standardized and the supervisor can more easily isolate the data that must be backed up on a regular basis.

Controlling how, when, and where users use the network could be called the fifth level of security. With the FCONSOLE utility the supervisor can observe the files accessed by users and see what workstations they are using. SYSCON can then be used to restrict the user to certain workstations, times, and directories.

Questions

1. Describe the four levels of security.
2. Describe what might be considered a fifth level of security.
3. Can any user change his or her password?
4. What trustee rights are automatically granted to any user?
5. A user has all trustee rights in a directory but still cannot access the files in it. What is preventing him from using the files?
6. A user checks her own Trustee Assignments list and finds that the only directory listed is her MAIL directory, yet she is able to use many different programs on the server. How can this be?
7. Where is a user's login script stored on the server?
8. How can the supervisor identify the workstation a user is logged into?
9. Ordinarily, which should be backed up more often, a database file or the NetWare system files?

Projects

Objective

The following projects provide additional practice in establishing security and trustee rights. Additionally, they provide more hands-on practice with the FCONSOLE utility and login scripts.

Project 1. FCONSOLE and Trustee Rights

1. Use the SYSCON utility to create a new user. Use your initials as the name of the user.
2. Select Trustee Assignments and write down the full MAIL directory path.
3. Give the new user Read and File Scan rights to the SYS:\LOGIN, SYS:\SYSTEM, and SYS:\PUBLIC directories. Do not give the user a login script.
4. Examine the trustee assignments of the account you have been using. Write down the full MAIL directory.
5. Exit the SYSCON utility.
6. Use the DOS COPY command to copy the file called LOGIN from the MAIL directory of the supervisor-equivalent account you have been using to the MAIL directory of the new account.
7. Login as the new user. Record the results with the SHIFT/PRINT SCREEN keys.
8. From another workstation, login under the supervisor-equivalent account.
9. Start the FCONSOLE utility.
10. Use the Connection Information menu to clear the new user account on the other workstation.
11. Use SHIFT/PRINT SCREEN keys to record the message that appears at the first workstation.
12. Exit FCONSOLE and start the SYSCON utility.
13. Delete the new user account.

Project 2. Practicing the Login Script Commands

1. Given the following directory structure, write the MAP commands needed to map the drive letters H:, I:, J:, and K: to the numbered directories. Do not attempt to perform these operations on the computer unless appropriate directories have been established.

```
F:\___|
        |-ACCOUNTS
        |  |
        |  |-RECEIVE (1)
        |  |-PAY (2)
        |
        |-PERSONEL
        |  |
        |  |-ARCHIVE
        |  |  |
        |  |  |-FULLTIME (3)
        |  |  |-PARTTIME
        |  |
        |  |-CURRENT
        |     |-FULLTIME
        |     |-PARTTIME (4)
```

2. Create a new user. Give the new user a login script that prints "Happy Birthday" on your birthday.

3. Using the network, create a directory structure similar to the following:

```
F:\___|
        |-(Your User Name)
                |
                |-SECURE
                |  |
                |  |-DATA
```

Using the SYSCON utility create a new user with all trustee rights to the directory (Your User Name) except Supervisory and Access Control. Use the Filer utility to make the contents of the SECURE directory inaccessible to the user. Use the SHIFT/PRINT SCREEN keys at each step and remove the directories and the user when you are finished.

5

Workstation Installation and Customization

Objectives

After completing this chapter you will

1. Know what files are required to link a workstation with a Novell 3.12 file server.
2. Know how these required files interact to cause a workstation to communicate with a file server.
3. Understand the use of login script variables to create a search path to DOS directories.
4. Understand the concept of remote reset.
5. Recognize the problems that can occur when using an AUTOEXEC.BAT file during remote reset.
6. Know how to create a boot image file.
7. Know how to use a BOOTCONF.SYS file.

Key Terms

AUTOEXEC.BAT
DOS
DOSGEN
LSL.COM
Remote Reset
Workstation Software

CONFIG.SYS
DOS Directories
IPXODI.COM
MAP
VLM.EXE

Introduction

In previous chapters, attaching workstations to the network was shown to be simple. Booting the workstation and loading Terminate and Stay Resident Programs LSL, the ODI-compliant (Open Data-Link Interface) NIC (network interface card) driver, IPXODI, and VLM programs sufficed to connect the workstation to a file server, but little was related regarding how these programs interact with each other and with the normal DOS workstation's CONFIG.SYS and AUTOEXEC.BAT. Also, some workstations can take advantage of a feature known as remote reset. This feature allows workstations to boot from the file server rather than from a diskette in drive A or a hard disk. All these features can be utilized if the workstation is customized, so a few techniques for accomplishing this are well worth learning.

Customizing NetWare

Network Drivers

Since the most common NetWare client is a DOS client, access to a Novell network requires the workstation to be booted with DOS. During the boot process, the CONFIG.SYS and AUTOEXEC.BAT files are executed. The AUTOEXEC.BAT file then calls the four previously mentioned programs to be loaded into memory in the workstation. The four programs are LSL.COM, the ODI-compliant (Open Data-Link Interface) NIC driver such as SMC8000 for some SMC Plus 10BaseT Network Interface Cards, IPXODI.COM, and VLM.EXE. Additionally, a network workstation configuration file called NET.CFG is referenced for configuration parameters for these four files.

The LSL.COM (Link Support Layer) program allows multiple network protocols to be loaded and have access to the NIC hardware. The NIC driver is designed to operate with only one type of network interface card, but it can communicate with more than one communications protocol such as IPX and TCP/IP simultaneously. Novell includes several standard ODI-compliant NIC drivers. Other non-standard drivers are usually shipped with the network interface card. IPXODI.COM provides Novell's IPX protocol, and TCPIP.COM provides Novell's TCP/IP protocol. The VLM.EXE program is the interface between DOS and the network. It monitors the operations of the user and directs commands to the network card that involve the network.

LSL.COM

The Link Support Layer, which is loaded first of the four network workstation files, actually acts as the traffic cop, directing traffic between the network interface card driver and the appropriate communications protocol stack, typically IPX, TCP/IP, or Appletalk. This program allows for simultaneous support of multiple communications protocols on one network interface card.

Network Interface Card Driver

The network interface card driver is a program which controls the network interface card and presents data to and takes data from the Link Support Layer program, LSL.COM. As mentioned earlier, this driver must be an ODI-compliant driver in order for it to communicate with LSL to support multiple communications protocols on the same NIC at the same time. Novell provides several ODI-compliant network interface card drivers on the distribution diskettes; other ODI-compliant network interface cards provide their drivers on diskettes included with the network interface card.

IPXODI.COM

IPXODI.COM provides support for the IPX protocol which allows the workstation to communicate with the file server. Additionally, IPXODI.COM automatically loads support for SPX (Sequenced Packet Exchange), which is the protocol which supports communication with print servers and such functions as RCONSOLE for remote file server console support. Note that the IPXODI.COM looks to the NET.CFG file for any special information regarding Interrupt setting, I/O setting, and memory setting for the network interface card. If there is no NET.CFG file, then IPXODI uses the default settings for the card, and the card must be physically set up accordingly.

NetWare DOS Requester

The NetWare DOS Requester is activated by running the VLM manager, a program called VLM.EXE, which loads a set of individual VLMs (Virtual Loadable Modules) to provide for such things as network file and print services. VLMs are the workstation equivalent of the NLMs on the file server because they are modular and can be loaded individually. The NetWare DOS Requester coexists with DOS, utilizes DOS tables and has a modular architecture which allows it to load only those VLMs which are needed by a given workstation. Additionally, VLM.EXE can be loaded in conventional, extended, or expanded memory for optimum memory usage. The specific list of VLMs to be loaded for a given workstation is given in the NetWare DOS Requester section of NET.CFG.

Customizing the Workstation Software Through NET.CFG, CONFIG.SYS and AUTOEXEC.BAT

NET.CFG, CONFIG.SYS, and AUTOEXEC.BAT work together to provide configuration parameters to support customized loading of LSL, the NIC driver, IPXODI, and VLM. We will examine the effects of each of these programs in the discussion which follows.

CONFIG.SYS is the standard configuration file which loads drivers and sets up other environment parameters for DOS. When used in conjunction with the NetWare DOS Requester type of workstation software, the command LASTDRIVE=Z: must be added to CONFIG.SYS. Since the NetWare DOS Requester coexists with DOS and utilizes DOS tables, this command is necessary so that all 26 drives are accessible.

AUTOEXEC.BAT, as used by DOS, provides a shorthand method for activating several programs on the workstation that could, if desired, be entered from the command line one by one. Under the NetWare DOS Requester scenario, AUTOEXEC.BAT is usually modified during the installation of the NetWare DOS Requester so that it changes directories to a directory called C:\NWCLIENT and then calls a batch file called STARTNET.BAT in the NWCLIENT directory. STARTNET.BAT then loads LSL, the NIC driver, IPXODI, and runs VLM, which then loads appropriate VLM files that are also typically installed in C:\NWCLIENT.

NET.CFG is a text file which provides configuration information for the workstation boot process. The major sections of configuration information are the Link Driver section and the NetWare DOS Requester section. A sample NET.CFG file is shown in Fig. 5-1.

The Link Driver section of the sample NET.CFG identifies the NIC driver, SMC8000 in Fig. 5-1, and indicates that the card is functioning using interrupt line 3, I/O address 300, memory address D0000, and Ethernet frame type Ethernet_802.3.

The NetWare DOS Requester section of the sample NET.CFG indicates that the drive letter for the first network drive is F. It is very important that the first network drive be specified; otherwise, the first network drive will be the first drive available after the VLM program identifies which drives are local to a given workstation. This means that for a workstation with a single C drive, the first network drive would, by default, be D: unless otherwise specified in the NET.CFG file. Since this drive would vary with workstations with differing numbers of local hard drives, it is far less confusing to specify the first network drive for all workstations to be F.

```
Link Driver SMC8000
  INT 3
  PORT 300
  MEM D0000
  FRAME Ethernet_802.3
NetWare DOS Requester
  FIRST NETWORK DRIVE=F
  Preferred Server=MYSERV
  USE DEFAULTS=OFF
  VLM = CONN.VLM
  VLM = IPXNCP.VLM
  VLM = TRAN.VLM
  VLM = BIND.VLM
  VLM = NWP.VLM
  VLM = FIO.VLM
  VLM = PRINT.VLM
  VLM = GENERAL.VLM
  VLM = REDIR.VLM
  VLM = NETX.VLM
  VLM = AUTO.VLM
```

Fig. 5-1 A sample NET.CFG file

The Preferred Server statement in NET.CFG causes the workstation to attempt to connect to a specific server upon executing the VLM program. Otherwise, execution of the VLM program causes the workstation to issue a "Get Nearest Server" to the network cable requesting the logically nearest file server to respond. For a variety of reasons, the nearest file server may or may not be the same each time the VLM runs. Therefore, the particular file server accessed by a workstation VLM without the Preferred Server option cannot be guaranteed. Customarily, the Preferred Server option is used and is set to the name of the file server to which the user normally needs access.

The USE DEFAULTS=OFF command indicates to VLM.EXE that the list of VLMs which follows is the list of VLMs and the load order of the VLMs which are to be loaded on the workstation. These files all have the extension of .VLM, and they are almost always located in the same directory as VLM.EXE, normally the C:\NWCLIENT directory.

DOS Directories

In a large network there may be many different types of workstations running many different versions of DOS. The utility programs for each of those DOS versions are sensitive to the version loaded into the computer. Each program, such as FORMAT.COM or CHKDSK.COM, checks which version the computer is running before it executes. For instance, if the FORMAT.COM program from MS DOS 3.1 was started on a computer running PC DOS 6.22 the program would print "Incorrect DOS version." on the screen and then halt.

The result is that if the DOS files for the workstations are to be loaded on the file server, a directory must be created for each of the types of DOS versions that might be used by the workstations. The most critical of the DOS files stored in this way is the DOS command interpreter COMMAND.COM. It is loaded by DOS when the computer is booted and must be frequently reloaded during normal operation. DOS uses the COMSPEC environment variable to record the location of this program. Ordinarily, the COMSPEC variable is set when the computer is booted. If, for instance, the computer was booted from a DOS disk in drive A:, the COMSPEC variable would probably be set to A:\COMMAND.COM. Unfortunately, the DOS disk must often be removed from drive A: to make room for other program or data disks. When DOS needs to reload COMMAND.COM, it will display the message "Insert diskette with COMMAND.COM and strike any key when ready" on the screen and wait for the user to respond.

Network workstations may be booted from a diskette, so setting the COMSPEC variable to point to a copy of COMMAND.COM on the file server can save a great deal of time for the user. The problem is of course setting it to point to the correct version of COMMAND.COM. NetWare provides facilities for doing just that. The login script variables OS, OS_VERSION, and MACHINE can be used to locate the DOS files at the time the user logs in to the network.

These variables are automatically set when the network drivers are loaded. Once set, they can be used by the login script to MAP network drive letters to appropriate directories. For instance, if an IBM PC running DOS version 3.3 were to login to the network, the OS variable would be set to MSDOS, the OS_VERSION variable would be set to V3.30, and the MACHINE variable would be set to IBM_PC. All the user accounts on the file server could have a line in their login scripts like this:

MAP S1:=SYS:\PUBLIC\%MACHINE\%OS\%OS_VERSION

The search drive, S1, would be mapped to a different directory on the file server for each different value of MACHINE, OS, and OS_VERSION. The supervisor need only ensure that there is a directory containing the correct DOS version for each workstation that logs in. After this line has been executed, the S1 can be used to set the COMSPEC variable.

COMSPEC=S1:COMMAND.COM

In actual practice these two lines would probably be placed in the System Login Script, where they would be executed for every user.

Remote Reset

In some environments, strict network security is required. In these situations, diskless workstations can be used to prevent most users from copying data from the server to a diskette on the workstation. The problem, of course, is to boot a computer with no disk drives. The solution is called remote reset, remote boot, or sometimes remote program load. With this feature, a computer can be booted from a file on a network drive rather than from a local disk drive.

Essentially, the workstation is tricked into thinking that the file on the server is a boot disk in drive A. Remote boot is also very helpful for workstations with only floppy disk drives since it eliminates the need for a customized boot diskette to be located near each workstation. Another advantage is that upgrades to a computer's DOS or the network drivers can be made from the network without the need for the supervisor to visit each workstation.

Setting up remote boot involves four steps:

1. The network card must be prepared for remote boot. Only certain network cards can support remote boot. These cards have a ROM (read only memory) chip that requests boot information from the server. Many network cards have sockets for remote boot ROM chips, but the chips are not usually sold with them. Most network cards that are capable of remote boot require a switch to be set on the card or a setup program to be run that sets the card to remote boot mode. It is imperative that the manual for the particular network interface card you are using be consulted to properly set up the card to remote boot.

2. A boot disk must be prepared for the workstation that is to be set for remote boot. DOS, the network drivers, and any other programs that are to be loaded when the computer boots must be copied to the disk. The proper AUTOEXEC.BAT, CONFIG.SYS, and NET.CFG files must be prepared and copied to the disk.

3. A program on the file server called DOSGEN must be used to copy all the data on the boot disk to a file on the server called a boot disk image file. The default name for this file is NET$DOS.SYS but it can be changed to something more meaningful such as ROOM1.SYS.

4. If more than one boot image file is needed, another file must be created that indicates which workstations are to use which boot image files. The file, which is named BOOTCONF.SYS, is simply a list of network addresses and the boot image file each needs.

Remote Reset Setup

The Network Card

Preparing the network card for remote boot will be different on each card. Some cards will require only a switch to be set on the card. Many cards have setup programs that are used to set the card to remote boot mode. Other cards will need a remote boot ROM to be inserted in a socket on the card.

The Boot Disk

Some special considerations must be made when preparing a boot disk for remote boot. The problem stems from the unusual behavior of the computer while it is using remote boot.

Without remote boot, the computer will search for a bootable disk. Assuming there is a disk in drive A:, the computer first loads the DOS system files and reads the CONFIG.SYS file for device drivers or other instructions. Next the AUTOEXEC.BAT file is executed. A network boot disk will have an AUTOEXEC.BAT file that loads the appropriate network drivers, LSL.COM, the NIC driver, IPXODI, and VLM.EXE, for example. Once these programs are loaded the next line in the AUTOEXEC.BAT file would be executed. Suppose the following lines are in the AUTOEXEC.BAT file.

```
LSL
SMC8000 (for an SMC 10Base T Network Interface Card)
IPXODI
VLM
LOGIN JSMITH1
```

Since the computer is booting off the A drive, drive A is the default drive. When the LSL instruction in AUTOEXEC.BAT is executed, the computer will first search only the root directory of drive A to locate and load this program. The same is true for the NIC driver SMC8000, IPXODI, VLM and LOGIN JSMITH1 instructions. Note that after the VLM program is loaded, drive letter F: is available to the user. When the LOGIN JSMITH1 instruction is executed, the default drive is still A, even though the workstation has been attached to the server.

The same sequence of events occurs when remote boot is used; however, the computer is "fooled" into reading the boot image file as if it were a disk in drive A. The difference comes after the VLM program is loaded. As soon as a formal connection is made to the file server, the remote boot process is abandoned and the default drive is left at drive F.

Even though the remote boot process is essentially over, the AUTOEXEC.BAT file is still executing. Unfortunately DOS has not stored the entire file in memory. Only a byte offset of the next instruction in the batch file is stored. With the remote boot process ended, the AUTOEXEC.BAT file is no longer available since it cannot be read from the boot image file. Additionally, DOS does not recognize that the default drive has been changed. The result is that the computer will attempt to read the next instruction in the AUTOEXEC.BAT from the F:\LOGIN directory.

If there were no more instructions in the file, that is, if VLM were the last line, the workstation would simply display the F:> prompt and be ready for the user to login. Often, however, additional instructions must be executed after the workstation is connected to a file server. In the example above, the command LOGIN JSMITH1 is intended to provide an automatic login at the workstation. To accommodate this one workstation, a copy of the AUTOEXEC.BAT file could be placed in the F:\LOGIN directory. This would not, however, be a satisfactory solution, since every workstation that uses remote boot and needs instructions executed after being connected to the server would encounter the same AUTOEXEC.BAT file.

Fig. 5-2 shows three different AUTOEXEC.BAT files. The first two represent files in the boot image prepared for workstations #1 and #2. The third is the file in the F:\LOGIN directory. After the VLM instruction in each of the workstation files is executed, those workstations are connected to the file server. They will be "fooled" into executing the next line in F:\LOGIN\AUTOEXEC.BAT on the server. The last line in workstation #1's AUTOEXEC.BAT, LOGIN JSMITH1, and the last line in workstation #2's AUTOEXEC.BAT, LOGIN SUSAN would be lost. Each would execute the CAPTURE command in F:\LOGIN\AUTOEXEC.BAT.

There are two solutions to this problem. The first, and most widely used, is to provide a different batch file for each boot disk. The second solution is to ensure that the F:\LOGIN\AUTOEXEC.BAT file will execute different instructions based on information received from the workstation boot image file.

```
Workstation #1
AUTOEXEC.BAT in boot image file
SET NEXT=LOGIN JSMITH1
REM *
LSL
PCN2L
IPXODI
VLM
%NEXT%

Workstation #2
AUTOEXEC.BAT in boot image file
SET NEXT=LOGIN SUSAN
REM ***
LSL
PCN2L
IPXODI
VLM
%NEXT%

On the file server
F:\LOGIN\AUTOEXEC.BAT
REM *****************
REM ***
LSL
PCN2L
IPXODI
VLM
%NEXT%
```

Fig. 5-3. Updated batch files.

drive letter F: is available to the user. When the LOGIN JSMITH1 instruction is executed, the default drive is still A, even though the workstation has been attached to the server.

The same sequence of events occurs when remote boot is used; however, the computer is "fooled" into reading the boot image file as if it were a disk in drive A. The difference comes after the VLM program is loaded. As soon as a formal connection is made to the file server, the remote boot process is abandoned and the default drive is left at drive F.

Even though the remote boot process is essentially over, the AUTOEXEC.BAT file is still executing. Unfortunately DOS has not stored the entire file in memory. Only a byte offset of the next instruction in the batch file is stored. With the remote boot process ended, the AUTOEXEC.BAT file is no longer available since it cannot be read from the boot image file. Additionally, DOS does not recognize that the default drive has been changed. The result is that the computer will attempt to read the next instruction in the AUTOEXEC.BAT from the F:\LOGIN directory.

If there were no more instructions in the file, that is, if VLM were the last line, the workstation would simply display the F:> prompt and be ready for the user to login. Often, however, additional instructions must be executed after the workstation is connected to a file server. In the example above, the command LOGIN JSMITH1 is intended to provide an automatic login at the workstation. To accommodate this one workstation, a copy of the AUTOEXEC.BAT file could be placed in the F:\LOGIN directory. This would not, however, be a satisfactory solution, since every workstation that uses remote boot and needs instructions executed after being connected to the server would encounter the same AUTOEXEC.BAT file.

Fig. 5-2 shows three different AUTOEXEC.BAT files. The first two represent files in the boot image prepared for workstations #1 and #2. The third is the file in the F:\LOGIN directory. After the VLM instruction in each of the workstation files is executed, those workstations are connected to the file server. They will be "fooled" into executing the next line in F:\LOGIN\AUTOEXEC.BAT on the server. The last line in workstation #1's AUTOEXEC.BAT, LOGIN JSMITH1, and the last line in workstation #2's AUTOEXEC.BAT, LOGIN SUSAN would be lost. Each would execute the CAPTURE command in F:\LOGIN\AUTOEXEC.BAT.

There are two solutions to this problem. The first, and most widely used, is to provide a different batch file for each boot disk. The second solution is to ensure that the F:\LOGIN\AUTOEXEC.BAT file will execute different instructions based on information received from the workstation boot image file.

```
Workstation #1
AUTOEXEC.BAT in boot image file
LSL
PCN2L (for IBM PC Baseband Card)
IPXODI
VLM
LOGIN JSMITH1
Workstation #2
AUTOEXEC.BAT in boot image file
LSL
PCN2L (for IBM PC Baseband Card)
IPXODI
VLM
LOGIN SUSAN
On file server
F:\LOGIN\AUTOEXEC.BAT
LSL
PCN2L
IPXODI
VLM
CAPTURE
```

Fig. 5-2. Different AUTOEXEC.BAT files.

Providing a different batch file for each boot disk is a little more involved than it would first seem. The computer booting up will need to return to the batch file after any programs in it are executed. For instance, if the batch file had a LOGIN statement in it, the computer would need to find the batch file after the LOGIN statement was executed. But the LOGIN script might have changed the current directory. For this reason the batch file being used by the computer during the remote boot process should exist in three places, in the boot disk image file, in the \LOGIN directory, and in the directory that the login script leaves as the default directory when it finishes.

To create the proper boot image file, a complete boot disk should be prepared. DOS, the network workstation programs (including VLMs), and an appropriate AUTOEXEC.BAT file should be placed on a disk. To accommodate all of the boot disk image files that might exist on the server, the AUTOEXEC.BAT file is divided into two batch files. AUTOEXEC.BAT simply starts another batch file with a unique name. On the boot disk, the AUTOEXEC.BAT file would have a single line such as JSMITH.BAT. The other file, JSMITH.BAT, would contain all the appropriate instructions for starting the workstation on the network. This file would also be the one that must be duplicated in all three locations mentioned above, the boot disk, the \LOGIN directory, and the default directory left after the login script executes.

The second solution to the problem of multiple boot image files involves the creation of an AUTOEXEC.BAT file on the file server that can accommodate different instructions depending on which boot image file calls it. Creating these batch files requires a better understanding of DOS batch files and the remote boot process.

In Fig. 5-3 all three AUTOEXEC.BAT files have been changed. Three new DOS batch file commands have been used, the SET command, the REM command, and the "%" symbol. The SET command places the text to the right of the "=" in the variable on the left of the "=". This variable is known as an environment variable and is stored in the workstation's memory. The REM command is called a remark and is used simply to put a comment in the file. It and any text that follows it on the same line are not executed by the computer. The "%" symbol is called a replacement symbol. In a batch file, the environment variable contained inside two "%" symbols is replaced with the contents of the variable. In workstation #1's file, for instance, the last line, %NEXT%, would be replaced with the contents of the variable NEXT, which is LOGIN JSMITH1.

In this case, however, the last line of workstation #1's AUTOEXEC.BAT file will never be executed. But the same replacement will take place when the last line of F:\LOGIN\AUTOEXEC.BAT is executed. The environment variable NEXT will still have the value in it from the first line in workstation #1's AUTOEXEC.BAT.

Followed from the beginning, this is what will happen to workstation #1.

1. When the workstation is turned on or re-booted, the network interface card requests boot information from the server.
2. The file server sends a copy of the boot image file to the workstation. That file is treated as if it were a disk in drive A of the workstation.
3. The workstation loads DOS and begins to execute AUTOEXEC.BAT.

Workstation #1

AUTOEXEC.BAT in boot image file

    SET NEXT=LOGIN JSMITH1

    REM *

    LSL

    PCN2L

    IPXODI

    VLM

    %NEXT%

Workstation #2

AUTOEXEC.BAT in boot image file

    SET NEXT=LOGIN SUSAN

    REM ***

    LSL

    PCN2L

    IPXODI

    VLM

    %NEXT%

On the file server

F:\LOGIN\AUTOEXEC.BAT

    REM ****************

    REM ***

    LSL

    PCN2L

    IPXODI

    VLM

    %NEXT%

Fig. 5-3. Updated batch files.

4. The first line, SET NEXT=LOGIN JSMITH1, creates a variable called NEXT and stores the value LOGIN JSMITH1 in it.

5. The second line, REM *, is a remark and is not executed.

6. The third, fourth, fifth, and sixth lines load the network drivers LSL, PCN2L, IPXODI, and VLM.

7. The instant VLM has loaded successfully, the workstation is attached to the file server and the boot image file is abandoned.

8. The workstation reads its next command from the file server in the file F:\LOGIN\AUTOEXEC.BAT. This is when the REM statements become important. The next command is not necessarily the fifth line in the batch file. It is the command located at the same byte offset as the next command in workstation #1's AUTOEXEC.BAT. There are 43 characters in workstation #1's AUTOEXEC.BAT file up to the end of the sixth line VLM. Adding a carriage return and line feed character to each line brings the total number of bytes to 55 through the end of the sixth line. The REM statements are used to ensure that the seventh line starts at byte offset 56 in each of the three files. The REM statement in the second line of workstation #2's file has two more asterisks in it than the similar line in workstation #1's file because the line SET NEXT=LOGIN SUSAN is two characters less than the line SET NEXT=LOGIN JSMITH1. The first two lines of F:\LOGIN\AUTOEXEC.BAT are there to occupy the space that the first two lines in each of the workstation's files use.

9. Since the byte offsets of the files are aligned properly, the next statement executed by workstation #1 is the fifth line in F:\LOGIN\AUTOEXEC.BAT. The %NEXT% is replaced with the value of the NEXT variable and LOGIN JSMITH1 is executed.

10. The login script for user JSMITH1 takes over and any instructions located there are executed.

The files in this example represent just one way in which environment variables can be used to make individual workstations work differently.

Using DOSGEN

Once created, the information on the boot disk must be converted to a special type of file known as a boot image. The file consists of all the information, including the DOS system files, the network driver programs, and the AUTOEXEC.BAT on the boot disk, converted to a form that the file server can store and send to the workstation when necessary. The NetWare utility program for doing this is called DOSGEN.EXE. The following syntax is used with DOSGEN:

DOSGEN drive [file name]

The drive specified must be a floppy disk drive on the local computer. The file name is optional but must end with a .SYS extension. If no file name is given, DOSGEN will convert the information on the disk to a file called NET$DOS.SYS. The boot disk itself is not changed. NET$DOS.SYS is also the default name that a workstation will use when remote booting. The DOSGEN program is located in the F:\SYSTEM directory on the file server, and all boot image files must be stored in the F:\LOGIN directory.

DOSGEN works with any bootable DOS diskette except DOS version 5 and higher. Novell has provided a program called RPLFIX.COM that is used to repair a DOS 5 or 6 boot image file already created with DOSGEN. This program, RPLFIX.COM (Remote Program Load Fix), is available on Novell's Compuserve forum Netwire or through a Novell authorized dealer.

BOOTCONF.SYS

Customizing each boot disk means that each workstation will need a separate boot image file. A file called BOOTCONF.SYS is used to store the names of all the boot image files and the network addresses where each will be used. BOOTCONF.SYS must be located in the F:\LOGIN directory and is a simple text file in the form:

    0Xnetwork number,node number=boot image file name

A typical line in BOOTCONF.SYS might look something like the following:

    0X00D22901,08005A6A34F1=ROOM1.SYS

BOOTCONF.SYS can contain as many lines as needed. When a workstation is using remote boot, BOOTCONF.SYS is searched for a line with that workstation's address. If the address is found, the boot image file specified is used. If the address is not found, the file NET$DOS.SYS is used.

Hands-on NetWare

In order to complete the tutorials in the remaining half of this chapter, the file server and a workstation should be ready to use.

1. The file server must be on.
2. The user account created in the previous chapter must still be available.
3. The network boot disk created earlier must be available.
4. A complete set of DOS diskettes must be available. DOS version 5 or higher must be used in some sections. The MEM command must be available for these sections.

5. The latest releases of the client workstation programs should be obtained, including LSL.COM, your NIC driver, IPXODI.COM, VLM.EXE, and all the *.VLM files. The latest versions of some of these programs are available through Novell's Compuserve forum Netwire or through a Novell authorized reseller.

6. In the examples below TYPE THE NAME OF YOUR ACCOUNT WHERE USER JSMITH IS USED. For instance, if the instructions read "Type LOGIN JSMITH", you should type LOGIN followed by the name of the account you created earlier.

Memory Usage

One of the most important concerns when attaching a DOS computer to any network is the amount of RAM that will be used by the network drivers. In some cases the network drivers use so much memory that application programs cannot run. This of course makes the network worse than useless. The amount of memory used by different networks varies widely from as much as 100K to as little as 10K. Also, the amount of memory used by a single network can vary depending on the options used and the way the drivers are loaded into memory. NetWare is no exception. Many different configurations are possible, and each leaves different amounts of conventional memory free. Conventional memory is all memory up to 640K. All DOS programs must use some of this area during some time in their operation. Other areas of memory, high memory, extended memory, and expanded memory, can only be used in addition to the 640K region, which is what makes it so critical. On a computer with 640K or less of memory, the choices are somewhat limited. The following tutorial demonstrates memory usage in these computers.

Computers with 640K or Less of RAM

In the following tutorial, a workstation with 640K of memory is used.

1. Boot the computer with a DOS diskette by placing the disk in drive A: and pressing the CONTROL, ALT, and DELETE keys simultaneously.

2. Enter the date and time as requested.

3. Type **CHKDSK** and press the ENTER key. The CHKDSK program will show the disk space information and memory usage similar to that in Fig. 5-4. The last two sets of numbers at the bottom show the total amount available to DOS and the amount currently unused. In this case the CHKDSK program shows 569,264 bytes of free memory with only DOS loaded.

4. Remove the DOS diskette from drive A and replace it with the network boot disk.

5. Type **LSL** and press the ENTER key.

6. Type the name of your NIC driver. In our example, this was PCN2L for an IBM PC Baseband card, and press the ENTER key.

7. Type **IPXODI** and press the ENTER key.

8. Type **VLM** and press the ENTER key.

9. With the network drivers loaded, return the DOS disk to drive A, type **CHKDSK**, and press the ENTER key. The CHKDSK program should report significantly less memory in the "bytes free" section. The missing memory is being used by the network drivers. Write down the figure shown for "bytes free" for comparison later.

The example above represents a worst-case situation in which all the drivers must be placed entirely in conventional memory. Many programs not originally intended to operate in a networked environment would not have enough memory to run. A computer with at least 1 megabyte of memory can be configured to preserve much more conventional memory.

```
A:\>chkdsk

    1,457,664 bytes total disk space
    1,439,232 bytes in 5 user files
       18,432 bytes available on disk

          512 bytes in each allocation unit
        2,847 total allocation units on disk
           36 available allocation units on disk

      655,360 total bytes memory
      569,264 bytes free

Instead of using CHKDSK, try using SCANDISK.  SCANDISK can reliably detect
and fix a much wider range of disk problems.  For more information,
type HELP SCANDISK from the command prompt.

A:\>
```

Fig. 5-4. Output produced by the CHKDSK program.

Computers with 1 Megabyte or More of Memory

DOS programs are typically limited to the 640K conventional memory region, but a number of methods have been created to use more. On a computer with 1 megabyte of memory, some of the 360K (actually 384K) above conventional memory (called high memory) can be used by DOS, if an appropriate extended memory manager program is implemented. Microsoft's

HIMEM.SYS device driver is the most readily available of these programs. The following instructions demonstrate how high memory can be used to save conventional memory.

Using HIMEM.SYS and Loading VLM.EXE with flags

1. Copy the HIMEM.SYS file to the network boot disk.
2. Edit the CONFIG.SYS file on the network boot disk, adding the following line:

    DEVICE=HIMEM.SYS

3. Boot the workstation with the network boot disk in drive A:.
4. Type **LSL** and press the ENTER key.
5. Type the name of your NIC driver and press the ENTER key. Remember, the example is using PCN2L for the IBM PC Baseband card, but you must type the name of the driver for your NIC.
6. Type **IPXODI** and press the ENTER key.
7. Type **VLM** and press the ENTER key
8. Replace the network boot disk with the DOS disk containing the CHKDSK program.
9. Type **CHKDSK** and press the ENTER key.

The number of bytes free should be significantly larger in this case than in the previous example with only LSL, the NIC driver, IPXODI, and VLM loaded. The extra space available in conventional memory is made possible by the VLM program loading primarily into the high memory region between 640K and 1 megabyte. Write down the figure shown for "bytes free" for comparison later.

DOS Versions 5 and 6

DOS versions 5 and 6 offer other ways to use the high memory area. Most of the DOS code itself, as well as any other memory resident programs such as network drivers can be loaded into the high memory area. The following exercises demonstrate the benefits in conventional memory savings using DOS 5 or 6 on a computer with at least 1 megabyte of memory. A bootable DOS disk will be needed.

1. Copy the LSL, the NIC driver, IPXODI.COM, VLM.EXE and the *.VLM files to the bootable DOS disks.
2. Copy the following files from the original DOS disks to the bootable disk: HIMEM.SYS, EMM386.EXE, CHKDSK.EXE, MEM.EXE, and MORE.COM.
3. Ensure that the DOS disk is in drive A and edit the CONFIG.SYS file adding the following lines:

    DEVICE=HIMEM.SYS

DEVICE=EMM386.EXE NOEMS
DOS=HIGH,UMB

The CONFIG.SYS file is being used in this case to load programs that will manage the high memory area and to load DOS into that area. The HIMEM.SYS device driver manages the use of all the memory above 640K. The EMM386.EXE program is being used to allow DOS programs access to the high memory area between 640K and 1 megabyte. The DOS command instructs DOS to load itself into the high memory area and to allow other programs to be loaded there as well.

4. Boot the workstation with the DOS disk by simultaneously pressing the CONTROL, ALT, and DELETE keys.
5. Enter the date and time as requested.
6. Type **LSL** and press the ENTER key.
7. Type the name of your NIC driver and press the ENTER key. Remember, the example is using PCN2L for the IBM PC Baseband card, but you must type the name of the driver for your NIC.
8. Type **LOADHIGH IPXODI** and press the ENTER key. LOADHIGH, which can be abbreviated LH, is a DOS command that attempts to load the program into the high memory area.
9. Enter **VLM /MX** to ensure that the VLMs will load into the memory between 640KB and 1 MB. Note that by default the VLMs will attempt to load in this area even without the switch.
10. Type **CHKDSK** and press the ENTER key. Compare the "bytes free" figure with the number obtained when using conventional memory only. This amount should be much larger.
11. Type **MEM /C | MORE** and press the ENTER key. The | MORE portion of this command is necessary only because the output from the MEM /C command will be longer than 25 lines displayed on the monitor.

This command displays memory usage in a more complete form than the CHKDSK command. The first screen shows programs running in conventional memory. MSDOS, HIMEM, EMM386, and COMMAND, LSL, and the NIC driver should be listed there.

12. Strike any key to advance to the next screen of output from the MEM /C command. A list of programs loaded into high memory should appear. SYSTEM, IPXODI, and VLM should be shown in high memory. The MSDOS shown in conventional memory and the SYSTEM shown in high memory are both portions of DOS code.

Remote Reset

With the remote reset feature, also called remote boot or remote IPL, a workstation can boot from a file on the server rather than from a diskette. This is extraordinarily beneficial in environments where there are many computers without a hard disk to boot from. The supervisor can avoid the tedium of maintaining a boot disk for each workstation which can become lost, damaged, or infected with a computer virus. Remote reset also makes possible a diskless workstation for use in environments where strict data security is required.

Remote reset is only possible when using network interface cards that are specifically designed for it. In addition, most network cards that can employ remote reset require a switch to be physically set on the card. Some network cards require the switch to be set using a program on a setup disk provided with the computer or the card. The following exercises assume the proper hardware settings have been made for remote boot. Remote reset will only work on a computer that has no other physical disk to boot from. Therefore, if the workstation being used to test remote boot has a hard disk, it must be configured as nonbootable.

Installing remote reset will require some cooperation between students using the server. Since there is only one BOOTCONF.SYS file and one AUTOEXEC.BAT file on the server, these files may need to be created only once or updated by an individual for all others. The BOOTCONF.SYS file will contain the network addresses of all the workstations using remote boot. Follow the instructions below to determine the address of the workstation you are currently using.

1. Type **LOGIN** and your user name. Then press the ENTER key. The password prompt should appear.

2. Type the password used for this account and press the ENTER key.

3. Type **FCONSOLE** and press the ENTER key. The FCONSOLE main menu should appear, similar to the one in Fig. 5-5.

4. Move the highlighted bar to the Connection Information option and press the ENTER key.

5. Type the name of your user account. The highlighted bar will move to your name. Press the ENTER key.

6. Use the ARROW keys to highlight the Other Information option and press the ENTER key.

7. The box displayed shows when and where this user logged in. Write down the number labeled Network Address. Remember to include the ":". The first eight digits of this number indicate the network being used. This is the same network number entered

when NetWare was installed. The last twelve digits identify the actual network card in the workstation being used. Later in this chapter, when this number is used, you must be using the same workstation.

8. Press the ESC key four times until the Exit FCONSOLE menu appears.
9. Press Y, then the ENTER key.
10. Type **LOGOUT** and press the ENTER key.

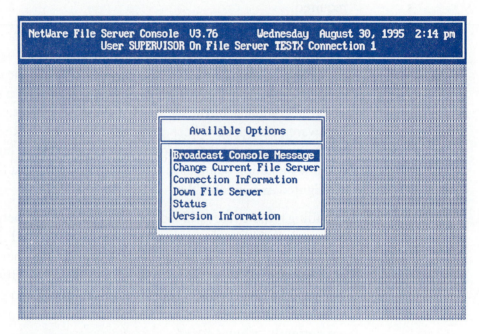

Fig. 5-5. FCONSOLE's main menu.

For this exercise the last eight digits of the node number will be used as the name for the boot image file. Ordinarily a name would be used that indicates the location or type of computer being used. For instance, the file might be called ROOM222.SYS or COMPAQ#1.SYS. The .SYS extension is required by NetWare. By using a portion of the node number as the name, the chance of accidental duplications of node numbers in the BOOTCONF.SYS file can be greatly reduced.

The next task is to create an appropriate AUTOEXEC.BAT file to be placed on the boot disk. Often a complementary AUTOEXEC.BAT needs to be placed in the F:\LOGIN directory on the file server. The file server AUTOEXEC.BAT must be usable by all the workstations using remote boot. Remember the necessity of a general purpose AUTOEXEC.BAT on the file server is considered to be a bug by Novell and may be fixed in the version of the network shell you are using. To simplify this exercise, a short AUTOEXEC.BAT file will be used that does not have any commands after the network shell is loaded. No file server AUTOEXEC.BAT will then be needed. Follow the steps below to create an AUTOEXEC.BAT file for the boot disk and to create a boot image file on the file server.

1. Boot the workstation with the network boot disk in drive A.
2. Enter the date and time as required.
3. At the A: prompt type the following lines exactly as shown, pressing the ENTER key after each line.

   COPY CON AUTOEXEC.BAT

   LSL

   PCN2L (substitute the name of your NIC driver)

   IPXODI

   VLM

4. Hold down the CONTROL key and press the Z key. Then press the ENTER key.
5. Type **AUTOEXEC.BAT** and press the ENTER key. This will test the AUTOEXEC.BAT file and load the network driver programs.
6. Type **F:** and press the ENTER key.
7. Type **LOGIN** followed by the name of your account and press the ENTER key.
8. Type your password and press the ENTER key.
9. To ensure that you are in the proper directory, type **CD\LOGIN** and press the ENTER key.
10. Verify that the disk in drive A is the network boot disk with the proper network driver programs, including configuration files such as CONFIG.SYS, AUTOEXEC.BAT, and NET.CFG.
11. Type **DOSGEN A:** followed by the last eight digits of the node number of the workstation you are now using followed by .SYS, then press the ENTER key. For example, if the network address written down earlier was 00D22901:08005A5A0123, the command would be DOSGEN A: 5A5A0123.SYS.

    An additional step is required for DOS 5 and 6 users. A program called RPLFIX.COM must be obtained from Novell's Compuserve forum Netwire or from a Novell authorized reseller.

    With the RPLFIX program on a disk in drive A:, type **A:RPLFIX** followed by the name of your boot image file. Then press the ENTER key. For instance, if your boot image file name is 5A5A0123.SYS, the command would be A:RPLFIX 5A5A0123.SYS.

12. A BOOTCONF.SYS file must be created to tell NetWare which boot image file is to be sent to which workstation. This file could be completely entered by an individual using the proper format to indicate the names of the boot image files. A complete BOOTCONF.SYS file might look something like the following.

0X00D22901,08005A6A3491=5A6A3491.SYS

0X00D22901,08007A6A44F1=7A6A44F1.SYS

0X00D22901,08005A6A348B=5A6A348B.SYS

0X00D22901,08005A6B14FC=5A6B14FC.SYS

0X00D22901,08005A6A3A11=5A6A3A11.SYS

0X00D22901,08005A6A24F7=5A6A24F7.SYS

0X00D22901,08005B6AF4E1=5B6AF4E1:SYS

0X00D22901,08005A6A34F2=5A6A34F2.SYS

The first two characters of each line, 0X, are required to indicate that the other characters represent a hexadecimal number. The next eight characters are the network number of the network being used. The characters between the ",'' and the "=" are the individual workstation node numbers, and, finally, the characters following the "=" are the names of the boot image files.

An alternate method of creating the BOOTCONF.SYS file would be to have each student append the line required for his or her workstation by using a command in the following format.

ECHO 0X00D22901,08005A6A3491=5A6A3491.SYS >> BOOTCONF.SYS

This command must be entered while still logged in under your supervisor-equivalent account and with F:\LOGIN as the current directory. The network address, node address, and boot image file name in the command above would be replaced with the numbers for your workstation.

Testing Remote Reset

With the BOOTCONF.SYS file created, the only step left is to test the remote reset.

1. Type **LOGOUT** and press the ENTER key.
2. Remove any disk that may be in disk drive A.
3. Boot the computer by pressing the CONTROL, ALT, and DELETE keys simultaneously.
4. The workstation should boot as if it were using the boot disk created earlier without prompting for the date and time.
5. To completely test the remote boot feature, type **F:** and press the ENTER key.

6. Type **LOGIN** followed by your account name and press the ENTER key.
7. If the login was successful, type **LOGOUT** and press the ENTER key.

Summary

The workstations on a network may have different types and amounts of memory. To take full advantage of the memory available, these differences must be taken into account when loading the network driver programs. DOS version 5 and 6 can also be used to increase available memory by loading the network driver programs into high memory.

Workstations may also use different versions of DOS. Each of the different versions must be loaded onto the file server with appropriate login script commands to make the DOS files available to the user.

Some network cards can take advantage of a NetWare feature called remote reset, which allows the workstation to boot from the file server rather than a floppy or hard disk. In this process, a fully customized boot disk is copied to a file on the server using a program called DOSGEN. If more than one boot image file is needed, a file called BOOTCONF.SYS is used to correlate the workstation with the boot image file.

Questions

1. How are VLMs on NetWare workstations similar to NLMs on NetWare file servers?
2. Where do VLMs, by default, attempt to load?
3. What is the purpose of the NET.CFG file, and where is it found on the workstation?
4. Why is the FIRST NETWORK DRIVE statement usually included in the NET.CFG file? What is the first network drive if this statement is left out?
5. Why is it important that the login script variables MACHINE, OS, and OS_VERSION have the proper values for a given workstation?
6. The remote reset process can abandon the AUTOEXEC.BAT file in the boot image file and use another. Where is this other copy of AUTOEXEC.BAT located?

7. What is the name of the program used to create a boot image file?
8. What information does the BOOTCONF.SYS file contain?

Projects

Objective

The following projects provide additional practice creating automated processes in order for users to access the network and to remotely boot a file. They enhance earlier hands-on exercises on these topics.

Project 1. Automating User Logins

1. Create a new user with the SYSCON utility. Use the appropriate login script variables to display the workstation type, operating system, and operating system version each time the user logs in. Do not give the user a password. Use the SHIFT and PRINT SCREEN keys to record the results.

2. Write the MAP command needed to ensure the correct version of DOS is used with a COMPAQ computer running MS DOS version 3.1. Assume the necessary directories are in place. Also write the MAP command needed to ensure the correct version of DOS is running regardless of the type of computer and version of DOS, assuming the necessary directories are in place.

3. Change the login script so that the SET command is executed during the login script. The SET command is an internal DOS command, not a program name. To execute an internal DOS command, use the following syntax:

    #COMMAND /C command name

    COMMAND is the DOS command interpreter COMMAND.COM. The /C tells COMMAND.COM to execute the internal DOS command that follows. Use SHIFT/PRINT SCREEN to record the results.

4. Using the DOSGEN program, create a boot image file that logs in the user created above. Use SHIFT/PRINT SCREEN to record the results.

Project 2. Creating a Remote Boot File

1. Create a remote boot file for your workstation. Use only one command in the AUTOEXEC.BAT file. That command should be the name of another batch file with a unique name that exists both on the boot disk and in the F:\LOGIN directory.

2. Modify the remote boot file above to login to a user account.
3. Create a login script that assigns the drive letter M: to one of three different subdirectories, MORNING, AFTERNOON, and EVENING, depending on the time of day.
4. Modify the login script of the account used above to start another program such as a word processor or the FILER utility.

Project 3. Modifying a NET.CFG File

1. Modify the NET.CFG file shown in Fig. 5-1 to support a WD-PLUS NIC. Configure the file with interrupt 4, I/O address 320, and memory address D0000, and enable it to load default VLMs.

6

Network Printing

Objectives

After completing this chapter you will
1. Understand the concepts of network printing.
2. Know how network printers can be attached to the network.
3. Understand the use of printing structures to direct data and control printers.
4. Know how to install a print server and print queue.
5. Be able to send data to a network printer.

Key Terms

Bridges	Boot Disk
CAPTURE	Print Server
PCONSOLE	PRINTCON
PRINTDEF	Queue
Remote Printing	Server Printing

Introduction

Often an important function of a network is printer sharing. Printing across a network involves loading special software on the workstation that remains resident along with the other network drivers. The software intercepts output that a normal application such as a word processor sends to the workstation's printer port. That data is then sent across the network to a printer attached to another computer. With a network, many users can send output to the same printer. Or, users may wish to select among different types of printers available on the network. NetWare has supported network printing since its earliest versions, but lacked many important features. Several third-party products offered capabilities that made network printing a much more valuable resource. With later versions of NetWare, however, some of these features have been introduced as separate utilities.

Printers can be attached to the network in several ways. They can be connected to the file server, to a NetWare bridge, to a dedicated print server, or to a remote print server. Each of these methods will be discussed here. In addition, several third party vendors have produced products that allow even more flexibility in printing.

To accommodate the many users and printers that might be on a network, Novell has created a number of structures that are used to control what gets printed and where it gets printed. These structures are print forms, print devices, print queues, and print job configurations.

Printing in a Novell Network

File Server Printing

NetWare networks are very centralized in that almost all activity is handled through the file server. Therefore, the file server is a natural place to begin network printing. In NetWare version 3.12, printing on printers attached to the file server requires setting up a print server which is loaded via running the PSERVER NLM (NetWare Loadable Module) either as part of the file server's AUTOEXEC.NCF or by loading the NLM manually from the file server's monitor once the file server has booted. The NLM is essentially another program that runs on the server in addition to NetWare.

Print Server Printing

It is often inconvenient for a variety of reasons to use a file server for printing. Perhaps most importantly, the users who may need access to the printer may not be users who should have access to the file server. In other words, it may be dangerous to have the file server where an unskilled individual might try to reboot it in an attempt to restart the printer or run some other software. Physical proximity to the server can also create a noise problem if the network supervisor, the file server, and a loud printer are all located in the same room. Another reason to avoid attaching the printers to the file server is simply that printers usually require a great deal of maintenance while file servers do not. A file server may run for months without being turned off or even touched. Frequent installation and removal of printers or printer ports could disrupt the file server. Additionally, it is often inadvisable to burden an already busy file server with the load of also running as a print server. A dedicated print server can be used to avoid these concerns by placing the printers, paper, cables, and noise in a separate location.

The print server can be any computer on the network with at least 360K of memory and up to five printer ports. The computer runs a program called PSERVER that sends the output to the printers attached to it. Since a print server requires only minimal hardware, it is a good investment to make if there are to be several network printers.

Remote Printing

A print server can direct data to sixteen different printers, but those printers do not need to be physically attached to it. In fact, only five printers can be locally attached to the print server. With the proper software loaded on another workstation, the workstation's printer becomes a network printer. Authorized users anywhere on the network can send data to be printed on the workstation's local printer with only a slight slowing of the normal operation of the workstation. The remote printer software is a memory resident program that uses approximately 9K of memory and allows other applications to run. It operates similar to the way the DOS PRINT command works, operating in the background while the workstation's user runs another application in the foreground, such as a word processor. Using remote printing, a printer that is usually accessed by a single workstation can be set up to be accessible by anyone on the network. The greatest disadvantage to this system is its vulnerability. If the user reboots or causes an operating system crash, the remote printing software will no longer be available and will have to be reloaded to continue printing.

Wherever the printer is located, the same tools can be used to access and control it. These tools or printing structures can be used to control all aspects of printing, such as which printer is to be used, what print style is to be used, and who will have access to the printer.

Print Forms

Print forms are the simplest of the printing structures. They represent the type of paper the printer will use. Fig. 6-1 shows a Form Definition dialog box in the Printer Definition utility program PRINTDEF. As seen here, the only important information to the printer is the length and width of the paper. The name of the form might represent much more to the printer operator. For instance, one form might be called CHECK and another BILL. While they may be the same size, they are definitely different.

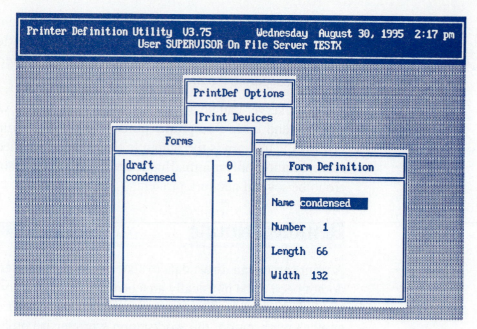

Fig. 6-1. The Form Definition dialog box.

Print Devices

Since each type and brand of printer may have a different set of control codes, NetWare uses the print device structure to define each printer. Fig. 6-2 shows the Print Device Options of the PRINTDEF program. The three options Edit Print Devices, Import Print Device, and Export Print Device refer to the use of printer definition files. When Import Print Device is chosen, the PRINTDEF program prompts the user for a directory. With the proper directory chosen, the program displays a list of printer definition files. Novell has provided files for most popular printers, and these files are normally stored in the PUBLIC directory. The arrow in the lower left corner of the Available .PDFs box indicates that more files are available than are shown. The files contain the codes that each printer uses for each of its functions. For instance, the CIT120D.PDF file contains the codes a Citizen 120D printer uses for bold, italics, and underline printing. Selecting one of these files causes it to be stored in a separate file, where the information can be used by the other printing structures.

The print devices can also be edited to provide more functions or to create completely new printer device files. After the Edit Print Devices option is selected, a box containing the Defined Print Devices shows the printers that have already been loaded. Fig. 6-3 shows the Edit Device Options menu that appears when one of the devices is selected. Both of the options listed represent control codes that might be sent to the printer. Device Modes refers to a set of codes that might be sent as a setup before printing, while Device Functions represents the specific codes sent for a single printer command. After selecting Letter Quality, the functions that make up the Letter Quality mode are displayed. In this case it is only one, also called letter quality. Fig. 6-4 shows the control codes for the function letter quality. This box is intended only to display the functions. To edit them, the Edit Print Functions option must be selected from the Edit Device Options menu.

The Printer Definition Utility, PRINTDEF, is used to create and edit print forms and print devices which control the printer. To control how the printers are used, separate utilities are used to create print queues and print job configurations.

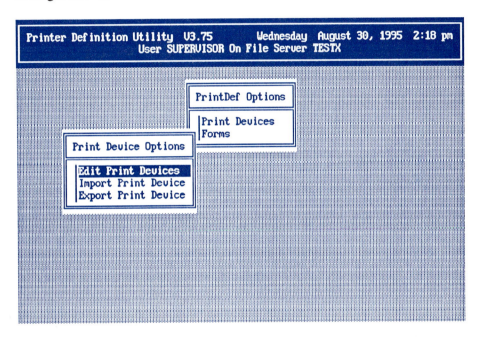

Fig. 6-2. Print Device Options menu.

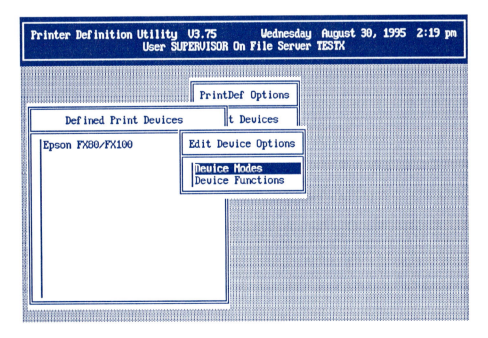

Fig. 6-3. Edit Device Options menu.

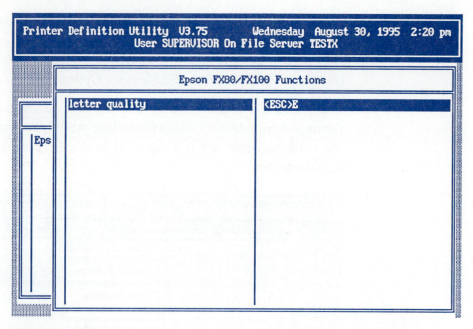

Fig. 6-4. Dialog box for the control codes for the letter quality function.

Print Queues

Obviously, if everyone on the network sent data to a network printer at once, problems would arise. A system had to be created to allow the data from each user to be stored and then printed when the printer becomes available. Print queues provide this function and more. The NetWare Print Console utility, PCONSOLE, is used to create and maintain print queues and print servers. Fig. 6-5 shows PCONSOLE's main menu. The first option, Change Current File server, simply allows the user to select another file server. The second option, Print Queue Information, displays a list of existing print queues. When a print queue is selected, the Print Queue Information menu appears. These options control the who, what, where, and when of the queue. The following is a description of each of the selections.

1. Current Print Job Entries. This option displays a list of the print jobs waiting to print from the selected print queue. A print job is any set of output sent to the printer. This term is easily confused with a print job configuration, which is a certain set of network printing options.

2. Current Queue Status. Shown in Fig. 6-6, the Current Queue Status box displays how many jobs are waiting to print and how many print servers are attached to the queue. The Operator Flags section allows the operator to turn certain features of the queue on and off. Most importantly, it allows the operator to turn off access to the queue altogether.

CHAPTER 6. NETWORK PRINTING

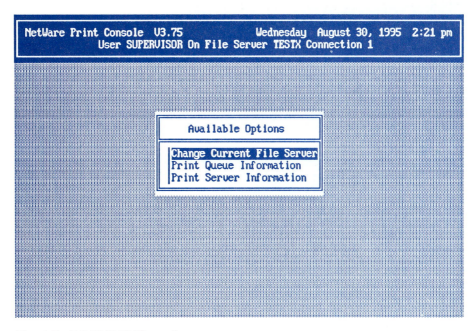

Fig. 6-5. PCONSOLE's main menu.

3. Currently Attached Servers. It shows the file servers attached to a queue.
4. Print Queue ID. This option displays the eight-digit hexadecimal number that represents the queue on the file server. The number can be used by custom programs to access and control the queue.

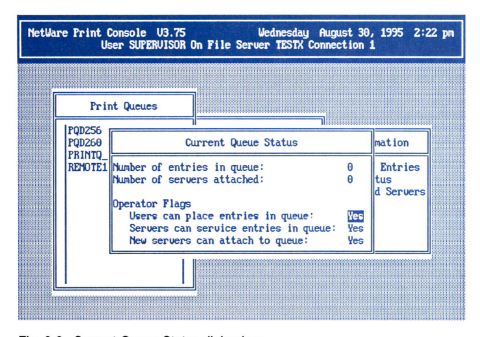

Fig. 6-6. Current Queue Status dialog box.

167

5. Queue Operators. Each print queue can be controlled by a different set of users. The queue shown in Fig. 6-7 has three operators, MJ, ROOT, and SUPERVISOR. Only these users can make changes to the queue or control jobs in the queue. The word "User" appears next to each name because groups can also be made queue operators.

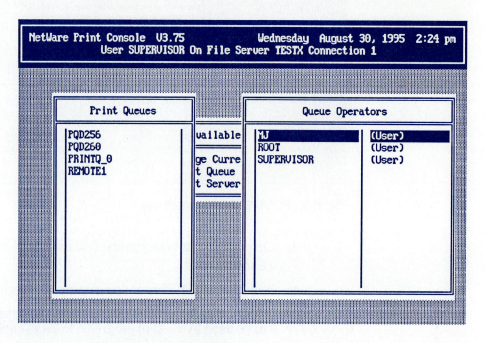

Fig. 6-7. A queue with three operators.

6. Queue Servers. Fig. 6-8 shows the box displayed after selecting Queue Servers. This queue is being serviced by the print server PSERV256. The message "Print Server" appears next to the name because file servers can also service print queues.

7. Queue Users. Each queue can be restricted to certain users or groups of users. This box shows the users and groups who have access to a queue.

The last item on PCONSOLE's main menu is Print Server Information. This item is, of course, quite important in network printing. However, to complete the topic of printing structures, another program, the Configure Print Jobs utility PRINTCON, must be considered.

Print Job Configurations

PRINTCON allows users to create print job configurations. Notice that this terminology refers to a printing structure, not to individual sets of data that have been sent to the printer. A print job configuration is a set of instructions that are used to create a certain type of output on a certain type of printer.

PRINTCON's main menu, shown in Fig. 6-9, has only three selections: Edit Print Job Configurations, Select Default Print Job Configuration, and Copy Print Job Configurations.

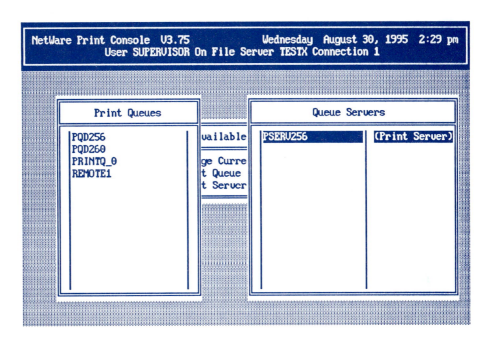

Fig. 6-8. Dialog box displaying a queue and its print server.

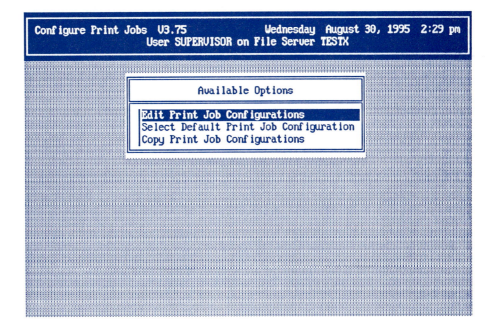

Fig. 6-9. PRINTCON's main menu.

1. Edit Print Job Configurations. When this option is selected, a list of existing print jobs appears. After one has been selected or a new one created, the Edit Print Job Configuration box appears. This is

where the power of the print job configuration becomes evident. Every printing option available under NetWare can be set to a specific value or in some cases left to be chosen automatically.

The options that can be set are as follows:

a. Number of copies. The user can specify how many times a certain set of data will be printed.

b. File contents. This option helps NetWare determine how to handle the data.

c. Tab size. Often in a text document, a tab character is used to represent a certain number of spaces. The number of spaces is then left to the printer to determine. This option tells NetWare to convert those tab characters into the specified number of spaces.

d. Suppress form feed. Another character often present in text files is the form feed character. It tells the printer to advance to the next page. Since NetWare can handle this function, too many form feeds may be sent to the printer. Suppressing the form feed character allows NetWare to fully control the page advance.

e. Notify when done. When this option is set to "Yes" a message is sent to the user after the data sent has been printed.

f. Local printer. Used with the CAPTURE command to specify which local parallel printer ports the user wishes to redirect to a network printer. Choices are 1, 2, or 3 for LPT1, LPT2, or LPT3.

g. Auto endcap. Output sent to a network printer is stored in the print queue first. The data is not printed until an ENDCAP message is sent. With the Auto endcap feature set to "Yes," output from a certain application is sent to the printer when that application finishes executing. In other words, a word processor such as WordPerfect can send data to the queue, but that data will not be sent to the printer until the user exits WordPerfect. With Auto endcap set to "No," the data would not be printed until the user issues an ENDCAP command.

h. File server. Displays the file server being used.
   i. Print queue. Shows which queue the data will be sent to.
   j. Print server. Shows which print server the data will be sent to.
   k. Device. Shows which device definition will be used, if any. When a device definition is used, it must be one which was set up using the PRINTDEF command.
   l. Mode. Shows which mode the device will be in. The mode is dependent on the device used. The available modes are also set up using the PRINTDEF command.
   m. Form name. Shows which form will be used.
   n. Print banner. A banner printed in extra large characters can be printed at the top of the output for identification. Normally when a banner is included, the name of the user and the file name are used in the banner. Here, the name of the user and the file name can be given different values. Printing banners wastes a sheet of paper for each print job in a small environment. In a large environment, the use of the print banner is highly recommended for separation of print jobs.
   o. Enable timeout/timeout count. Used to set the number of seconds to wait after an application has finished sending output to the printer before sending that data on to the print server. If TIMEOUT=0 and AUTO ENDCAP have been selected, printing begins only when the user exits from the application creating the printer output.
2. Select Default Print Job Configuration. PRINTCON's second main menu option allows the user to specify a certain print job configuration to be always used unless another is specified.
3. Copy Print Job Configurations. Print job configurations allow individuals to customize how their output will be printed by the network. Unfortunately, the configuration must be set up for each user and cannot be extended to a group as with most NetWare functions. However, the Copy Print Job Configurations option allows print job configurations to be copied to other users one user at a time.

NetWare offers print forms, print devices, print queues, and print job configurations to allow the process of printing on the network to be completely customized. These features are useless, of course, without printers attached to the network and a means for sending data to them.

Attaching the Printer

The printers can be attached to the network in essentially three different ways: on a print server (which may be the file server or a dedicated workstation), to a NetWork bridge, and on a workstation as a remote printer. By far the most versatile method for attaching printers to the network is to install a print server. The print server is simply a computer running a program called PSERVER.EXE. This program directs the data that has been queued on the file server to the printers that are managed by the print server. The printers may be attached to the print server or they may be attached remotely to workstations. The PCONSOLE program is used again to configure print servers. Fig. 6-10 shows the print servers already available on the file server. Selecting one of them displays the Print Server Information menu, as shown in Fig. 6-11. Each of its options is explained below.

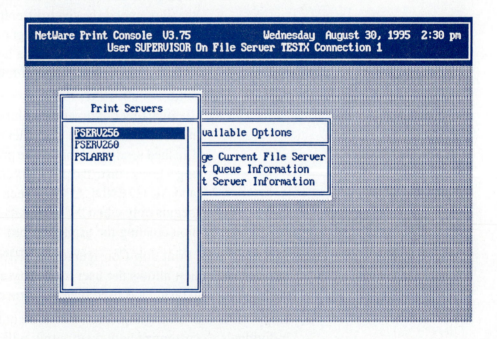

Fig. 6-10. Print servers available to users.

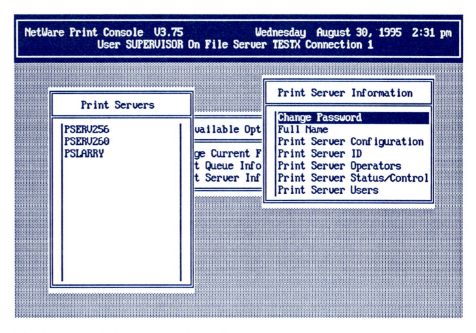

Fig. 6-11. The Print Server Information menu.

1. Change Password. A password can be set on the print server to prevent unauthorized changes.

2. Full Name. The Full Name option can be used to provide a more descriptive name for the print server.

3. Print Server Configuration. This option displays another menu as shown in Fig. 6-12. Its four options are as follows:

   a. File Servers to Be Serviced. This option displays the file servers this print server will accept print jobs from. The current file server does not need to be listed.

   b. Notify List for Printer. Printers require frequent maintenance. A print server can detect when a printer goes off-line and notify a user. The Notify List for Printer option is used to set which users will be notified about problems with each printer.

   c. Printer Configuration. When selected, this option displays a list of the sixteen printers that can be managed by a single print server. By selecting any of these, a Printer Configuration box appears. These options tell the print server how the printer is physically attached to either the print server or to a remote workstation.

   d. Queues Serviced by Printer. When this option is selected, a list of defined printers appears. Selecting a printer shows which print queues send data to that printer and allows the user to add a print queue to a given printer by pressing the INS key and then selecting the queue to be attached.

4. Print Server ID. This option simply displays the NetWare Object Identification number.

5. Print Server Operators. This option displays a list of users or groups authorized to change the status of the print server selected. Users can be added to or deleted from this option.

6. Print Server Status/Control. This option displays status and allows some control over the print server.

7. Print Server Users. This option displays a list of users and groups allowed to send data to the selected print server. Users can be added or deleted with this option.

The PRINTDEF, PCONSOLE, and PRINTCON utilities are used to manipulate how data is to be sent to the available network printers. Sending the data to be printed can be accomplished in four ways: using the PCONSOLE utility, using a command line utility called NPRINT, using a command line utility called CAPTURE, or by using an application program designed to use network printers.

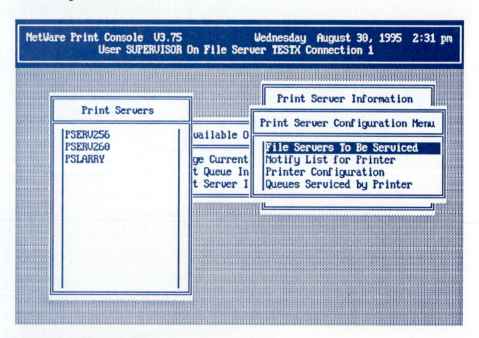

Fig. 6-12. Print Server Configuration menu.

Printing with PCONSOLE

The PCONSOLE program provides much of the control needed for network printing, including manipulating the jobs waiting to be printed. With it, print jobs can be added to or deleted from the print queue. Selecting Current Print

Job Entries in the Print Queue Information menu of PCONSOLE displays the print jobs printing or waiting to be printed. Pressing the INSERT key allows the user to select a file to be printed. This method of sending data to be printed assumes that a file has been created that contains any special characters that may be needed for underlining, boldface fonts, or other special effects. Such a file is known as a print file. Many application programs allow their output to be sent to a print file.

Printing with NPRINT

The NPRINT utility also requires a print file to already exist. A command of NPRINT THISFILE would send the file called THISFILE to the default print queue. The NPRINT program has several command line options that allow the print forms, print queues, and print job configurations to be specified.

Printing with CAPTURE

Almost any application can be used with network printers using the CAPTURE program. It is a memory resident program that intercepts data that the workstation sends to its printer ports, and redirects that data to a print queue. The CAPTURE program can be used in three different ways: in conjunction with the ENDCAP program, with the AUTO ENDCAP feature, or with the TIMEOUT feature.

The ENDCAP program is used to turn off redirection of the printer data. It essentially unloads the CAPTURE program from memory and places the data in the print queue. Notice that the data is only stored, not put in the queue, until the ENDCAP program is run. This way a user may send data to the network printer in many separate pieces. When the ENDCAP command is given, all the data is placed in the queue.

With the AUTO ENDCAP feature of the CAPTURE program enabled, the printer output data is sent on to the print queue when the application which created the print job terminates. For instance, if a user wants to send data to a network printer using a word processor, he or she would first run the CAPTURE program, then start the word processing program. Any printing that is done from the word processing program is stored until the user exits the word processing program. It is only then that the data is placed in the print queue.

Using the TIMEOUT feature allows the user's data to be sent to the print queue while the user is still in the application program. A timeout period is given in seconds and tells the CAPTURE program when to send the data that it has captured on to the print queue. The CAPTURE program waits the time specified after the last output has been captured before placing the data in the print queue.

Suppose a spreadsheet program is being used with the TIMEOUT feature set to 15 seconds. When the user requests a chart to be printed, the output is stored, and a timer starts counting after the last byte is captured. If the user prints another chart less than 15 seconds later, the data will continue to be stored. The data will be sent to the print queue only when a time longer than 15 seconds passes between print requests.

Making the timeout period too short may break up data that should be printed together. For instance, it may take longer than 15 seconds for the second chart in a single report to be calculated. Someone else's data could be placed in the queue between the first and second charts.

Making the period too long may cause data that the user intended to be printed separately to be printed together instead. If the user wanted the charts to be printed separately, he or she would have to watch the clock until the 15 seconds had passed before printing the second chart. This is not usually a problem since most applications would advance to the next page before printing the second time. A period longer than a few seconds may also be a source of frustration for the user. Even when only one person is sending data to be printed, he or she must wait for the data to be captured, wait the timeout period, then wait for the print server to start processing the data in the queue. These delays can add up to a long enough time that the user may wonder if there is a problem with the printer.

The last and easiest way to send data to a network printer is to use an application program that is designed to send its output to a print queue on a NetWare network.

Hands-on NetWare

In order to complete the following exercises, the file server and at least two workstations should be ready to use.

1. The file server should be on.
2. The accounts created earlier should be available.

Configuring the Print Server and Print Queue

The long list of steps below create a new print server and a new print queue. These operations can be carried out at any workstation which is logged into the network.

1. Boot the workstation.
2. The network driver programs should have been loaded by the AUTOEXEC.BAT file. If they were not, type **LSL** and press the ENTER key. Then type the name of your network card driver and press ENTER. Next type **IPXODI** and press ENTER. Then type **VLM** and press the ENTER key.
3. Type **F:** and press the ENTER key.
4. Type **LOGIN** followed by your supervisor-equivalent login name and press the ENTER key.
5. Type the password for this account, and press the ENTER key.
6. Type **CD\PUBLIC** and press the ENTER key
7. Type **PCONSOLE** and press the ENTER key.
8. Select Print Server Information by using the cursor keys to highlight that option and pressing the ENTER key.
9. Press the INSERT key. A box requesting a new print server name should appear, as shown in Fig. 6-13. Here the print server name LASER has been added.

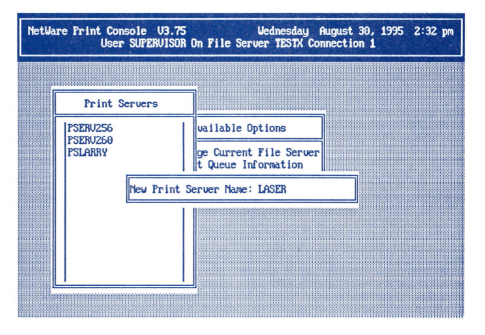

Fig. 6-13. Dialog box to request a new print server.

10. Type **PS** followed by your login name. For instance, if your login name is JSMITH, type PSJSMITH and press the ENTER key. The PS is simply used to indicate Print Server; it is not a required prefix.
11. With the new name highlighted, press the ENTER key.

12. Select Print Server Configuration in the Print Server Information box by using the cursor keys to highlight that option and pressing the ENTER key.

13. Select Printer Configuration in the Print Server Configuration menu by highlighting that option with the cursor keys and pressing the ENTER key. Your screen should appear similar to Fig. 6-14.

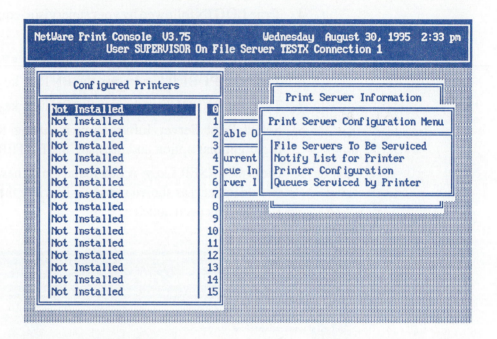

Fig. 6-14. Printer Configuration option

14. With the first Not Installed message highlighted, press the ENTER key.

15. Move the cursor to the field labeled Name: and type **PRINTER 0** and press the ENTER key. Press the ENTER key again on the Defined elsewhere option.

16. A list of possible printer ports should be displayed as they are in Fig. 6-15. Use the cursor keys to highlight the printer port your printer is attached to. The first one on the list, Parallel, LPT1, is the most common. This means that the printer is attached to the LPT1 port on the workstation to be used as a print server.

17. With the correct printer port highlighted, press the ENTER key.

18. If the printer port you selected was Serial, additional options will have to be set. Only if you have selected a Serial port, use the cursor keys to move to the fields labeled Baud rate:, Data bits:, Stop bits:, Parity:, and Use X-On/X-Off: and place the correct values in each.

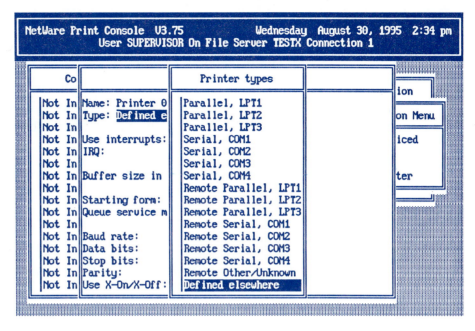

Fig. 6-15. List of printer ports.

19. Press the ESC key to leave the Printer 0 configuration menu.
20. Press the Y and ENTER keys to save the changes.
21. Press the ESC key twice to return to the Print Server Information box.
22. Use the cursor keys to highlight Print Server Operators and press the ENTER key.
23. Press the INSERT key.
24. Type the name of your user account. The highlighted bar should move to your name. Highlight the correct account name with (User) displayed in the right column and press the ENTER key.
25. Press the ESC key to return to the Print Server Information box.
26. Highlight Print Server Users and press the ENTER key.
27. Verify that the group EVERYONE has been made a user of this print server and press the ESC key.
28. Press the ESC key twice to return to PCONSOLE's main menu.

When creating a new print server and print queue combination, something of a chicken and egg problem arises. You cannot finish configuring the print server without the print queue, and you cannot finish configuring the print queue without the print server. The reason for this complexity is that one queue can send data to several print servers and one print server can receive data from several queues. The following instructions create a new print queue and assign it to the new print server.

29. Highlight the Print Queue Information Option and press the ENTER key.
30. Press the INSERT key.
31. Type **Q**, followed by your account name, and press the ENTER key. For instance, if your account name is JSMITH, type QJSMITH and press the ENTER key. The "Q" is simply used to indicate a queue. It is not a required prefix.
32. With the new print queue name highlighted, press the ENTER key. The Print Queue Information box should appear as shown in Fig. 6-16.

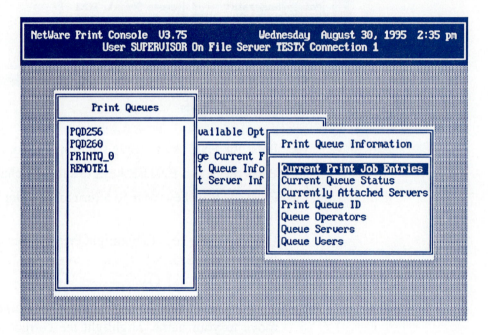

Fig. 6-16. The Print Queue Information menu

33. Highlight Queue Servers and press the ENTER key.
34. Press the INSERT key to view the list of available servers, as shown in Fig. 6-17.
35. Type the name of your print server and press the ENTER key. Your print server's name is PS, followed by your account name.
36. Press the ESC key.
37. Highlight Queue Operators and press the ENTER key.
38. Press the INSERT key.
39. Type the name of your user account. The highlighted bar should move to your name, but it will stop when it reaches the group of the same name. Highlight the correct account name with (User) displayed in the right column and press the ENTER key.

Chapter 6. Network Printing

40. Press the ESC key to return to the Print Queue Information box.
41. Highlight Print Queue Users and press the ENTER key.
42. Verify that the group EVERYONE has been made a user of this print queue and press the ESC key.

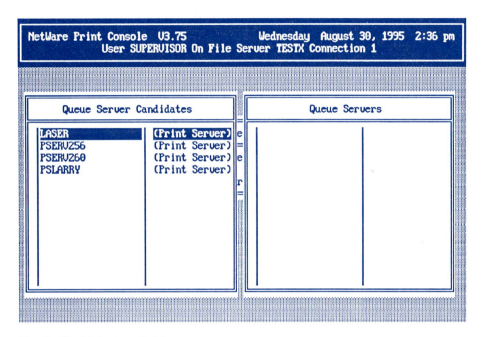

Fig. 6-17. List of available servers.

43. Press the ESC key twice to return to PCONSOLE's main menu.
44. Highlight Print Server Information again and press the ENTER key.
45. Type the name of your print server and press the ENTER key. Your print server's name is PS, followed by your account name.
46. In the Print Server Information box, move the cursor down to the Print Server Configuration option and press the ENTER key.
47. In the Print Server Configuration menu, move the cursor down to the Queues Serviced by Printer option and press the ENTER key.
48. Press the ENTER key with the printer you defined earlier highlighted.
49. Press the INSERT key to view the list of available queues.
50. Type the name of your print queue and press the ENTER key. Its name is Q followed by the name of your account.
51. Since several queues can be assigned to a single server, a priority number can be given to each queue. This feature permits a special queue to be created for "rush" print jobs. Press the ENTER key to accept the priority shown.

181

52. Press the ESC key six times until the Exit PCONSOLE prompt appears.
53. Press the Y and ENTER keys. The print server is now ready for operation.
54. Type **LOGOUT** and press the ENTER key to end this session.

Running PSERVER

With the Print Server software loaded onto the file server hard disk and configured using the PCONSOLE program, the print server can be started by running the PSERVER program on any workstation. The following operations start the print server.

1. A new line must be added to the NET.CFG file on the workstation in order for the print server to operate properly. Ensure that the NET.CFG file is in the default directory. Type **ECHO SPX Connections=60>>C:NET.CFG** and press the ENTER key. The >> symbol in the command appends SPX Connections=60 to the existing NET.CFG file.
2. Boot the workstation again. The network driver programs should have been loaded by the AUTOEXEC.BAT file.
3. Type **F:** and press the ENTER key.
4. Type **LOGIN** followed by the name of your non-supervisor-equivalent account and press the ENTER key. This account name was created using your first initial, last name, and a 1. For instance, if your supervisor-equivalent account was called JSMITH, the non-supervisor account was called JSMITH1.
5. Type the password for this account and press the ENTER key.
6. Type **CD\PUBLIC** and press the ENTER key.
7. Type **PSERVER** followed by the name of your print server and press the ENTER key. Your print server's name is PS followed by your account name. PSERVER's screen should appear as in Fig. 6-18.
8. The status of the printer is displayed in the upper left corner of the screen. Press any key to display the status of the eight other possible printers. Press any key again to return to the first eight printers.

```
         Novell NetWare Print Server V3.76
              Server PSERV256 Running
```

0: Epson FX80/FX100 Waiting for job	4: Not installed
1: Not installed	5: Not installed
2: Not installed	6: Not installed
3: Not installed	7: Not installed

Fig. 6-18. PSERVER display

Sending Output to the Print Server

The Print Server is up and running. All that remains is to test it. Leave the print server software running and move to another workstation. Follow the directions below to send data to the print server.

1. Boot the workstation and login to the network using your supervisor-equivalent login name.

2. Type **NPRINT A:NET.CFG /Q=** followed by the print queue created earlier. Then press the ENTER key. For example, if your supervisor-equivalent account is JSMITH, the command would be NPRINT A:NET.CFG /Q=QJSMITH.

3. In a few moments the contents of the NET.CFG file should print on the printer attached to the print server. Note that this method of network printing does not interfere with the use of the printer on the workstation.

4. Type **CAPTURE /Q=** followed by the print queue name and **/NA**. Then press the ENTER key. For instance, the command might look like CAPTURE /Q=QJSMITH /NA. The CAPTURE program loads into memory and remains resident. The /NA option indicates that the auto endcap feature is disabled.

5. Type **COPY A:NET.CFG LPT1:** and press the ENTER key. Ordinarily, this DOS command would send the contents of the NET.CFG file to the local printer. With the CAPTURE program loaded, the output is stored until the ENDCAP command is issued.

6. Type **ENDCAP** and press the ENTER key. The contents of the NET.CFG file will print at the print server in a few moments.

7. To end this session, type **LOGOUT** and press the ENTER key. The print server can be turned off or rebooted.

Configuring the Print Server for Remote Printing

Additional printers can be connected to the print server, even printers that are not physically attached to it. With a program called RPRINTER running on a workstation, the workstation's local printer becomes a network printer. Use the directions below to configure the print server for a remote printer, restart the print server, and start the RPRINTER program on a workstation.

1. Boot the workstation and login to the network using your supervisor-equivalent login name.

2. Type **PCONSOLE** and press the ENTER key.

3. Move the cursor to Print Server Information and press the ENTER key.

4. Type the name of your print server. Press the ENTER key when the proper name is highlighted.

5. Move the cursor to the Print Server Configuration option and press the ENTER key.

6. Move the cursor to the Printer Configuration option of the Print Server Configuration Menu and press the ENTER key. A list of printers attached to this print server should appear as it does in Fig. 6-19.

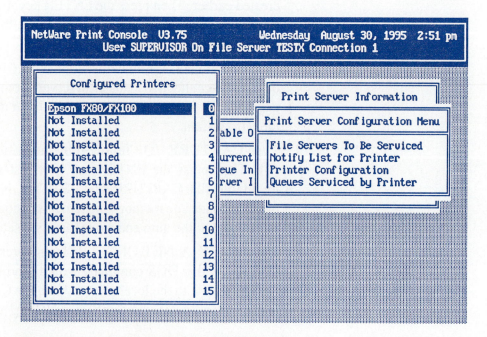

Fig. 6-19. List of printers attached to the server.

7. Move the cursor to the first available Not Installed message and press the ENTER key.

8. Move the cursor to the Name: and type **Remote printer** and press the ENTER key. Press the ENTER key again to select the Defined elsewere option.

9. Move the cursor to the Remote Parallel, LPT1 option in the Printer types box, as shown in Fig. 6-20. Then press the ENTER key.

10. Press the ESC key until the Save Changes menu appears.

11. Press the Y and ENTER keys.

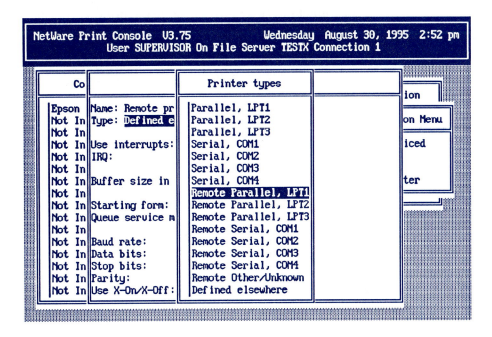

Fig. 6-20. Selecting a port for the printer.

12. Press the ESC key four times to return to PCONSOLE's main menu of available topics.

13. Highlight the Print Queue Information option and press the ENTER key.

14. Press the INSERT key to enter a new print queue name.

15. Type **R** followed by your account name and press the ENTER key. For instance, user JSMITH would type RJSMITH and press the ENTER key.

16. With the new print queue name highlighted, press the ENTER key.

17. Move the cursor to highlight Queue Servers and press the ENTER key.

18. Press the INSERT key to view the list of available servers.

19. Type the name of your print server and press the ENTER key. Your print server's name is PS, followed by your account name.
20. Press the ESC key.
21. Move the cursor up to highlight Queue Operators and press the ENTER key.
22. Press the INSERT key.
23. Type the name of your user account. The highlighted bar should move to your name. Highlight the correct account name with (User) displayed in the right column and press the ENTER key.
24. Press the ESC key to return to the Print Queue Information box.
25. Highlight Queue Users and press the ENTER key.
26. Verify that the group EVERYONE has been made a user of this print queue and press the ESC key.
27. Press the ESC key twice to return to PCONSOLE's main menu.
28. Highlight Print Server Information again and press the ENTER key.
29. Type the name of your print server and press the ENTER key. Your print server's name is PS, followed by your account name.
30. In the Print Server Information box, move the cursor to the Print Server Configuration option and press the ENTER key.
31. In the Print Server Configuration menu, move the cursor down to the Queues Serviced by Printer option and press the ENTER key.
32. Move the cursor down to the remote printer defined as Printer 1 earlier and press the ENTER key.
33. Press the INSERT key to view the list of available queues.
34. Type the name of your remote printer queue and press the ENTER key. The remote printer queue name is R followed by your account name.
35. Press the ENTER key to verify the Priority.
36. Press the ESC key six times until the "Exit PCONSOLE" menu appears.
37. Press the Y and ENTER keys.

Running PSERVER with a Remote Printer

The print server now has the capability of supporting a remote printer anywhere on the network. Any workstation that loads the RPRINTER program and selects the proper print server and printer will operate as the remote print server. The following steps restart the print server, which will control the remote printer.

1. Boot the print server workstation and login to the network using your non-supervisor-equivalent account. This account name was created using your first initial, last name, and a 1. For instance, if your supervisor-equivalent account was called JSMITH, the non-supervisor account was called JSMITH1.
2. Type **CD\PUBLIC** and press the ENTER key.
3. Type **PSERVER** followed by the name of your print server and press the ENTER key. Your print server's name is PS, followed by your account name.

Running RPRINTER

With the new improved version of the Print Server program running, move to a new workstation that has a local printer. Follow the instruction below to install the RPRINTER program.

1. Boot the workstation attached to the printer that you are going to use.
2. Login using your supervisor-equivalent login name and press the ENTER key.
3. Type **RPRINTER** and press the ENTER key. The remote printer program should display a list of print servers.
4. Type the name of your print server and press the ENTER key. The remote printers available for that print server should be displayed.
5. Select the name of your remote printer by pressing the ENTER key. The message "*** Remote Printer "Printer 1" (printer 1) installed **" indicates that the RPRINTER program has been successfully installed.

Sending Output to the Remote Printer

The printer attached to the workstation can still be used by the workstation, but data being sent to the workstation by the print server will also be printed. Two methods can be used to test this situation. One is to have another student at another workstation send data to the remote printer. The other method is to use a network printing utility to send data to the same workstation as a remote printer. The following steps will work equally well at another workstation or at the same workstation. These instructions assume the workstation is still logged in.

1. Type **NPRINT C:NET.CFG /Q=** followed by the remote print queue created earlier, then press the ENTER key. For example, if your supervisor equivalent account is JSMITH, the command would be
   NPRINT C:NET.CFG /Q=RJSMITH.

2. In a few moments the contents of the NET.CFG file should print on the printer attached to the remote print server. Note that this method of network printing does not interfere with the use of the printer on the workstation.

3. Type **CAPTURE /Q=** followed by the remote print queue name and /NA, and then press the ENTER key. For instance, the command might look like

    CAPTURE /Q=RJSMITH /NA.

    The CAPTURE program loads into memory and remains resident. The "/NA" stands for No Autoendcap.

4. Type **COPY C:NET.CFG LPT1:** and press the ENTER key. Ordinarily, this DOS command would send the contents of the NET.CFG file to the local printer. With the CAPTURE program loaded, the output is stored until the ENDCAP command is issued.

5. Type **ENDCAP** and press the ENTER key. The contents of the NET.CFG file will print at the remote print server in a few moments.

6. To end this session, type **LOGOUT** and press the ENTER key. The print server can be turned off or rebooted.

Summary

One of the network features that is most often used is sharing printers. A Novell network allows printers located on the file server, on a dedicated print server, or on a remote print server to be accessed by any user or group with authorization. Print forms, print devices, print queues, and print job configurations are all tools that can be used to control how and where data is to be printed. Data can be sent to a network printer in four ways: with the PCONSOLE utility, with the NPRINT command, with the CAPTURE command, or with an application program designed to send data to a network printer.

Questions

1. What is considered to be the most versatile way to attach a printer to the network?
2. Can a print form be used to specify which printer will be used?
3. Can a print device be used to define a special font such as bold?
4. Can a print job configuration be used by a group?

5. How many printers can be attached to a print server?
6. If a print server has only one printer port, but two printers attached, where is the second printer?
7. Can a single print queue feed data to more than one printer?
8. In what ways is a remote printer vulnerable?

Projects

Objective

The following projects provide additional practice with the basic network printing facilities of NetWare. Additionally, the second project provides more hands-on training in creating print queues and sending print jobs across the network.

Project 1. Basic Network Printing

1. Use the PRINTDEF utility to ensure that the driver for the printer attached to the print server created earlier is available on the system. The driver will need to be imported only once for the file server being used.
2. Use the PRINTDEF utility to create a print form called 132_COL that uses a form width of 132 columns. The form will need to be created only once for the file server being used.
3. Use the PRINTCON utility to create a print job configuration called CONDENSED that specifies the print device, the print mode, and the print form. Use the print device name of the printer attached to your print server, the condensed mode of that printer, and the 132-column form.
4. Use the NPRINT utility to print the AUTOEXEC.BAT file on your workstation with the print job CONDENSED. The syntax of the NPRINT command is

    NPRINT filename /J=print_job_name

Project 2. Advanced Network Printing

1. Create a print queue with a unique name on an existing print server. Be sure to include your user name as a print queue operator.
2. Set the printer to OFF LINE. Send a file to the print queue. Then use the PCONSOLE utility to remove the file from the queue. Put the printer back on line.
3. Try the same operation as above, but send your data to a classmate's print queue. You should not be able to remove the print job.

Project 3. Setting up a Print Server with One Locally Attached Printer and Two Remote Printers

1. Following instructions given in the Hands-On section of this chapter, modify your print server to have one more remote printer.
2. Assign a new queue to this printer and test its operation.

7

Customizing NetWare

Objectives

After completing this chapter you will
1. Understand the benefits of using menus.
2. Know two techniques to create menus.
3. Know different techniques to make LANs more accessible to users.

Key Terms

Application Software   Batch File
Menu   Network Software
Server   Submenu
Variables

Introduction

Assuming Novell NetWare has been installed correctly, appropriate users and login scripts have been created, and all network printing functions needed have been installed, there is only one item missing—application software. The primary purpose of the network is to deliver the software that users need to their workstations. All other setup means nothing to the users if they cannot easily access the word processors, databases, spreadsheets, and other programs they need to do their jobs.

With the 3.12 version of NetWare, Novell supplies a subset of the popular SABER menu for its menu utility. This menu system is greatly improved over the menu utility in previous versions of NetWare. It can be used to produce attractive, easy to use menus that blend smoothly with the other Novell utilities. Although the new menu system works in almost all cases, it is also still possible to use DOS batch files to serve as menus. It is also possible to purchase other programs designed specifically to operate as NetWare menus.

The software that is to be accessed by these menus falls into three categories: network incompatible, network compatible, and network aware. Network incompatible software is software that cannot be run from the file server. It might, however, still need to be called from the workstation's local hard disk in a menu system. Network compatible programs have no difficulty running on the file server, but they do not take advantage of the network for services such as network printing or mail. Programs that do take advantage of these services are known as network aware.

Customizing NetWare

All programs in a NetWare file server should be made easy to access by all users. The process for accessing network-based software consists of the following steps.

1. The user workstation must automatically attach to the file server that contains the shared programs.
2. A drive must be mapped to the directory where the required program resides.
3. The mapped drive should be made the default drive.
4. The command required to start a program must be given.
5. After the program is exited, the drive letter mapped in step 2 needs to be deleted.
6. The user logs out of the file server that contains the shared software.

These steps are difficult to perform by most users and are cumbersome to use on a continuous basis. One solution is to create a batch file and place it in the SYS:PUBLIC directory where all users can have access to it.

An example of a typical batch file to start a copy of Lotus 123 from a server named SERVER2 may consist of the following lines.

```
ATTACH SERVER2/GUEST
MAP H:=SERVER2/SYS:SHARESOF\LOTUS123
H:
LOTUS
MAP DEL H:
LOGOUT SERVER2
```

In this example, the first line attaches a user who has the login name GUEST to the server whose network name is SERVER2. A drive H is mapped to the directory that stores Lotus 123, and the program is executed with the command LOTUS. When the user exits the program, the drive mapping is deleted, and the user is logged out of the server SERVER2.

Batch Files

Batch files are used when shared programs are stored on special servers to which the user must attach in order to run the programs. Although network managers create much more complicated batch files, the above example illustrates the use of such a file to access programs stored in a network file server.

Although batch files protect the user from needing to know the intricacies of NetWare commands to attach to file servers and map directories, the use of menus further enhances the usability of the network. Using menus provides easy access to shared software for new or inexperienced users.

Novell has a menu-building system that can be used for most situations and needs. Many commercially available programs can also be used for this purpose. With menus, users can start the equivalent of batch files by selecting a letter or a number from a list of choices. The menu then transfers execution to the batch file equivalent. When the batch file terminates executing, control is returned to the menu, and it is automatically re-displayed on the screen. Creating menus requires extra effort from the network administrator, but in the long run menus tend to increase network usage by making users feel comfortable with the hardware. The use of menus reduces or eliminates the user's need to learn commands and limits the amount of information that must be presented on the screen at any given time.

Novell Menus

A Simple Menu

Novell provides a set of menu programs with NetWare 3.12 called MENUMAKE.EXE and NMENU.EXE that can be used to compile and execute custom menus. Both MENUMAKE and NMENU.EXE reside in the SYS:\PUBLIC directory. The program set uses ASCII script files which are then compiled with MENUMAKE to create a compiled version which is then run with NMENU to display menus similar to those used in the NetWare utilities. The script file can be written with any ASCII text editor. For example, suppose an ASCII text file called START.SRC contains the following:

MENU 1,Available Options
  ITEM Syscon
    EXEC SYSCON
  ITEM Filer
    EXEC FILER
  ITEM Exit
    EXEC EXIT

The command MENUMAKE START would compile the menu and create a file called START.DAT. The command NMENU START would then load and execute the START menu program as shown in Fig. 7-2.

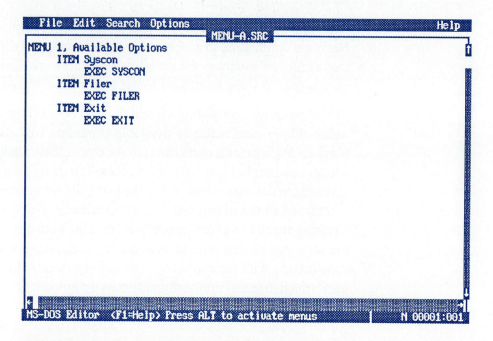

Fig. 7-1. Simple menu created using the DOS editor

Submenus

The START menu example above is, of course, a very simple menu. The Novell 3.12 menu system is capable of producing much more complex menus through the use of submenus. Suppose the file START.SRC is expanded to indicate the submenu "Other Options," as shown in Fig. 7-3. The main menu display is shown in Fig. 7-4.

The third option in the Main Selections menu executes something called "Other Utilities." The definition for the menu "Other Utilities" is further down in the same script file. The submenu definition does not have to immediately follow the line that calls it. For instance, if all the options in the Main Selections menu were submenus, all three definitions would be listed at the bottom of the file. See Fig. 7-5 for the effect of executing the submenu.

Chapter 7. Customizing NetWare

Fig. 7-2. The screen display of the simple menu created using the Novell 3.12 menu system.

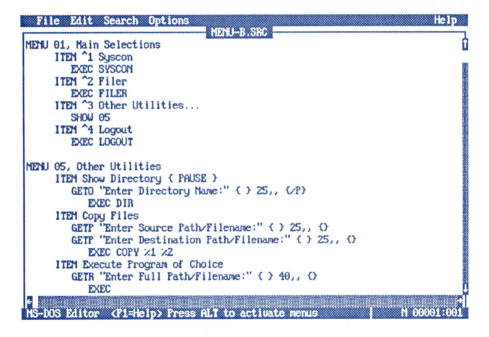

Fig. 7-3. A Novell 3.12 menu with a submenu.

Menu Commands

There are two types of menu commands: organization commands and control commands. Organization commands do just what one would expect; they provide organization for the menu. Control commands direct actions that are taken as a result of selecting a menu option.

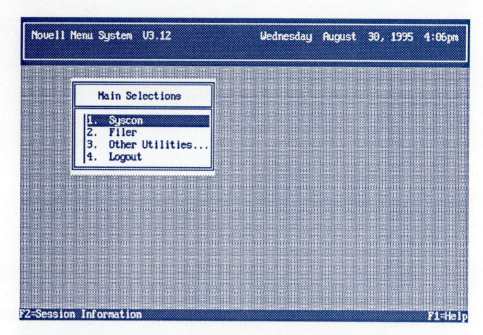

Fig. 7-4. The main menu of a Novell menu with a submenu.

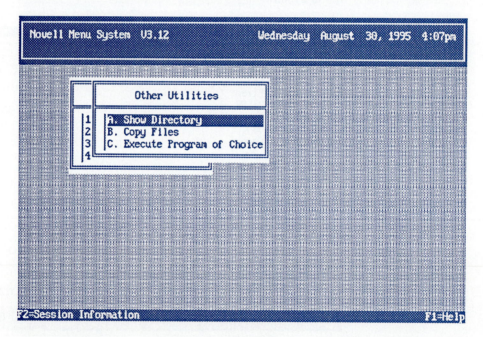

Fig. 7-5. A Novell 3.12 submenu as executed

Organization Commands

There are only two organization commands, MENU and ITEM. The MENU command identifies the menu, its name, and its number. For example,

> MENU 1,MAIN

defines menu 1 and indicates that the title of the menu is MAIN. The general syntax for this command is

> MENU menuno,titleofmenu

where menuno is the number of the menu and titleofmenu is the title of the menu.

Each ITEM command identifies a selection within a menu. Normally, the menu program automatically assigns a letter to each menu selection from A to Z, but the menu display can be altered to have numbered items by using the ^ option in the ITEM statement as shown in Fig. 7-3.

For example, the command

    ITEM ^1 Syscon

causes an item numbered

    1. Syscon

to be displayed as a choice on the menu.

The MENU and ITEM command together form the structure for the menu.

Control Commands

A control command causes action to occur. These commands include EXEC, LOAD, SHOW, GETO, GETR, and GETP.

The EXEC command causes commands to be executed. Any command entered after EXEC would be executed as a result of the user's choosing the ITEM command associated with that EXEC. For example, in the simple menu, the program SYSCON is executed as a result of the user's choosing ITEM A on the menu, which is identified as Syscon and which is followed immediately by the EXEC SYSCON command.

Each EXEC command belongs to the ITEM command above it and executes after all other control commands used by that ITEM command.

There are also three special versions of the EXEC command:

    EXEC EXIT permanently unloads the menu from memory and leaves the user at the DOS prompt.

    EXEC DOS temporarily unloads the menu, leaving the user at the DOS prompt. The user can return to the menu by typing EXIT.

    EXEC LOGOUT unloads the menu and logs the user out of the system.

For those familiar with the NetWare 3.11 menu system which allowed for exiting the menu by pressing the ESC key, it is important to remember that the Novell 3.12 menu does not allow that. Each menu must have either an EXEC EXIT or an EXEC LOGOUT command in order to exit from the menu. An example of the EXEC LOGOUT command is shown in Fig. 7-6.

```
F:\PUBLIC>logout
SUPERVISOR logged out from server TESTX connection 1.
Login time:   Wednesday  August  30, 1995  2:05 pm
Logout time:  Wednesday  August  30, 1995  4:07 pm


F:\>
```

Fig. 7-6. Example of EXEC LOGOUT.

The LOAD command allows for the loading of submenus from other files. This command is normally used only in very large menus.

The SHOW command is used to display a submenu whose script code is listed later in the file containing the main menu. The syntax of SHOW 05 as in the submenu shown executing in Fig. 7-5 causes the menu numbered 05 to be displayed on top of the main menu and for control to be transferred to this submenu.

The GETx commands request input from the user which is then appended to the end of the next EXEC command prior to executing the EXEC command.

There are three GETx commands; GETO, GETR, and GETP.

GETO requests optional input from the user. The associated EXEC command will execute even if the user enters no input. An example of the GETO command during execution is shown in Fig. 7-7. Note that pressing the Enter key causes acceptance of the information that the user enters, but the user must press <F10> to continue menu execution.

GETR requests required input from the user which is appended to the end of the next EXEC command before the EXEC command is executed. When a GETR command is used, the user must provide input for the menu to continue to execute. An example of the GETR command in execution is shown in Fig. 7-8.

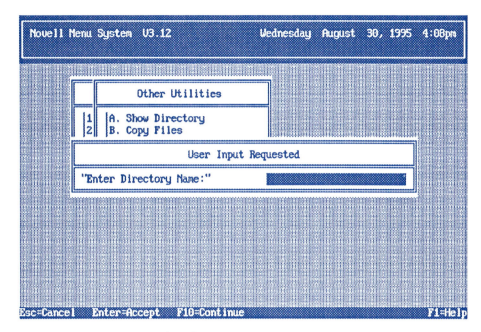

Fig. 7-7. Example of the GETO command.

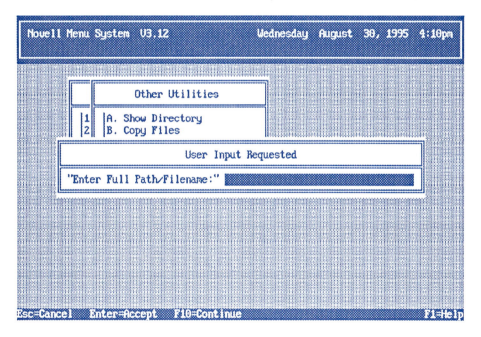

Fig. 7-8. Example of the GETR command.

GETP requests parameter input from the user. The first GETP command stores the user input into a variable called %1, the second GETP stores the user input into a variable called %2, and so on. The variables %1, and %2 can be used in one or more EXEC commands which follow. An example of the GETP command is shown in Fig. 7-9. In this figure, the user has entered f:\public\menu-b.src for the Source Path/Filename and pressed the Enter key to accept this entry. Then the user has entered f:\public\temp\menu-b.src for the Destination Path/Filename. Again, the user must press the <F10> key for menu execution to continue.

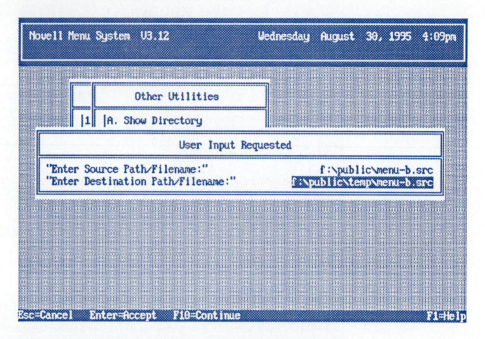

Fig. 7-9. Example of the GETP command.

The syntax of the GETx command is

    GETx userinstruction {prepend} length, prefill, SECURE {append}

The userinstruction parameter instructs the user what type of information to enter. Information entered in the userinstruction field must be surrounded by double quotes (" "). During execution of all GETx commands, the menu program waits for the user to press <F10> prior to proceeding. If the user fails to enter anything, the prefill value is used. Otherwise, the prepend string is added to the beginning of the user input, and the append string is added to the end of the user input. If the SECURE parameter is filled in, the user's input is overwritten on the screen with * characters rather than being displayed. The length designator determines the maximum length of the entry that the user can make.

Menu Rules

Several rules must be observed when creating a legal Novell 3.12 menu program. These include:

1. Each user instruction prompt should be limited to 1 line.
2. Each GETO, GETR, or GETP must be between the ITEM line and its associated EXEC line.

3. A menu may include a maximum of 100 GETx commands per ITEM.
4. The person creating the menu must have appropriate rights to create the menu's .DAT program that results from running MENUMAKE.
5. The user must have Read and File Scan rights to the SYS:\PUBLIC directory where the NMENU program resides, a search drive to SYS:\PUBLIC, and Write and Create rights to the directory from which the user starts the menu to accommodate the temporary files which are created as a result of menu execution.

Batch File Menus

Novell's menu system allows the supervisor to create menus that match the NetWare Utilities, but it doesn't fit all situations. In a diverse environment where there may be dozens of programs available on the file server, loading and unloading memory resident programs becomes quite important.

General-purpose resident programs such as Sidekick can consume a large amount of memory, too much for some other programs to run in what is left. In addition, memory resident programs often collide with each other or with the primary application, causing a system crash. For example, many programs require a mouse and a memory resident mouse driver program, but others such as Microsoft Windows are capable of running without a memory resident mouse driver program and may crash if one is present. If the user is not permitted to install memory resident programs as they are needed and remove them when possible, he or she will be forced to logout and reboot the workstation frequently, causing frustration and delays.

Fortunately, complex menus can be created using only DOS batch commands. Consider the batch file, MYMENU.BAT below.

```
@ECHO OFF
IF "%1" == "" GOTO SCREEN
IF "%1" == "a" GOTO A
IF "%1" == "A" GOTO A
IF "%1" == "b" GOTO B
IF "%1" == "B" GOTO B
IF "%1" == "c" GOTO C
IF "%1" == "C" GOTO C
ECHO %1 is not a valid menu option.
goto screen
:A
CAPTURE
```

```
CD Z:\SHARESOF\WORDSTAR
WORDSTAR %2
CD\
ENDCAP
GOTO SCREEN
:B
CD Z:\SHARESOF\LOTUS
 LOTUS %2
GOTO SCREEN
:C
CD Z:\SHARESOF\WP
WP %2
GOTO SCREEN
:SCREEN
CLS
ECHO Type MENU followed by:
ECHO _____
ECHO   A    for WordStar
ECHO   B    for Lotus
ECHO   C    for WordPerfect
ECHO _____
```

This batch file starts one of three different programs when the user types MYMENU A, MYMENU B, or MYMENU C. The menu screen itself is displayed when the user types MENU. Any DOS commands can be used to start the program or prepare for it. For example, the WORDSTAR option includes the CAPTURE and ENDCAP commands. The %1 in the first few lines of the batch file represents the item typed immediately after the word MENU. The %2 in the lines that call the application programs represents the second item typed after the word MYMENU. For instance, if the user types MYMENU A LETTER.DOC, the WORDSTAR program would execute with the word LETTER.DOC as its parameter. Notice that no PATH statement is used and no MAP statement is used. Instead, the search drive Z, which is assumed to have been mapped earlier, is moved to point to the appropriate directory. When a search drive is created, it starts at the end of the alphabet to choose an available drive letter, in this case drive letter Z. By simply changing the directory that drive letter Z points to, the search path is changed as well.

Hands-on Creating Menus

The Novell Menu System

The following instructions offer practice in using the Novell menu program.

1. Boot the workstation, and login using your supervisor-equivalent user name.

2. Type **MD** followed by your account name and press the ENTER key. For instance if the account name is JSMITH, the command would be MD\JSMITH followed by the ENTER key. then type **CD** followed by your account name.

3. A menu file can be created with any ASCII text editor or by using the DOS COPY CON command. If you do not have an appropriate text editor, type COPY CON MYMENU.SRC and press the ENTER key.

4. Type the lines shown in Fig. 7-10, either immediately following the COPY CON MYMENU.SRC command or in your text editor. Type each line exactly as it appears, pressing the ENTER key at the end of each line as shown in Fig. 7-10.

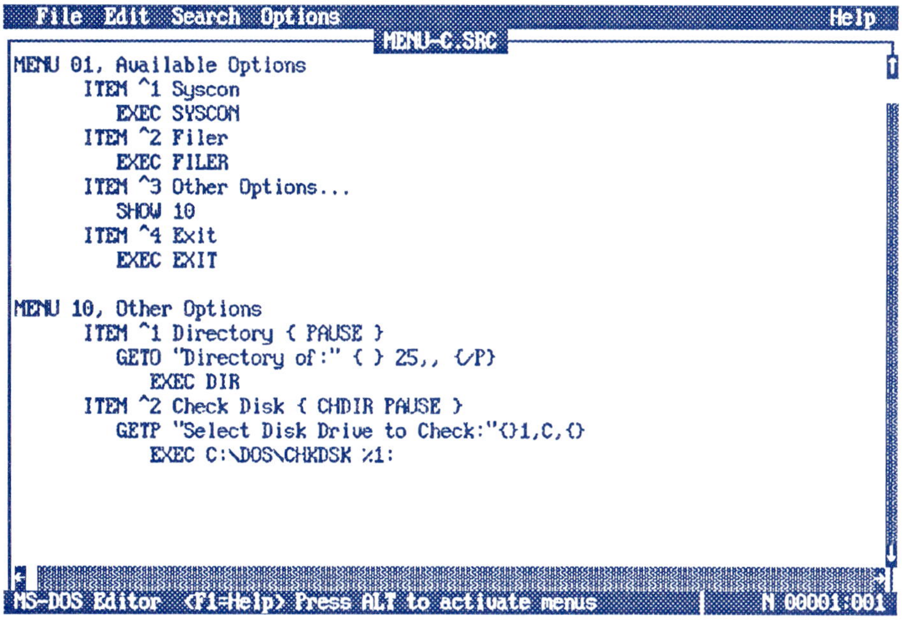

```
File  Edit  Search  Options                                    Help
                        MENU-C.SRC
MENU 01, Available Options
     ITEM ^1 Syscon
          EXEC SYSCON
     ITEM ^2 Filer
          EXEC FILER
     ITEM ^3 Other Options...
          SHOW 10
     ITEM ^4 Exit
          EXEC EXIT

MENU 10, Other Options
     ITEM ^1 Directory { PAUSE }
          GETO "Directory of:" { } 25,, {/P}
               EXEC DIR
     ITEM ^2 Check Disk { CHDIR PAUSE }
          GETP "Select Disk Drive to Check:"{}1,C,{}
               EXEC C:\DOS\CHKDSK %1:


MS-DOS Editor  <F1=Help> Press ALT to activate menus    N 00001:001
```

Fig. 7-10. Hands-on menu source code.

5. If you are using the COPY CON MYMENU.SRC command, hold down the CONTROL key and press the Z key and then press the ENTER key. If you are using a text editor, save the file under the name MYMENU.SRC.

6. Type **MENUMAKE MYMENU** and press the ENTER key to create MYMENU.DAT. Then, type NMENU MYMENU to activate the menu as shown in Fig. 7-11.

7. With the Syscon option highlighted, press the ENTER key. Syscon's main menu should appear.

8. Press the ESC key, then the Y and ENTER keys. You should return to your menu.

9. Press the DOWN ARROW key two times and then the ENTER key. The Other Options menu should appear as it does in Fig. 7-12.

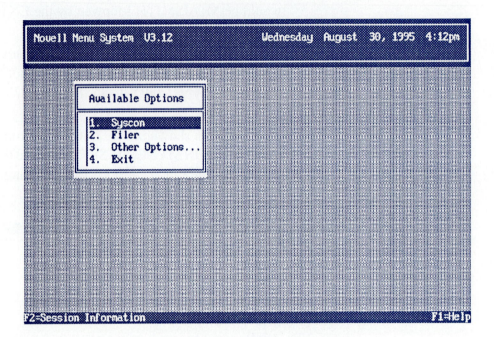

Fig. 7-11. Available Options menu created by MYMENU.

10. Highlight the Check Disk option and press the ENTER key. The "Select Disk Drive to Check:" prompt should appear as in Fig. 7-13.

11. If your computer has a C: drive, then type C:, and press the ENTER key. The CHKDSK program should run and display data about your C: drive. If your machine does not have a C: drive, then enter A: and make sure that there is a diskette in the A: drive of your machine.

12. Press a key to return to the menu program.

13. Press the ESC key to return to the Available Options menu.

14. Select Exit and press the Enter key.

15. To end this session, type **LOGOUT** and press the ENTER key.

CHAPTER 7. CUSTOMIZING NETWARE

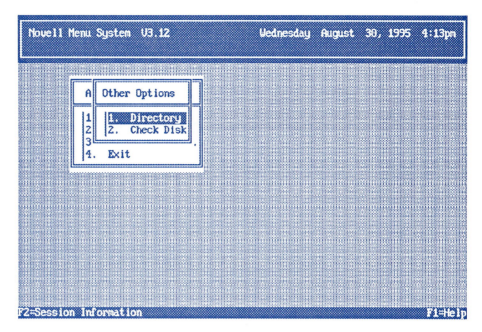

Fig. 7-12. Other Options submenu created by MYMENU.

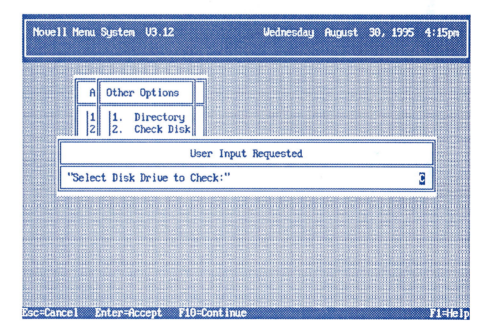

Fig. 7-13. User Input Requested box for Check Disk Option

Batch Files

The following steps demonstrate how some of the same features can be built into a batch file rather than the Novell menu program. It is often necessary to use batch files, even if they are not as attractive as the menus created with MENUMAKE and NMENU.

205

1. Boot the workstation, and login using your supervisor-equivalent login name.
2. Type **CD** followed by your account name and press the ENTER key. For instance if the account name is JSMITH, the command would be CD\JSMITH followed by the ENTER key.
3. The batch file can be created with any ASCII text editor or by using the DOS COPY CON command. If you do not have an appropriate text editor, type COPY CON M.BAT and press the ENTER key.
4. Type the following lines, either immediately following the COPY CON M.BAT command or in your text editor. Type each line exactly as it appears, pressing the ENTER key at the end of each line.

```
@ECHO OFF
 IF "%1" == "" GOTO SCREEN
IF "%1" == "a" GOTO A
IF "%1" == "A" GOTO A
IF "%1" == "b" GOTO B
IF "%1" == "B" GOTO B
IF "%1" == "c" GOTO C
IF "%1" == "C" GOTO C
ECHO %1 is not a valid menu option.
PAUSE
GOTO SCREEN
:A
SYSCON
GOTO SCREEN
:B
FCONSOLE
GOTO SCREEN
:C
CHKDSK %2 %3
PAUSE
GOTO SCREEN
:SCREEN
CLS
ECHO Type M followed by:
ECHO _____
```

ECHO	A	Syscon
ECHO	B	Fconsole
ECHO	C:	Chkdsk
ECHO	_____	

5. If you are using the COPY CON M.BAT command, hold down the CONTROL key and press the Z key. Then, press the ENTER key. If you are using a text editor, save the file under the name M.BAT.

6. Press M and press the ENTER key. A menu should appear at the top of the screen.

7. Type **M A** and press the ENTER key. Syscon's main menu should appear.

8. Press the ESC key and then press the ENTER key. The batch file menu should be displayed.

9. To end this session, type **LOGOUT** and press the ENTER key.

Summary

The efficiently installed network is useless without easy access to the application programs it is intended to deliver. Often this implies that a menu system is needed to allow users to select the programs they need. Novell supplies a program that can be used to create such menus, but there are times that batch files must be used.

Most programs can be put into one of three categories: network incompatible, network compatible, and network aware. The network incompatible software might be installed on the workstation's local hard disk where it could be included in the menu system. Network compatible programs are often the easiest to install but are the most dangerous from a legal perspective, because a copy of the software must be purchased for each user accessing the program on the server. Network aware software often eliminates the legal issue by using the network to restrict the number of users accessing it. Network aware programs can also offer features such as electronic mail and can provide easier network printing.

Questions

1. Can a menu created with MENUMAKE.EXE and run with NMENU.EXE have submenus?
2. What is the difference between the executions of the following two GETx commands?

    GETP "Enter directory name" { } 25,,{ }

    GETO "Enter directory name" { } 25,,{ }

    Assume that each GET command is followed by EXEC DIR.
3. What is the most common problem that makes a program incapable of running on the file server?
4. What can be done to force a program that looks for its files on drive C to operate on the file server?
5. What is the difference between the LOAD command and the SHOW command?
6. If the Novell menu system cannot be used, what are two other ways menus might be created?

Project

Objective

The following project provides additional practice for subjects already learned and in creating menus using Novell NetWare's menu facility.

Creating Directories and Menus

1. A company has three divisions: Sales, Manufacturing, and Business Services. The Sales division has two departments: Accounting and Transportation. The Manufacturing division has three departments: Accounting, Transportation, and Quality Control. The Business Services division has three departments: Accounting, Personnel, and Secretarial. Each division stores its own data but they share all the software possible. Draw a directory structure that might be suitable for this company's file server.
2. In this company, the Business Services division collects all the data it needs from the other divisions directly from their directories. The other divisions, however, should not be able to read each other's data or modify Business Services' data. Write the trustee rights that should be given to a typical user from each of the divisions.

3. Use the MENUMAKE and NMENU programs to create and execute a simple menu which allows the user to choose to run SYSCON or the SESSION utility. What command must also be included as a third choice in this menu?

4. Use the MENUMAKE and NMENU programs to create and execute a menu that provides access to at least three other programs and one submenu. Make the menu/submenu utilize GETO, GETR, and GETP.

# 8

Microsoft Windows 3.1 and Networking

Objectives

After completing this chapter you will

1. Be familiar with the process of installing software in a network.
2. Understand the different modes that applications may have when working in a network.
3. Be familiar with the installation process of Windows 3.1.
4. Understand the different options in installing Windows 3.1.
5. Be familiar with some of the problems associated with running Windows 3.1 and Novell NetWare.

Key Terms

Application Software
MS-DOS
Network Security
Trustee Rights

File Attributes
Network Applications
Server
Windows

Introduction

Personal computers derive their usefulness from the software that they are capable of running. This software includes word processors, spreadsheets, databases, graphics, and others. Local area networks enhance the usefulness of the personal computer. Therefore, it is important to understand the capability of the personal computer in running applications in a local area network environment.

One type of software system that many network users are using is Microsoft Windows. Microsoft Windows is a graphical environment for IBM personal computers and compatibles running under the MS-DOS operating system. Windows creates a new working environment on top of MS-DOS, thus shielding the user from having to memorize operating system commands.

It is important to understand that Windows is not a replacement for MS-DOS. It is just a graphical shell that becomes the interface between the computer and the user. Additionally, individuals who plan to use Microsoft Windows should have some knowledge of the basic input/output operations performed by the computer.

Microsoft Windows 3.1 contains many features that can be used to navigate through a network environment and to perform many functions that used to be done from the DOS command prompt. When a network and Windows are properly installed, Windows will automatically make a network connection and related menu items appear on the Windows menu. These menus can then be used to assist network administrators with network management and related activities such as printing.

Using Application Software in a Network

Benefits

There are many reasons for using network versions of software on a local area network. Some of the most compelling are

1. Sharing of software.
2. Sharing of data.
3. Sharing system resources.
4. Security and backups.
5. Easier maintenance and upgrades.

Sharing Software

Imagine an office that has 20 employees, all using personal computers with word processing, spreadsheet, and database software. If each user is to have individual copies of software, there must a legally purchased copy of each package for each user.

Another solution is to purchase network versions of all software products and install a single copy of each on a local area network connecting all users. Purchasing a network version of a software product is, in many situations, less expensive than buying individual copies for each user.

Additionally, there isn't the need to keep track of 20 copies of the same software product. Only one copy needs to be administered, maintained, and updated.

Sharing Data

With network copies of software programs, the data generated by one user can be used by other users in a "transparent" mode. That is, all users can work with the same data file as if it were their own. With individual copies of software, data generated on one workstation must be physically moved from one machine to another. In the case of sales, inventory departments, and others, this type of data transfer creates problems with outdated versions of files and with duplication of efforts and data.

Sharing System Resources

Network versions of software also save on hard disk space. Instead of using space on multiple users' hard disks, the software can be placed on the network server's hard disk. This allows the software and data to be shared by everyone in a local area network.

Security and Backups

Individual copies of software on multiple workstations are difficult to safeguard from unauthorized individuals. It is relatively easy to go to a person's desk and damage or change data files.

Using the security resources of a network, software can be safeguarded by installing passwords, trustee rights, and file attributes. This enhances the safety of data files and programs in a manner that is almost impossible with individual software.

With multiple users working with stand-alone programs, backing up software becomes a difficult task. Users are not always prompt when it comes to backing up important software and data. Using the network resources, software and data can be backed up from a single location with a minimal amount of effort. This also enhances security since the latest copy of a file is assured when using the latter method.

Easy Maintenance and Upgrades

In many situations users of a particular package do not have the latest updates or modifications. Sometimes this is due to a lack of time to install software upgrades, and other times there is a lack of funding to purchase the latest release of a product.

If network software is used, only one upgrade copy of the software needs to be installed and/or modified to get the latest features. Also, in large corporations with many users, the cost of upgrading a network version of a software product can be substantially less than purchasing individual copies of the same program.

Choosing Servers

If the network consists of only one server, then the choice of where to install shared software is easy. However, if multiple servers are available, a decision must be made as to which server will hold the shared software.

There are several possibilities for multiple server networks. Assume that a network consists of three servers. One possibility is to purchase three copies of the software and install one on each server. Another possibility is to purchase a fourth server and place all shared software on it. Or all shared software can be installed in one of the servers and let users of the other servers attach themselves to the one that has the software (see Fig. 8-1).

Each of these approaches has its pros and cons. If a copy is purchased for each server, then the expense of the extra copy may be higher than having a network version of the software and a license for all possible users. Additionally, there is the need to keep security and maintenance of the same software product on multiple servers.

Placing all shared software on a single server may prove to be too much for a computer acting as the server. Too many users can slow the response time of the server to unacceptable levels.

Acquiring an individual server on which to place all shared software is the most elegant solution. However, in many situations this is not economically feasible.

A final possibility is to spread all shared software among the available servers. This allows the purchase of a single network version of a software product along with a license for the number of users involved. This method also allows the load created by the shared software to be spread evenly among all available servers (see Fig. 8-2).

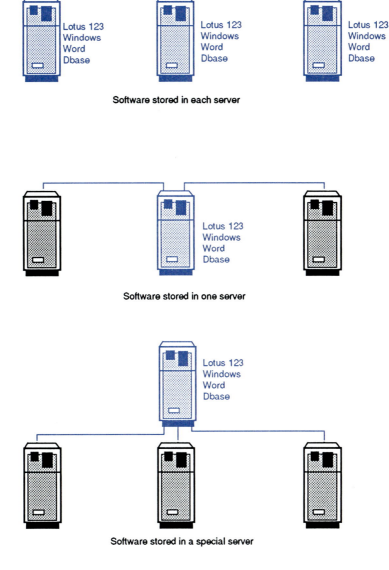

Fig. 8-1. Possible combinations of shared servers.

Choosing a Directory for Shared Software

In addition to choosing the server where the shared software is to reside, the directory structure of this server must be determined. There are several possibilities. One is to place all shared programs under the main or root directory. The other possible solution is to create a directory under the root directory and name this subdirectory SHARESOF, PROGRAMS, or something that indicates its purpose (see Fig. 8-3 for two such subdirectories).

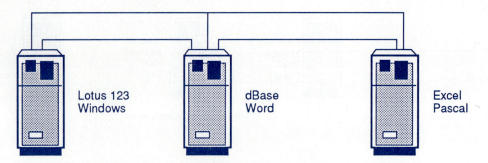

Fig. 8-2. Dividing software evenly among three servers.

The first solution is usually not the best approach. One problem is that the root directory may become cluttered as new programs are added to the server. This makes the task of maintenance and backup more difficult since each shared program name must be identified during backups using some backup schemes.

The second method is the better one. During backup procedures the entire shared software subdirectory can be backed up with a single command. Additionally, establishing security rights over one subdirectory is easier than over multiple subdirectories.

A more complex task is when some software is supposed to be "public domain" and other software is to be secured. The words "public domain" mean that all programs or data in the subdirectory are available to all users for use at their workstation, and there are no restrictions imposed on how they use it. Even though such software is shared, it should not share a parent directory with programs and data that require large measures of security.

Accessing Shared Programs

Several NetWare tools allow a system manager to determine the access rights and privileges of the network users. As a rule, users should be able to work with networked software as if it were an individual program on their workstation. They should be able to change certain software parameters, such as type of printer, in the same manner as if they had a personal copy of the program. Also, users should be able to create data files and store them without the need to learn complex network commands. All of this should take place with the shared programs safeguarded from accidental deletions or deliberate alterations by users without the proper authorization.

A list of all users must be made, specifying their software needs, hard disk space, requirements, and rights. Also, for each data file and software program, attributes such as Shareable or Read Only need to be identified. This also must be performed for all subdirectories and the programs stored inside of them.

When a program is Shareable, its parent directory should also be Shareable. The parent directory attributes typically determine what can be done with the programs and files stored inside of it.

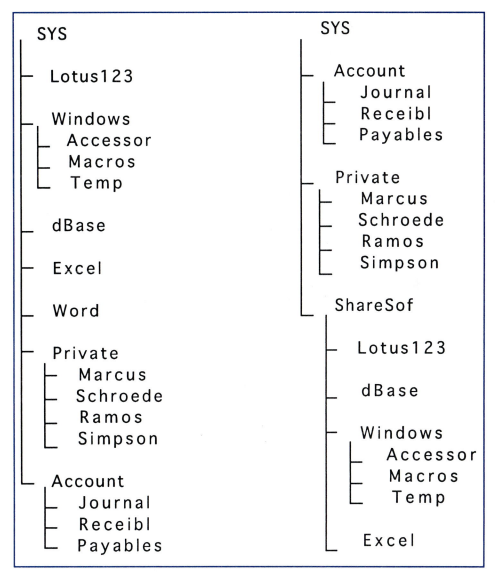

Fig. 8-3. Directory structure for shared programs.

Granting NetWare Rights

Most shared network software comes with documentation that indicates in detail the types of rights to provide to program users. If a list is not available, the network administrator must decide what rights to provide.

The goal is to provide users access to the program without allowing them to change or delete the files that make up the program. If the software package to be installed provides no documentation, then a possible model is to place the software in the SYS:PUBLIC directory. This directory contains program files that all users must be able to run but not change.

All users on a NetWare system have, by default, Read and File Scan rights to the SYS:PUBLIC directory. If the shared software to be installed provides little or no information as to the rights to provide to programs and files, the rights of Read and File Scan can be provided as a first try. The programs should then be tested to make sure that they perform correctly. If errors are encountered, a trial and error procedure of assigning rights may have to be undertaken until the proper rights are provided.

Group Rights

If a large number of users have the same rights, such as a class in a college, a group can be created instead of creating individual users. Then group rights can be provided that affect all the users that belong to the group. For example, if an accounting class needs access to an accounting package, and no one else needs to use the programs, a group ACCOUNTING can be created. When a user who is a member of the ACCOUNTING group logs in, he or she will be granted all rights for the group and access to the programs accordingly. This eliminates the need to grant rights to several dozen accounts, thus reducing the overhead of the network and making maintenance less difficult for network administrators.

Many network administrators create a group for each program that requires some type of access control. Each group is then given rights to its corresponding program. Finally, users are placed in the appropriate groups.

Program File Attributes

Files in a NetWare-based network can be given any of the file attributes outlined in earlier chapters. Generally, most files are made Shareable and Read Only. Files that are Shareable are available to multiple users at the same time. If a file is not Shareable and a user is accessing the file, other users must wait for the first user to finish using the file before they can gain access to it. In other words, it can be used by only one user at a time.

Making a program Read Only protects it from accidental deletion and modification, even by users who have delete privileges, such as the supervisor.

Another type of file attribute is Execute Only. This attribute can be given to executable files in order to prevent them from being copied. While this attribute is on, users can execute the program but cannot copy it to their own disks or subdirectories.

Using Application Programs in a Network Environment

Most software written for IBM compatibles can be divided into three categories: network incompatible, network compatible, and network aware.

Network incompatible software cannot be used at all while it is stored on a file server. Usually the problem involves the program's use of low-level operations to control the disk drive or access its own files. These low-level operations access the hardware of the computer directly, rather than using the DOS function calls that NetWare has redirected to the file server. Other problems can arise when the program is simply incompatible with the resident network driver programs, although this situation is rare. In that case the program cannot be run on a computer that is attached to the network. When the software can be run with the network drivers loaded, but not on the network, it is necessary to install it on the workstation's hard disk. A complete menu system would also offer selections to the user to run this software, as well as network software.

Network compatible software includes all programs that can be run on the network, even though they might not be network specific versions. Many programs have no install options that indicate what drive letter the program is running on. These programs can simply be copied to a network directory. Others, such as older versions of WordStar, can be installed on any drive letter A - Z using the appropriate install procedures. This is often the easiest type of program for the network supervisor to install. Still others may be programmed to always look on a certain disk drive for their files, for instance on drive C. In this case, the NetWare MAP command can be used to map drive letter C to the appropriate network directory. The programs in this category must be handled very carefully in regard to federal copyright laws. Under almost all license agreements accompanying the software, one copy of the software must be owned for each user accessing the program at the same time.

Network aware programs have been written to detect and sometimes take advantage of a network. Many programs released in the last few years are designed specifically to detect that they are running on a network and to allow only one user to access them. This prevents users from illegally using more copies of the software than they own. Usually, special multiuser versions of such programs are available that allow five, ten, or some other number of users to access the software simultaneously. The multiuser versions are always more expensive than single-user versions, of course. But they are less expensive than an equal number of single-user copies. Other programs are written to take advantage of the network environment. These programs offer electronic mail, quick messages, easy use of network printers, or network use of a common database.

Installing Microsoft Windows

To install Windows on a Novell network, a shared copy of the program can be placed in the network. Then copies of some Windows files need to be placed on user disks. This is done by using the command SETUP /X where X is one of three switches that the installer will have to choose from. These switches are as follows:

1. /a. This is the Windows Administrative Setup. When this option is used, Windows files are copied to a network server so users can run the Setup program from the network.

2. /n. This is the Windows Network Setup. When this option is used, the setup system sets up a workstation to run a shared copy of Windows. In this case only a few of the Windows system files are copied to the workstation's hard disk. The rest of the files reside in the server's hard disk. The files copied to the user's workstation allow the user to customize the Windows environment.

3. /h. This is the Windows Automated Setup. This option allows the automated or easy installation of Windows by invoking an automated Setup routine.

Before installing Windows on a network, make sure that any network messaging services and TSRs used for sending messages are turned off. This type of application can cause the Setup program to fail during installation.

Using the Setup /a Option

By using the Setup /a (Windows Administrative Setup) option, the system administrator can place Windows files on a network server. However, this option doesn't create a usable copy of Windows. This option only transfers files from the Windows disks to the server's hard disk. All the files copied are expanded, renamed, and placed on the server's disk as read-only files. This is done so they can be accessed by more than one user or application at a time.

To use this option:

1. From the user's workstation, connect to the network where the copy of Windows is going to be installed. Make sure that you have the rights to perform this operation.

2. Insert Windows 3.1 disk #1 into drive A and set the drive pointer to this drive.

3. Type Setup /a and press the ENTER key.

4. Follow the instructions on the screen.

5. After the installation is complete, mark all Windows files as shareable.

To copy Windows to another network drive that is part of the same network as the one where Windows was just installed, you can run the setup procedure using the /a option from the shared directory that was previously created.

After all Windows files are placed on a network server, users can connect to that server and install Windows in their workstations by running Setup /n from their workstations. However, at this point the network administrator must decide whether to allow users to share Windows from the network server, or copy all Windows files to their workstation using the Automated Setup option.

Using the Setup /n Option

Users can set up their workstations so they have access to a shared copy of Windows by running Setup /n. By using this option, some of the Windows files are copied to the user's hard disk. The directory where some of the Windows files are placed is a personal directory for the user that must be present in order to run Windows.

By maintaining their own copies of these files, users can customize the Windows environment without affecting the shared files located in the network and used by all individuals working with Windows.

To set up a shared copy of Windows on a workstation:

1. From the user's workstation, connect to the network where the copy of Windows is going to be installed. Make sure that you have the rights to perform this operation.
2. Change to the network directory where Windows is located.
3. Type Setup /n and press the ENTER key.
4. Follow the instructions on the screen.

This option copies only the files that pertain to the user's system, such as the group (GRP) and initialization (INI) files.

Using the Setup /h Option

This option uses the information stored in a system settings file to install Windows without much user intervention. The installation is performed quickly and easily. This option is usually preferred if there are many workstations to set up or if users will be performing their own installations.

To use the Automated Setup option:

1. Create a system settings file for each workstation configuration and place the files in a directory where users have access to it and can open, read, and copy the file to the workstation.
2. From the workstation, the users can set up Windows by typing Setup /h and pressing the ENTER key.

If a shared copy of Windows is to be installed using this option, then

3. Type Setup /h:[drive:\path]\filename /n, where filename is the name of the system configuration settings file that contains the details required by the installation program.

Windows comes with a system setting file called SETUP.SHH that can be found in disk #1 of the Windows system disks. The sections in this file are

1. [sysinfo]. This determines if a System Configuration screen will appear during Setup.
2. [configuration]. Determines the various devices on the user's system.
3. [windir]. Determines where to put the Windows files.
4. [userinfo]. Determines the user and company name.
5. [dontinstall]. Determines which Windows components shouldn't be installed.
6. [options]. Determines various options such as setting up existing applications, starting the Windows tutorial, and loading the README files.
7. [printers]. Determines the printer to be used by Windows.
8. [endinstall]. Determines if Setup will modify the CONFIG.SYS and AUTOEXEC.BAT files and if the system is to be rebooted after the installation of Windows.

The basic SETUP.SHH file is displayed below. These settings can be customized to the environment where it will be used.

```
[sysinfo]

;

; Use this section to specify whether you want Setup to display the

; System Configuration screen. Specify "yes" to display the screen and "no"

; if you don't want the screen displayed. (The default value is "no".)

;

; You may want to display and review the System Configuration screen so

; that you can confirm the configuration settings before continuing with

; Setup.

showsysinfo=yes
```

```
[configuration]
;
; Use this section to specify the various devices on your system. You can
; find the values for each variable in the SETUP.INF file. If you omit an
; entry, Windows uses the detected or default device.
;
; If you are updating Windows, some of these entries will be ignored and
; Windows will use the devices that are already installed. If you want to
; force the update and override the installed device, precede the value
; with an exclamation point (!), for example, display = !vga. Only the
; Machine, Display, Mouse, and Network devices require an exclamation point
; for overriding the installed device during an upgrade.
; Machine profile string from [machine] section of SETUP.INF
machine = ibm_compatible
; Display profile string from [display] section of SETUP.INF
display = vga
; Mouse profile string from [pointing.device] section of SETUP.INF
mouse = ps2mouse
; Network profile string from [network] section of SETUP.INF
; followed by version profile string from the appropriate
; [xxxxxxx.versions] section which identifies the network version.
```

; The following example will setup Windows using

; "Microsoft LAN Manager version 2.0 Enhanced".

network = lanman/01020000

; Keyboard profile string from [keyboard.types] section of SETUP.INF

keyboard = t4s0enha

; Language profile string from [language] section of SETUP.INF

language = enu

; Keyboard Layout profile string from [keyboard.tables] section of SETUP.INF

kblayout = nodll

[windir]

;

; Use this section to specify where to put Windows files. If a previous

; version of Windows is already set up in the specified directory, Setup

; will update it. If you do not specify a directory, or if the specified

; directory is not valid, Setup displays a dialog box asking you to specify

; the directory in which you want to set up Windows.

c:\windows

[userinfo]

;

; Use this section to specify the user and company name. The first line

; specifies the user's name. This line is required. The second specifies

; the company name, and is optional. Both names can be up to 30 characters

; long and must be enclosed in double quotation marks (" ") if they include

; blank spaces.

;

; If you do not specify a user name, a dialog box appears during Setup asking

; for the user's name.

;

; If you are setting up Windows across a network, the [userinfo] section

; will be ignored.

;

"John Q. Public"   ; User Name   (30 chars MAX) (required)

"Microsoft Corporation"   ; Company Name (30 chars MAX) (optional)

[dontinstall]

;

; Use this section to specify components that you do not want to set up

; on your system. By default, all components will be installed. If you do

; not want to set up a particular component, include it in this section.

accessories   ; Do NOT install accessories

readmes   ; Do NOT install readme files

games   ; Do NOT install games

screensavers   ; Do NOT install screen savers

bitmaps   ; Do NOT install bitmaps

[options]

;

; Use this section to specify whether you want to set up applications

; during Setup, and/or start the Windows Tutorial at the end of Setup.

; If you don't want any of these options, you can omit this section.

;

; If you choose to set up applications, you can either set them up

; interactively during Setup (you choose which applications you want to ; set up,) or you can specify that you want Setup to automatically set up ;all applications found on your hard disk.

;

; If you specify both "setupapps" and "autosetupapps", all applications ; on your hard disk will be set up.

;

setupapps   ; Setup applications already on hard disk

autosetupapps   ; Set up all applications on hard disk

tutorial   ; Start Windows Tutorial at the end of Setup

[printers]

;

; Use this section to specify any printers you want to set up. You specify

; a printer description and a port. Values for the printer description

; variable are listed in the [io.device] section of the CONTROL.INF file.

; Values for the port variable are listed in the [ports] section of the

; WIN.INI file.

;

; The printer description must be enclosed in double quotation marks (" ; ")

; if it contains blank spaces. The port value must appear exactly as it ;does in the WIN.INI file. If you do not want to set up a printer, omit ;this section.

;

"HP LaserJet III",LPT1:

[endinstall]

;

; Use this section to specify whether you want Setup to make modifications

; to the CONFIG.SYS and AUTOEXEC.BAT files and whether you want Setup to

; exit to DOS, restart Windows, or restart your system when it has finished

; installing Windows.

;

; The "configfiles" entry specifies whether Setup should modify the

; CONFIG.SYS and AUTOEXEC.BAT with the necessary changes, or whether Setup

; should save the proposed changes in separate files called CONFIG.WIN and

; AUTOEXEC.WIN in your WINDOWS directory. If you choose the latter, you ;must make the changes yourself.

;

; You can specify one of the following entries.

;

; configfiles = modify   ;writes modifications back to source.

; configfiles = save   ;saves changes to alternate (*.win) ;files.

;

; If you do not specify a "configfiles" entry, the CONFIG.SYS and

; AUTOEXEC.BAT files will be modified by Setup.

```
;
; The "endopt" entry specifies what happens at the end of Setup. You can
; specify one of the following entries.
;
;      endopt = exit          ; Setup exits to DOS
;      endopt = restart       ; Setup restarts Windows
;      endopt = reboot        ; Setup reboots your computer
;
; If you do not specify an "endopt" entry, a dialog box appears at the end
; of Setup asking the user to choose from the three options.
;
; If you are using the network option for setting up Windows (Setup /n), ;the reboot option is not valid. Setup will exit to DOS instead of rebooting
; your system.
;
configfiles = save
endopt      = restart
```

Accessing Windows

Users can access Windows applications easier by placing entries in the SETUP.INF file that indicate the application and the access mechanism for a specific program. The SETUP.INF file is included with Windows and becomes a permanent file in the shared Windows directory.

By placing entries in the SETUP.INF file, applications can be added to the Program Manager's groups and their settings can also be modified or customized. In this manner, if an application needs to be added to the user's Program Manager window, a title and the path for the application must be placed in the SETUP.INF file.

In addition to the title and path, an icon file name or icon number may also be included in the SETUP.INF file entry for a program application. If an icon is not specified, the displayed icon will be one from the application file.

The SETUP.INF file also has a network section that can be identified by looking for the keyword [network] within the file. This section contains information for specific versions of network drivers and specific network sections that describe SYSTEM.INI entries and other information for specific networks such as Novell NetWare.

Guidelines for Using Windows on a Novell Network

Using Windows on a Novell network is simplified by following these steps:

1. Start the network first; then start Windows. That is, make sure that the workstation is attached to the network server, and that the user is logged in.
2. Personal files should not be kept in a shared file directory.
3. Always use the same network drive letter used when Windows was installed. If Windows was installed in drive H, use drive H when trying to access Windows.
4. When attaching to a printer, always use the same port for that specific printer.

By following these guidelines, using Windows in a Novell network becomes a much simpler task.

When running Novell NetWare, Windows Setup copies NETX.COM (although it is not used with the NetWare DOS Requester version of the client software), IPXODI.COM, TBMI2.COM, IPX.OBJ, and LSL.COM to the WINDOWS directory, even if VLMs are actually used.

If Windows is running from a shared copy on the network, these five files are located in the shared network directory. Before running Windows, the following steps should be taken.

1. Install the NetWare DOS Requester and allow it to modify the Windows configuration files.
2. IPXODI.COM and LSL.COM should be upgraded to the version provided.
3. Increase the number of files in the CONFIG.SYS to 60.
4. Turn SHOW DOTS to ON in SHELL.CFG or NET.CFG.
5. When mapping a connection in File Manager use the MAP ROOT function. This simulates the MS-DOS SUBST command which sets the root of a given drive to a directory designated by the user instead of setting it to the true root of the volume. For example, instead of the usual command in the AUTOEXEC.BAT file of
MAP F:=IO\SYS:HOME\ACC

you should provide the mapping as

MAP ROOT F:=IO\SYS:HOME\ACC

6. Make sure that the entry

LOAD=NWPOPUP.EXE

is added to the [Windows] section of the user's WIN.INI file. This entry automatically starts the NetWare popup utility.

7. Care should be taken when running Printer Assistant with Windows 3.1 and Novell NetWare. Some Windows applications print garbage mixed with correct output when this TSR is in use.

If the system administrator needs to have a greater depth of knowledge about Windows 3.1 and the different options that can be set in it, an inexpensive product from Microsoft called the Microsoft Windows Resource Kit should be obtained. This is an in-depth coverage of Windows installation and operating procedures for stand-alone and network implementations. At a price under $20 it is one resource that a system administrator working with Windows should not be without.

Hands-on Installing Microsoft Windows

Installing Microsoft Windows 3.1

To install shared software on a Novell network, you should login as the supervisor or a supervisor-equivalent user.

1. Type **LOGIN SUPERVISOR** and press the ENTER key.
2. Type the password required to login as the supervisor.

We are going to install Windows as a shared program to be used by all network users. Therefore, a good place to put the Windows files is a subdirectory that branches off from the root directory or one that branches off from the PUBLIC directory. For this exercise we will take the latter approach.

We may decide later to install additional shared software; therefore, we will create a subdirectory called SHARESOF. The subdirectory SHARESOF will contain subdirectories for each shared application that may need to be installed.

3. Type **CD\PUBLIC** and press the ENTER key.
4. Type **MD SHARESOF** and press the ENTER key.

CHAPTER 8. MICROSOFT WINDOWS 3.1 AND NETWORKING

This creates the shared directory where all the applications subdirectories will reside.

5. Type **CD SHARESOF** and press the ENTER key.
6. Type **MD WINDOWS** and press the ENTER key.

This creates the Windows subdirectory.

7. Type **CD WINDOWS** and press the ENTER key.
8. Insert the Microsoft Windows 3.1 Disk 1 in disk drive A:
9. Type **A:SETUP /A** and press the ENTER key.
10. Windows will ask for a directory in which to install. Type **F:\PUBLIC\SHARESOF\WINDOWS** for the directory name.
11. Insert the remaining disks as prompted.

Installing Windows on Users' Disks

Microsoft Windows is now installed in the file server under the subdirectory Windows. The actual path to the Windows files is

F:\PUBLIC\SHARESOF\WINDOWS

Users will need only a few of the files residing in the above directory in order to use the application. These files will be copied to the user's directory or their hard disk. To prepare Windows in a user directory or hard disk follow these steps:

1. Login to the network with the user name and password.
2. Type **CD\PUBLIC\SHARESOF\WINDOWS** and press the ENTER key.
3. Type **SETUP /N** and press the ENTER key.
4. Press the ENTER key. The computer will respond with a default path and directory suggesting where files should reside.
5. Type the path and name of the directory where Windows will be installed. In this example we assume that the user has a hard disk on his or her workstation. Therefore, type **C:\WINDOWS** and press the ENTER key.
6. Continue to follow the installation instructions displayed on the screen by the setup program. You will need to verify the equipment that the setup program thinks you have and plan to use with Windows. If there are no hardware problems, Windows will install some required files on the user's disk and the installation will stop normally.

To facilitate using the Windows program, an entry should be made in the login script for this user. This entry will map a search drive to the Windows subdirectory. This helps in accessing the shared files required to run the application.

7. Logout of the user account and login as a supervisor-equivalent user.
8. Type **SYSCON** and press the ENTER key.
9. Highlight User Information from the SYSCON menu and press the ENTER key.
10. Highlight the name of the user to receive the changes in the login script and press the ENTER key.
11. Highlight Login Script and press the ENTER key.
12. Type

    MAP S4:=SYS:\PUBLIC\SHARESOF\WINDOWS

    Press ESC and highlight Yes when asked if you want to save the changes.
13. Press the ESC key three times.
14. Highlight Yes when asked if you want to exit SYSCON.

Windows is now installed. To access it, type C: and press the ENTER key. Then type CD\WINDOWS and press the ENTER key. Finally, type WIN and press the ENTER key.

To make it a little easier, a batch file like the one below can be placed in the PUBLIC directory and be given the attributes Shareable and Read Only. The batch file is as follows:

    C:
    CD\WINDOWS
    WIN
    F:

Summary

Microsoft Windows is a graphical environment for IBM personal computers and compatibles running under the MS-DOS operating system. Windows creates a new working environment on top of MS-DOS, thus shielding the user from having to memorize operating system commands.

Microsoft Windows 3.1 contains many features that can be used to navigate through a network environment and to perform many functions that used to be done from the DOS command prompt. When a network and Windows are properly installed, Windows will automatically make a network connection and related menu items appear automatically on the Windows menu. These menus can then be used to assist network administrators with network management and related activities such as printing.

To install Windows on a Novell network, a shared copy of the program can be placed in the network. Then copies of some Windows files need to be placed on user disks. This is done by using the command SETUP /X during the installation process. In this case the /X option refers to one of three switches that the installer will have to choose from. These switches are as follows:

1. /a. Windows Administrative Setup.
2. /n. Windows Network Setup.
3. /h. Windows Automated Setup.

Questions

1. Why use Windows 3.1 in a Novell network?
2. What are the options when installing Windows on a network?
3. What are the network drivers provided with Windows?
4. What is the purpose of the SYSTEM.INF file?
5. Which of the installation options is best for the normal user?

Projects

Objectives

These projects are designed to provide the student with hands-on practice installing software applications using Novell NetWare.

Project 1. Installing Microsoft Excel on the File Server

Excel is a spreadsheet developed by Microsoft Corporation to run under the Microsoft Windows environment. Before Excel can be installed, a shared version of Windows needs to be present on a network file server. Excel can be installed in a directory on the file server. Then it can be executed on any computer that has access to this file directory.

To install Excel on a Novell network server, the Microsoft Excel Setup program needs to be executed. When the Setup program asks for the name of a directory where Excel is to be installed, the name of a shareable directory has to be provided to the program.

All files in the new directory can have the attributes of Shareable, Execute, and Read Only. This will allow multiple network users to access the program simultaneously.

In addition to using Novell's network security mechanisms to protect documents generated by Excel, users can provide additional safeguards using one or more of the following methods:

1. Allow only authorized users to open a document. This is done by saving the document with a password using the Save As command. Only people who are given the password can access the document.

2. Prevent unauthorized editing of a document. Using the Format Cell Protection command, lock the cells. Then using the Options Protect Document command, give the document a password for further security.

3. Hide cells by setting the column width or row height to zero for the columns containing the cells to be protected.

Project 2. Installing Microsoft Word for Windows on the File Server

Microsoft Word for Windows is a word processor that runs under the Microsoft Windows environment. The Word program files can be stored in a shareable directory on the file server. Any workstation that has access to the directory can run the Word program.

For Word to work properly, its setup program inserts an entry into the file WIN.INI that indicates the Word options. Word also has its own version of WIN.INI. It is called WINWORD.INI. This file contains the settings for some Word menus and utilities.

Microsoft Word for Windows looks for WINWORD.INI in the directory specified in WIN.INI, the Word directory, or the directory from which Word was executed. If it doesn't find one, it will create it.

Appendix A. Workstation Utilities

Novell NetWare version 3.12 provides workstation utilities which can be used for a variety of purposes, from monitoring users on the network to limiting disk space on a volume. An explanation of several significant utilities follows.

USERLIST

This utility displays information about all of the users currently logged onto the network. The information displayed varies depending on the selection flags which are used when the command is executed.

The syntax for USERLIST is:

USERLIST fileservername/username /flags

Both the fileservername and the username are optional, and, if omitted, the command refers to all users on the current file server.

Common flag options and their meanings are:

/A   lists network and node addresses for all users as shown in Fig. A-1

/C   provides a continuous listing of users at regular intervals

no flag lists network users without network and node addresses

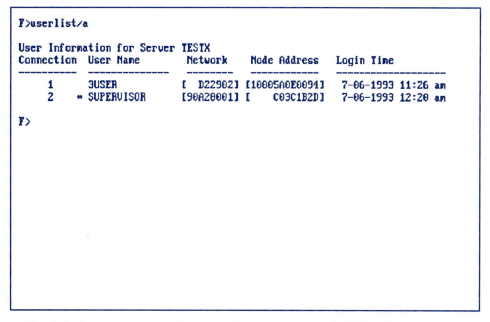

Fig. A-1. Output generated by executing the command USERLIST /A.

LISTDIR

The LISTDIR command shows a hierarchial view of the directory structure below the path indicated in the command. Information displayed varies depending on the flags entered with the command.

The syntax of LISTDIR is:

LISTDIR pathname /flags

The pathname is the path of the directory which is to be used as the highest level of the tree of the directories to be displayed. If the pathname is omitted, the current directory is assumed to be the top level directory.

Common flags and their meanings are:

/A   lists all information possible with this command as shown in Fig. A-2

/S   list all subdirectories

/D   lists creation date

/T   lists creation time

/E   lists effective rights per directory for the user running the command

/R   lists inherited rights mask of all subdirectories in a directory

```
F>listdir f:\public /a

The sub-directory structure of TESTX/SYS:PUBLIC
Date       Time    Inherited    Effective    Directory
-----------------------------------------------------------
 6-24-93   8:50p   [SRWCEMFA]   [SRWCEMFA]   ->DATA
 6-24-93   8:51p   [SRWCEMFA]   [SRWCEMFA]   -> 9USER
 3-23-93   7:04p   [SRWCEMFA]   [SRWCEMFA]   ->LECTURES
 6-26-93  10:12a   [SRWCEMFA]   [SRWCEMFA]   ->USERS
 6-26-93  10:13a   [SRWCEMFA]   [SRWCEMFA]   -> 9USER
5 sub-directories found

F>
```

Fig. A-2. Output generated by executing the command LISTDIR.

NDIR

This is the network directory command. This command is similar to the DIR command in DOS, but it provides more information than the regular DOS directory command.

The syntax is:

NDIR pathname /options and flags

The pathname can be a specific pathname or it can be a pathname with a wildcard designator such as * or ?

Multiple options or flags can be specified, each flag preceded by a / character. Common flags and their meaning are:

/SORT sortparameters

causes the directory to be sorted according to the information given in the sortparameters

/REV /SORT sortparameters

causes the directory to be sorted in reverse order according to the information given in the sortparameters

/HELP displays the options available for the NDIR command

Sortparameters available are:

OW	sort by owner
SI	sort by size
UP	sort by date last modified
CR	sort by creation date
AC	sort by date last accessed
AR	sort by date last archived

Several display format options are also available. These are:

/RIGHTS	lists the inherited and effective rights
/DATES	lists for each file the creation date, the date last modified, date last archived, and date last accessed

Several common restriction options are:

/SUB	instructs the command to search all subdirectories below the directory specified in the path command
/DO	displays only directories meeting search criteria
/FO	displays only file names meeting search criteria

For example,

NDIR *.EXE /SUB

which is entered while the current directory is SYS:PUBLIC list all files ending with the .EXE extension in all subdirectories under the current directory. Similarly,

NDIR *.EXE /SUB /SORT OW

when entered from the current directory SYS:PUBLIC lists all files ending with .EXE extension, sorted in ascending order by owner as shown in Fig. A-3.

```
TESTX/SYS:PUBLIC

Files:              Size        Last Updated    Flags                   Owner
-----------------   --------    -------------   -----------------       ---------
ATTRIB      EXE     15,796      5-09-91 12:00p  [Rw-A-------------]     N/A
PKUNZIP     EXE     20,006     12-20-92  2:04a  [Rw-A-------------]     N/A
COLORPAL    EXE     50,176     10-20-87  9:33a  [Ro-A-----------DR]     SUPERVISO
UNZIP       EXE     23,044      6-11-91  6:00a  [Rw-A-----------DR]     SUPERVISO
NCD         EXE     82,105      8-05-91  6:01a  [Rw-A-----------DR]     SUPERVISO
MAKLOCAL    EXE     11,008      3-11-90  7:22p  [RoS------------DR]     TESTX
BREQUEST    EXE     18,060      2-12-91  5:25p  [RoS------------DR]     TESTX
BROLLFWD    EXE     31,430      2-20-91  1:54p  [RoS------------DR]     TESTX
BCONSOLE    EXE     48,686      2-01-91 10:09a  [RoS------------DR]     TESTX
WBROLL      EXE     26,760      8-20-90 10:11a  [RoS------------DR]     TESTX
NFOLIO      EXE    194,139      8-14-90  0:00   [RoS------------DR]     TESTX
13T020      EXE     77,071      8-14-90  0:00   [RoS------------DR]     TESTX
VIEWER      EXE     75,495      8-14-90  0:00   [RoS------------DR]     TESTX
HELP        EXE     14,825      6-07-90  9:41a  [RoS------------DR]     TESTX
20UPDATE    EXE     41,045      8-14-90  0:00   [RoS------------DR]     TESTX
PCONSOLE    EXE    233,687      2-11-91  6:57a  [RoS------------DR]     TESTX
PRINTCON    EXE    160,823      1-26-91  7:58a  [RoS------------DR]     TESTX
PSTAT       EXE     28,921      2-02-91 10:55a  [RoS------------DR]     TESTX
PRINTDEF    EXE    192,203      2-11-91  4:52p  [RoS------------DR]     TESTX

Strike any key for next page or C for continuous display...
```

Fig. A-3. Output generated by executing the command NDIR.

NCOPY

NCOPY is the network copy command. It is similar to the DOS COPY and XCOPY commands with two significant differences. First, if the users wants to copy files from one directory to another on the file server, the entire operation is accomplished on the file server without having to involve memory on the local workstation. Second, NCOPY displays the source and destination directories during the copy process, a further verification that the desired copy procedure is occurring.

For example, the command

NCOPY F:\LOGIN*.* F:\LOGINBU*.*

causes all of the files in the LOGIN directory to be copied to a directory named LOGINBU on the file server. Note that the files are displayed as they are copied.

CHKDIR

The CHKDIR command on the network is similar to the CHKDSK command in DOS. It displays information about a volume or a directory, as shown in Fig. A-4.

The syntax is:

CHKDIR pathname

where pathname is optional and is the current directory if not specified. This command displays information regarding maximum storage capacity of a volume or a directory on which space limitations have been placed.

```
F>CHKDIR

Directory Space Limitation Information For:
TESTX\SYS:PUBLIC

    Maximum        In Use      Available
    39,040 K       38,124 K      916 K    Volume Size
                    9,460 K      916 K    \PUBLIC
F>
```

Fig. A-4. Output generated by the command CHKDIR.

CHKVOL

The CHKVOL command displays information regarding total volume space, including file server name, volume name, total volume space, space used by files, file allocation tables and directory tables, space in use by deleted files which have not been purged, space remaining on the volume, and space available to the user currently running the utility, as shown in Fig. A-5.

```
F>CHKVOL

Statistics for fixed volume TESTX/SYS:

Total volume space:                     39,040  K Bytes
Space used by files:                    38,128  K Bytes
Space in use by deleted files:             600  K Bytes
Space available from deleted files:        600  K Bytes
Space remaining on volume:                 912  K Bytes
Space available to SUPERVISOR:             912  K Bytes

F>
```

Fig. A-5. Output generated by the command CHKVOL.

The syntax is:

CHKVOL volumename

where volume name is optional and is the current volume if not specified.

RENDIR

RENDIR renames a directory on the file server.

The syntax is:

RENDIR olddirectoryname newdirectoryname

While this command renames the directory itself, it does not affect user trustee assignments which may have referenced the old directory name. These trustee assignments must be manually changed through SYSCON. RENDIR also does not change any references to the old directory name which may have existed in either the System or User Login scripts.

VOLINFO

VOLINFO show the space and number of directory entries allocated and the space and number of directory entries free per volume on the file server.

The syntax is:

VOLINFO

To terminate VOLINFO, the user must press the ESC key and then select "Yes" and press ENTER to exit VOLINFO, as shown in Fig. A-6.

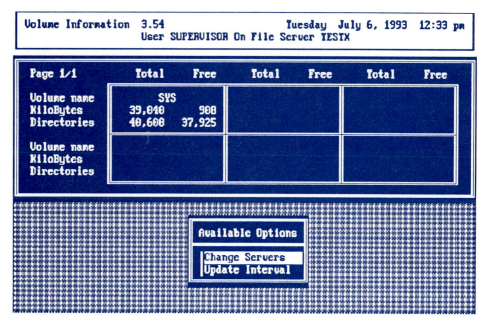

Fig. A-6. Exiting from VOLINFO.

SLIST

SLIST displays the names of all file servers which can logically be "seen" by the current file server. These are the file servers available to the user if the user has the appropriate user ID and password on the target file server. File servers not listed by SLIST are not available to the user from the current workstation.

The syntax is:

SLIST

TLIST

TLIST displays a list of all users and groups which have explicit trustee rights to the current directory.

The syntax is:

TLIST

A sample display of the results of having entered TLIST in a directory called \USERS is shown in Fig. A-7.

```
F:\USERS>TLIST

TESTX\SYS:USERS
User trustees:
    3KAY                                    [ R    F ]
    6WILL                                   [ R    F ]
    9MARY                                   [ R    F ]
No group trustees.

F:\USERS>
```

Fig. A-7. Output generated by the command TLIST.

GRANT

The GRANT command allows a user with the Access Control right to a directory to give any rights that he or she has except access control or supervisory to another user. This is useful when a user needs another user to have access to his or her directory. Care must be taken in using this command, however, because this command effectively hides from the supervisor the fact that another user has rights to a given directory.

The syntax is:

GRANT listofrights FOR fileorpath TO userorgroup

For example,

GRANT R F FOR SYS:\USERS TO LISA grants the Read and File Scan rights for the directory called USERS to a user called LISA.

REVOKE

REVOKE is the reverse of the GRANT command. It allows a user to rescind rights he or she has previously granted to another user.

The syntax is:

REVOKE listofrights FOR fileorpath FROM userorgroup

For example,

REVOKE R F FOR SYS:\USERS FROM LISA rescinds the Read and File Scan rights previous granted to user LISA.

REMOVE

The REMOVE command removes a user or a group from the trustee list for a given directory or file. Note that REMOVE is used to remove a user or a group from trustee rights which were explicitly given through SYSCON.

The syntax is:

REMOVE userorgroup FROM path

where userorgroup is the name of the user or group which is to be removed from the list of explicit trustees from the path specified. The effects of this command may be immediately shown by running the TLIST command on the path in question just prior to and just after the REMOVE command is executed.

SALVAGE

The SALVAGE command may be used to recover files which were accidentally deleted, provided that the space they occupy has not already been used by another file and provided that the directory has not been purged via the PURGE command. The user running the SALVAGE command must have the Create right to the directory being salvaged.

The syntax is:

SALVAGE

For example, if the files in \USERS have just been erased, entry of the SALVAGE command will cause a SALVAGE screen to be displayed as shown in Fig. A-8.

SECURITY

The SECURITY command shows a list of possible security violations including such things as users whose password is the same as their user ID, users with supervisory equivalence, and users with no login script.

This function is invoked by entering

SECURITY

and will produce output similar to Fig. A-9.

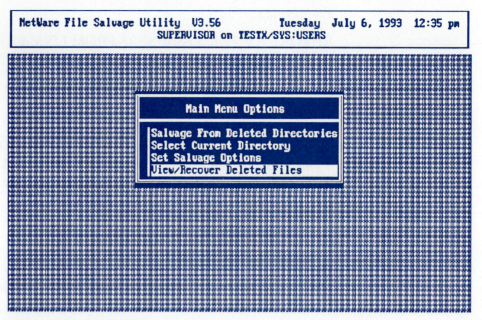

Fig. A-8. SALVAGE menu.

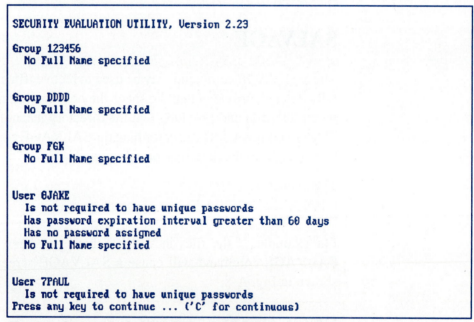

Fig. A-9. Output of the SECURITY command.

To print the list of possible security violations, it is possible to redirect the output of the SECURITY command to the print device as in:

SECURITY >PRN:

MAKEUSER

The MAKEUSER command allows a supervisor, a supervisor-equivalent user, or a workgroup manager to create, modify, and process a script, much like a batch file, to add users to the network. These script files are ASCII text files which have the .USR extension and contain keywords needed to create a user account. If there is an error in a MAKEUSER script, a nondescriptive error message will be displayed, but the script will not continue processing until the user has corrected the error. A sample script is shown in Fig. A-10. Representative MAKEUSER keywords, all similar to options available while creating a user with the SYSCON utility, are:

#ACCOUNT EXPIRATION mm/dd/yy

#ACCOUNT balance,lowerlimit

#CONNECTIONS number

#CREATE username

#HOME_DIRECTORY path

#LOGIN_DIRECTORY path

#MAX_DISK_SPACE vol,number

#PASSWORD_LENGTH length

#PASSWORD_PERIOD days

#PASSWORD_REQUIRED

#REM

#RESTRICTED_TIME day,start,end

#STATIONS network,station

#UNIQUE_PASSWORD

```
#ACCOUNT EXPIRATION 07/31/96
#ACCOUNT BALANCE 3000,100
#CONNECTIONS 1
#CREATE JUSER
#HOME_DIRECTORY SYS:\JUSER
#PASSWORD_LENGTH 5
#PASSWORD_REQUIRED
#UNIQUE_PASSWORD
```

Fig. A-10. Login Script.

Hands-on Workstation Utilities

USERDEF

The USERDEF command allows the supervisor, supervisor-equivalent users, and workgroup managers to create and edit templates to process users. Instead of creating a .USR file from MAKEUSER, which references several other files such as LOGIN DIRECTORY, USERDEF provides a means to use templates with different parameters for different user accounts. One typical use of USERDEF is to define templates by functional area such as department and then to use these templates in setting up individual user accounts.

Using USERDEF, you will create a template called TJSMITH, where you will substitute your user ID for the JSMITH, and then you will use that template to create a new user called JSMITHT where you will again substitute your user ID for the JSMITH.

1. Type **USERDEF** and press the ENTER key.

The main menu of the USERDEF utility will be displayed as in Fig. A-11.

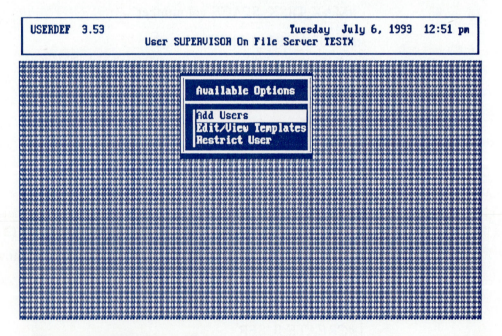

Fig. A-11. USERDEF Main Menu.

2. Use the arrow keys to move the cursor to Edit/View Templates and press the ENTER key.

A list of existing templates is displayed on the right side of the screen.

3. Press the INS key to add a template.
4. Enter the name of your template, such as TJSMITH, and press the ENTER key. A screen showing the available options for the new template is displayed as in Fig. A-12.

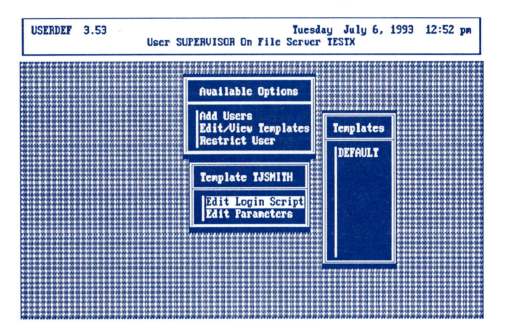

Fig. A-12. Available Options for Template in USERDEF.

5. Point to Edit Login Script and press ENTER. The default login script is displayed. Delete the last line of this login script and modify the mapping for S2: to point to the location where COMMAND.COM is stored.
6. Press ESC, select Yes, and press ENTER to accept the edited login script.
7. Scroll down to the Edit Parameters Option and press the ENTER key. A parameter screen similar to Fig. A-13 is displayed.
8. Scroll down to change the parameters as shown in Fig. A-14.
9. Press ESC, select Yes, press ENTER or press ESC two times to get back to the main USERDEF menu.
10. Point to the Add Users selection and press the ENTER key.

A list of templates is displayed. Scroll down to your template and press ENTER. A list of users is shown.

11. Press INS to add a user. Enter Full Name for the new user JSMITHT (where you substitute your user ID for JSMITH) and press the ENTER key two times.
12. Enter JSMITHT (where you substitute your user ID for JSMITH) for the Login Name and press the ENTER key.

13. Press the ESC key, select Yes to create the user and press the ENTER key two times.
14. Press ESC five times to return to the Exit USERDEF screen.
15. Select Yes and press ENTER to exit USERDEF.
16. Using SYSCON, examine the user just created. Notice that, with the exception of trustee rights to the new user's mail directory, trustee rights specific to this user must still be assigned through SYSCON.

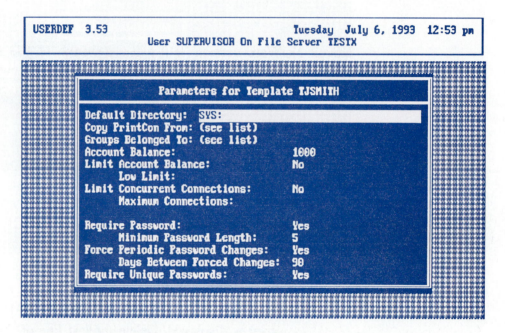

Fig. A-13. Blank Parameters for Template screen.

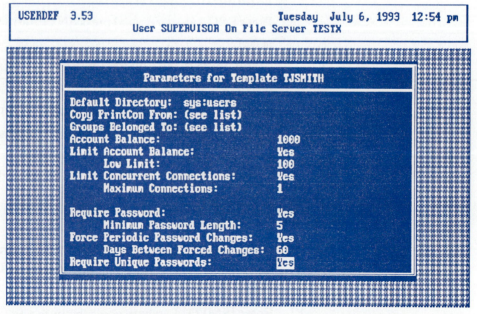

Fig. A-14. Parameters for Template screen for template being created.

Appendix B. File Server Utilities and Remote Management

Novell NetWare version 3.12 offers a wealth of file server utilities for management of the network. All of these utilities are executed at the file server console, and some allow the user to take over control from a workstation and execute the utility from the workstation rather than the console. Console commands are similar to internal DOS commands in that they are part of SERVER.EXE and provide the operator ways to monitor and control file server activity. NetWare Loadable Modules provide additional functions to the already running NetWare operating system.

NetWare Loadable Modules

With NetWare 3.12, Novell has moved to a modular approach to its operating system. The program SERVER.EXE loads the core of the operating system itself, and additional functionality is then provided by the loading of NetWare Loadable Modules. These modules can be run and then unloaded when no longer needed, thus freeing RAM for other uses without having to down the file server.

NetWare 3.12 uses NetWare Loadable Modules to provide disk drivers, LAN drivers (NIC drivers), Name Space Modules to support non-DOS naming conventions, and NLM utilities to oversee and modify configuration options. The syntax for loading these modules is:

LOAD [path]nlm_name[parameter list]

For example, one could load the LAN driver for an NE2000 network interface card by entering the following command on the file server console:

LOAD NE2000

One could then unload the driver when no longer needed by entering:

UNLOAD NE2000

NetWare Loadable Modules have different extensions, depending on their function. Some of the common extensions are explained next.

Type of NLM	Extension
Disk drivers	.DSK
LAN drivers	.LAN
Name space modules	.NAM
NLM utilities	.NLM

All NLMs are typically stored in the SYS:SYSTEM directory, which normally has limited access for security purposes.

NetWare Loadable Modules provide a significant design improvement over earlier versions of NetWare. Revisions to the network operating system in NetWare 2.x versions require the supervisor to down the file server and go through the lengthy process of reconfiguration, often called the generation process. Then, once the operating system has been generated, the supervisor must load it onto the file server from the file server console station.

With NLMs, the supervisor need merely load and unload appropriate modules to affect changes to the operating system with no need for downing the server or for regenerating the actual operating system. Obviously, this approach provides the supervisor with greater flexibility in operating system configuration.

Console Commands

Console commands are part of SERVER.EXE, and they allow the supervisor or console operator to perform various tasks in network management. There are four major categories of console commands:

1. Screen display management
2. Installation of NetWare
3. Maintenance of the operating system
4. Configuration information

All console commands must be entered on the console or on a remote workstation which is used as a console.

Some of the more commonly used console commands and their syntax are described in the following sections.

BROADCAST

This command takes the form:

BROADCAST "message to be broadcast" [[TO] username|connection number] [[and|,] username|connection number . . .]

Example:

BROADCAST "Please logout for 20 minutes"

This command causes the text entered between the double quotes to be sent to all active workstations on the network or to specific workstations if the optional "TO" clause is used. Care should be taken in using this command because the message delivered to the workstation suspends processing on the workstation until the user presses CTRL/ENTER to clear the message from the screen display.

```
:broadcast "SAMPLE BROADCAST MESSAGE SENT TO ALL USERS"
:
```

Fig. B-1. Sample BROADCAST command.

SEND

This command functions the same as the BROADCAST command.

CLEAR STATION

CLEAR STATION j

Example:

CLEAR STATION 2

This command allows the operator to clear the currently active session at a given connection number. The connection numbers assigned by NetWare to active stations can be seen by entering USERLIST /A. This function is especially useful when the operator is trying to perform some system-wide function which requires the users to logout, and one or more user fails to logout. Using this command, the operator can clear the connection, thus causing an automatic logout.

DISABLE LOGIN/ENABLE LOGIN

When it is desired that no users login during a time period, the operator can enter the DISABLE LOGIN command on the file server console. This command prevents new users from logging in until the operator enters the ENABLE LOGIN command. It is important to recognize that entry of the DISABLE LOGIN command does not affect users currently logged in. If current users must logout, the operator may broadcast a message requesting that users logout voluntarily. When users fail to logout voluntarily, the CLEAR CONNECTION command may be used to force logout.

Also, if the supervisor account is locked due to apparent intruder detection, the account can be reenabled by entering ENABLE LOGIN on the file server console. The ENABLE LOGIN command has no effect on the lockout status of other accounts.

DOWN

This command causes the file server's operating system to terminate operation in an orderly fashion. It is entered from the file server console. If users are currently logged in and currently have active files open, a warning message to this effect will be displayed, and the operator will again be asked whether or not to proceed with the downing of the file server. It is always a good idea to persuade users to logout in an orderly fashion rather than downing the file server with active files open. Index files and even the FAT table can be damaged by downing the file server with network files open (see Fig. B-2).

```
:down
File PCONSOLE.HLP in use by user 1USER on station 3
File SYS$ERR.DAT in use by user 1USER on station 3
File SYS$MSG.DAT in use by user 1USER on station 3
File RCONSOLE.HLP in use by user SUPERVISOR on station 6
File SYS$ERR.DAT in use by user SUPERVISOR on station 6
File SYS$MSG.DAT in use by user SUPERVISOR on station 6
**** WARNING **** There are active files open.
Down server? n
```

Fig. B-2. Attempting to DOWN a server with files open.

SET TIME

The time for the file server may be set using this command. Note that this time does not take into account the effect of daylight savings time; therefore, the time must be reset manually when daylight savings time goes into effect and when it goes off (see Fig. B-3).

```
:set time 17:40
Time set to Tuesday  July 6, 1993  5:40:36 pm
:
```

Fig. B-3. Setting time on the file server console.

CONFIG

The configuration of the network is displayed on the file server console screen upon entry of this command at the : file server console prompt.

DISPLAY SERVERS

Other servers that can be "seen" by the given file server are displayed on the file server screen upon entry of this command as shown in Fig. B-4.

```
:display servers
   00000371      6    05506371      6    005525253C01  7    CLASSROOM    6
   TESTX         1
There are 5 known servers
:
```

Fig. B-4. Display servers.

MODULES

This command displays on the file server console screen various types of information regarding the modules loaded on the file server. This command is very useful when the operator is trying to determine how the file server is currently configured. (See Fig. B-5)

```
:modules
RSPX.NLM
   NetWare 386 Remote Console SPX Driver
   Version 1.30    February 9, 1991
   Copyright 1991 Novell, Inc.  All rights reserved.
REMOTE.NLM
   NetWare 386 Remote Console
   Version 1.31    February 13, 1991
   Copyright 1991 Novell, Inc.  All rights reserved.
PCN2L.LAN
   IBM PCN II & Baseband LAN Driver  v1.06 (910207)
   Version 1.06    February 7, 1991
NMAGENT.NLM
   Network Management NLM
   Version 1.11    February 6, 1991
PS2ESDI.DSK
   Netware 386 PS/2 ESDI Device Driver
   Version 3.11    February 12, 1991
   Copyright 1991 Novell, Inc.  All rights reserved.
```

Fig. B-5. Ouput generated by the MODULES command.

Other NLMs

Novell NetWare version 3.12 provides an abundance of additional NLMs for various functions. Especially significant are those described in the following sections.

INSTALL

This command is entered as:

LOAD INSTALL

This NLM was already explored in the chapter on installation. Note that in version 3.12, the installation process is accomplished by first loading a "generic" network operating system using SERVER.EXE and then by using this operating system to load INSTALL.NLM. Various other NLMs are loaded during the installation process and are added to STARTUP.NCF and AUTOEXEC.NCF so that they can be loaded each time the file server is brought up.

MONITOR

The syntax for this command is:

LOAD MONITOR

This utility is the most powerful management utility in NetWare 3.12. As shown in Fig. B-6, many of the functions of MONITOR are functions which were offered by the FCONSOLE utility in earlier versions of NetWare. In addition to displaying connection, disk, and LAN information, MONITOR provides statistics regarding resource usage. This utility is used to track memory usage and usage of the LAN system itself.

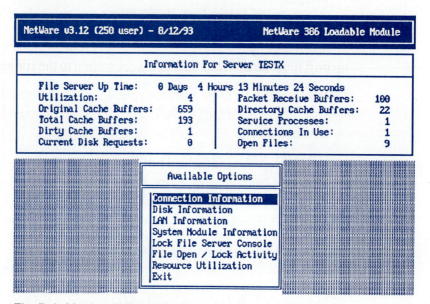

Fig. B-6. Monitor Utility Main Menu.

Additionally, the operator can monitor processor usage by entering

LOAD MONITOR -P

UPS

It is highly recommended that every file server be protected by an uninterruptible power supply (UPS) which provides power to the file server when wall current goes off. The UPS utility links the file server to the UPS so that the file server can do an orderly shutdown when power from the UPS is about to run out.

STREAMS

This NLM provides a shared interface which allows multiple protocols to function on a NetWare network. Streams is implemented by loading the following NLMs in order:

    STREAMS

    IPXS and SPXS

    CLIB

    TLI

APPENDIX B. FILE SERVER UTILITIES AND REMOTE MANAGEMENT

Remote Management

The remote management facilities of NetWare 3.12 provide the operator with the ability to manage NetWare file servers remotely. With this facility, a single operator or supervisor can manage multiple file servers from one site by causing the workstation to act as a file server console.

Remote management can be accomplished by executing RCONSOLE.EXE or ACONSOLE.EXE from the workstation. RCONSOLE is used when the workstation is physically connected, either directly or through bridges or routers, to the file server to be managed. ACONSOLE is used when a dial-up port must be used to attach the workstation to the file server to be managed.

If RCONSOLE is to be used for remote management, the following NLMs must have been loaded on the file server to be managed:

REMOTE.NLM

RSPX.NLM

RCONSOLE can then allow the operator to perform all of the tasks normally available on the file server console itself. It also allows the operator to scan directories and copy files to (not from) the managed file server.

ACONSOLE provides an asynchronous console connection. REMOTE.NLM and RS232.NLM must have been loaded on the file server to be managed for ACONSOLE to work. Then, ACONSOLE provides remote management functions similar to RCONSOLE.

Hands-on File Server Utilities

We will practice the use of various console commands ranging from BROADCAST to DISABLE LOGIN to DISPLAY SERVERS. These commands must be entered on the file server console, so it is important that only one student be entering commands at a time. It is, of course, possible to run these commands from a workstation using RCONSOLE, but it is still very important that only one student be entering commands at a time.

Prior to entering any of these commands, it is imperative that the file server be brought up and that the file server console prompt of : be displayed. Also, it is important for at least one user to be logged in at a workstation.

Sending a Message

1. Enter **SEND "This is a sample message with the SEND COMMAND"** and press ENTER.

Note that the "TO" clause is optional, and the assumption is that the operator wishes to broadcast to EVERYONE when the "TO" clause is missing.

2. Go to the workstation which is logged in and observe the effect. There should be a message on the bottom of the screen similar to that shown in Fig B-7.

3. Press Ctrl and Enter on the workstation to clear the message

```
:send "This is a sample message with the SEND COMMAND" to 12user
Broadcast was sent to 1 station
:
```

Fig. B-7. Results of SEND a message to all users.

Disabling and Enabling Login

1. Make sure that a workstation is logged into the file server prior to disabling login. This workstation should still be able to function after the entry of the DISABLE LOGIN command on the file server console.

2. Enter **DISABLE LOGIN** on the file server console and press ENTER.

3. Go to another workstation and attempt to login. The login attempt should be unsuccessful as shown in Fig. B-8.

4. Go to the workstation which is already logged in and enter a directory command or any other command. This station should still be logged in and operational.

5. Logout on the active workstation.

6. Attempt to login on the same workstation with the same login ID. This attempt should be unsuccessful because login has been disabled.

```
F>login testx\supervisor
TESTX/SUPERVISOR: The supervisor has the bindery locked or SYS volume is not mou
nted.
```

Fig. B-8. Attempt to login after Login has been disabled on file server console.

To enable Login

1. Enter **ENABLE LOGIN** on the file server console.

2. Go back to the station on which login was just unsuccessful and attempt to log in. The login should now be successful.

Displaying the Servers and Modules in Use

1. Enter **DISPLAY SERVERS** on the file server console and press ENTER.

A display similar to Fig. B-9 should be shown on the file server console.

To display the modules in Use

1. Enter **MODULES** on the file server console

A display similar to Fig B-10 should be shown on the file server console.

```
:display servers
   00000371      6    05506371      6    005525253C01   7   CLASSROOM    6
   TESTX         1
There are 5 known servers
:
```

Fig. B-9. Display Servers.

```
:modules
RSPX.NLM
   NetWare 386 Remote Console SPX Driver
   Version 1.30    February 9, 1991
   Copyright 1991 Novell, Inc.  All rights reserved.
REMOTE.NLM
   NetWare 386 Remote Console
   Version 1.31    February 13, 1991
   Copyright 1991 Novell, Inc.  All rights reserved.
PCN2L.LAN
   IBM PCN II & Baseband LAN Driver  v1.06 (910207)
   Version 1.06    February 7, 1991
NMAGENT.NLM
   Network Management NLM
   Version 1.11    February 6, 1991
PS2ESDI.DSK
   Netware 386 PS/2 ESDI Device Driver
   Version 3.11    February 12, 1991
   Copyright 1991 Novell, Inc.  All rights reserved.
:
```

Fig. B-10. Modules loaded on File Server.

Downing a File Server

1. First, make sure there is at least one user logged in and using a file of some sort.
2. Enter **DOWN** on the file server console and press ENTER.

A warning message should be displayed on the file server console.

3. Press the N key to terminate the DOWN process
4. Cause all active sessions on this file server to logout

5. Enter **DOWN** on the file server console and press ENTER. A message regarding exiting to DOS will appear on the screen after the system has been shut down.
6. Enter **EXIT** and press ENTER to exit to DOS.
7. Reboot the file server by pressing CONTROL, ALT, DELETE.

Appendix C

Vendors of Gateways and Related Products

Access Server
Novell Inc. Comm. Products
890 Ross Dr.
Sunnyvale, CA 94089
800-453-1267

C-Slave/286 and XBUS4/AT
Alloy Computer Products Inc.
165 Forest St.
Marlboro, MA 01752
508-481-8500

Chatterbox4000
J&L Information Systems Inc.
9600 Topanga Canyon Blvd.
Chatsworth, CA 91311
818-709-1778 FAX: 818-882-9134

ComBridge
Cubix Corp.
428 Sandalwood
Carson City, NV 89706
800-829-0550 FAX: 702-888-1001

FlexCom
Evergreen Systems Inc.,
120 Landing Ct.
Suite A
Novato, CA 94945
415-897-8888 800-383-7797

MultiComAsyncGateway
Multi-Tech Systems Inc.
2205 Woodale Dr.
Mounds View, MN 55112
800-328-9717 FAX: 612-785-9874

Telebits ACS
Telebit Corp
115 Chesapeake Terr.
Sunnyvale, CA 94089
408-745-3004 FAX: 408-745-3872

386/Multiware
Alloy Computer Products Inc.
165 Forest St.
Marlboro, MA 01752
508-481-8500

Vendors of EBBS and Related Products

Accunet
The Major BBS
Galacticom Inc.
4101 SW 47th Ave., #101
Fort Lauderdale, FL 33314
305-583-5990

Oracomm-Plus
Surf Computer Services, Inc.
71-540 Gardess Rd.
Rancho Mirage, CA 92270
619-346-1608

PCBoard
Clark Development Co.
3950 S. 700 East, #303
Murray, UT 84107
800-356-1686

RemoteAccess
Continental Software
195 Adelaide Terr.
Perth, Australia, 6000
USA contact 918-254-6618

Searchlight
Searchlight Software
Box 640
Stony Brook, NY 11790
516-751-2966

TBBS
eSoft Inc.
15200 E. Girard Ave., #2550
Aurora, CA 80014
303-699-6565

Vendors of Routers, Bridges, and Related Products

Eicon Router for NetWare
Eicon Technology Corp.
2196 32nd Ave.
Montreal, Quebec H8T 3H7 Canada
514-631-2592 800-80-EICON

G/X25 Gateway & Bridge 64
Gateway Communicatons Inc.
2941 Alton Ave.
Irvine, CA 92714
800-367-6555

LAN2LAN/Mega Router
Newport Systems Solutions Inc.
4019 Westerley Pl, #103
Newport Beach, CA 92660
800-368-6533

Microcom LAN Bridge 6000
Microcom Systems Inc.
500 River Ridge Dr.
Norwood, MA 02062
800-822-8224 FAX: 617-551-1968

NetWare Link/X.25
Novell Inc.
122 East 1700 South
Provo, UT 84606
800-638-9273 FAX: 801-429-5155

NetWare Link/T1
Novell Inc.
122 East 1700 South
Provo, UT 84606
800-638-9273 FAX: 801-429-5155

POWERbridge
Performace Technology
7800 IH 10, W. Suite 800
Lincoln Center
San Antonio, TX 78230
800-327-8526 FAX: 210-979-2002

Vendors of E-Mail Products

Beyond Mail
Beyond Inc.
38 Sidney St.
Cambridge, MA 02139
617-621-0095

cc:Mail Gateway
Lotus Development Corp.
800 El Camino Real W.
Mountain View, CA 94040
800-448-2500 FAX: 415-961-0215

@Mail
Beyond Inc.
38 Sidney St.
Cambridge, MA 02139
617-621-0095

MailMAN
Reach Soft. Corp.
330 Portrero Ave.
Sunnyvale, CA 94086
408-733-8685

Microsoft Mail for PC Networks
Microsoft Corp.
1 Microsoft Way
Redmond, WA 98052
206-882-8080

Microsoft Mail
Microsoft Corp.
1 Microsoft Way
Redmond, WA 98052
206-882-8080

Office Works Comm. Option
Data Access Corp.
14000 SW 119 Ave.
Miami, FL 33186
800-451-3539

WordPerfect Office
Novell, GroupWare
1555 N. Technology Way
Orem, UT 84057
800-861-2507 FAX: 801-228-5176

3+Open Mail
3Com Corp.
5400 Bayfront Plaza
Santa Clara, CA 95052
800-638-3266 FAX: 408-764-5001

Vendors of Fax Gateways and Related Products

FaxPress 2000
Castelle
3255-3 Scott Blvd.
Santa Clara, CA 95054
800-289-7555 FAX: 408-492-1964

GammaFax CPD
GammaLink
1314 Chesapeake Ter.
Sunnyvale, CA 94089
408-744-1400 800-329-4727

Facsimile Server
Interpreter, Inc.
11455 West 48th Ave.
Wheat Ridge, CO 80033
800-232-4687

NetFax Board
All the Fax, Inc.
917 Northern Blvd.
Great Neck, NY 11021
800-289-3329

Vendors of Network Management Products

PreCursor
The Alridge Co.
2500 City West Blvd., Suite 575
Houston, TX 77042
800-548-5019

StopCopy Plus
BBI Computer Systems
14105 Heritage Lane
Silver Spring, MD 20906
301-871-1094

Stop View
BBI Computer Systems
14105 Heritage Lane
Silver Spring, MD 20906
301-871-1094

SiteLock
Brightwork Development, Inc.
766 Shrewsbury Ave.
Jerral Center West
Trenton Falls, NJ
800-552-9876

Certus LAN
Certus International
13110 Shaker Sq.
Cleveland, OH 44120
800-722-8737

Saber Meter
Saber Software Corp.
5944 Luther Ln., Suite 1007
Dallas, TX 75225
800-338-8754 214-361-8086

EtherPeek
AG Group
2540 Camino Diablo, Suite 200
Walnut Creek, CA 94596
510-937-7900 FAX: 510-937-2479

LocalPeek
AG Group
2540 Camino Diablo, Suite 200
Walnut Creek, CA 94596
510-937-7900 FAX: 510-937-2479

NetPatrol Pack
AG Group
2540 Camino Diablo, Suite 200
Walnut Creek, CA 94596
510-937-7900 FAX: 510-937-2479

Net Watchman
AG Group
2540 Camino Diablo, Suite 200
Walnut Creek, CA 94596
510-937-7900 FAX: 510-937-2479

ARCserve for NetWare 286
Cheyenne Communications
3 Expressway Plaza
Roslyn Hts., NY 11577
800-243-9462 FAX: 516-627-2999

ARCserve for NetWare 386
Cheyenne Communicatons
3 Expressway Plaza.
Roslyn Hts., NY 11577
800-243-9462 FAX: 516-627-2999

Network Supervisor
CSG Technologies, Inc.
530 William Penn Place
Suite 329
Pittsburgh, PA 15219
800-366-4622

Retrospect Remote
Dantz Development Corp.
1400 Shattuck Ave., Suite 1
Berkeley, CA 94709
415-849-0293

LANVista 100
Digilog, Inc.
2360 Maryland Rd.
Willow Grove, PA 19090
800-344-4564 FAX: 215-830-9444

PhoneNET Manager's Pack
Farallon Computing, Inc.
2470 Mariner Sq. Loop
Alameda, CA 94501-1010
510-814-5000 FAX: 510-814-5020

NetWare Early Warning System
Frye Computer Systems, Inc.
19 Temple Place, 4th Floor
Boston, MA 02118
800-234-3793 FAX: 617-451-6711

NetWare Management
Frye Computer Systems, Inc.
19 Temple Place, 4th. Floor
Boston, MA 02118
800-234-3793 FAX: 617-451-6711

LANWatch
FTP Software, Inc.
100 Brickstone Sq., 5th Floor
Andover, MA 01810
800-282-4387 FAX: 508-794-4488

LANprobe
Hewlett-Packard Co.
5070 Centennial Blvd.
Colorado Springs, CO 80919
719-531-4000 800-452-4844
FAX: 719-531-4526

Network Advisor
Hewlett-Packard Co.
5070 Centennial Blvd.
Colorado Springs, CO 80919
719-531-4000 800-452-4844

OpenView
Hewlett-Packard Co.
5070 Centennial Blvd.
Colorado Springs, CO 80919
719-531-4000 800-452-4844

ProbeView
Hewlett-Packard Co.
5070 Centennial Blvd.
Colorado Springs, CO 80919
719-531-4000 800-452-4844

LANanlyzer
Novell, Inc.
122 East 1700 South
Provo, UT 84606
800-453-1267

Lantern
Novell, Inc.
122 East 1700 South
Provo, UT 84606
800-453-1267

Lantern Service Monitor
Novell, Inc.
122 East 1700 South
Provo, UT 84606
800-453-1267

Access/One
Ungermann-Bass, Inc.
3900 Freedom Cir.
Santa Clara, CA 95052
800-873-6381

NetDirector
Ungermann-Bass, Inc.
3900 Freedom Cir.
Santa Clara, CA 95052
800-873-6381

LattisNet Advanced Network Management
Synoptics Communication, Inc.
Box 58185
Santa Clara, CA 95052
408-988-2400

LattisNet Basic Network Management
Synoptics Communication, Inc.
Box 58185
Santa Clara, CA 95052
408-988-2400

LattisNet System 3000
Synoptics Communication, Inc.
Box 58185
Santa Clara, CA 95052
408-988-2400

Network Control Engine
Synoptics Communication, Inc.
Box 58185
Santa Clara, CA 95052
408-988-2400

Vendors of Network Operating Systems and Related Products

LANtastic
Artisoft, Inc.
2202 N. Forbes Blvd.
Tucson, AZ 85745
800-233-5564 FAX: 520-670-7101

LANsoft
ACCTON Technology Corp.
1962 Zanker Rd.
San Jose, CA 95112
800-926-9288 FAX: 408-452-8988

VINES
Banyan Systems, Inc.
120 Flanders Rd.
Westboro, MA 01581
508-898-1000 800-222-6926
FAX: 508-898-1755

PC/NOS
Corvus Systems, Inc.
160 Great Oaks Blvd.
San Jose, CA 95119
800-426-7887

LANsmart
D-Link Systems, Inc.
5 Musick
Irvine, CA 92718
714-455-1688 800-326-1688
FAX: 714-455-2521

OS/2 Ext. Ed.
IBM Corp.
Old Orchard Rd.
Armonk, NY 10504
800-426-2468

EasyNet NOS/2 Plus
LanMark Corp.
Box 246, Postal Station A
Mississauga, ON
CD L5A 3G8
416-848-6865

LAN Manager
Microsoft Corp.
One Microsoft Way
Redmond, WA 98052
800-426-9400 206-882-8080

NetWare
Novell, Inc.
122 East 1700 South
Provo, UT 84606
800-453-1267 FAX: 801-429-5155

Commercial Information Services

BIX
One Phoenix Mill Lane
Peterborough, NH 03458
800-227-2983

Compuserve
Box 20212
Columbus, OH 43220
800-848-8199

Dialog Information Service, Inc.
3460 Hillview Ave.
Palo Alto, CA 94304
800-334-2564

General Videotext Corp.
Three Blackstone St.
Cambridge, MA 02139
800-544-4005

GEnie
401 N. Washington St.
Rockville, MD 20850
800-638-9636

NewsNet
945 Haverford Rd.
Bryn Mawr, PA 19010
800-345-1301

Prodigy Services Co.
445 Hamilton Ave.
White Plains, NY 10601
800-776-3449

Quantum Computer Services
8619 Westwood Center Dr., Suite 200
Vienna, VA 22182
800-227-6364

SprintMail
12490 Sunrise Valley Dr.
Reston, VA 22096
800-736-1130

Public Communication Networks
Accunet
AT&T Computer Systems
295 N. Maple Ave.
Basking Ridge, NJ 07920
800-222-0400

CompuServe Network Services
CompuServe Inc.
5000 Arlington Centre Blvd.
Columbus, OH 43220
800-848-8199

IBM Information Network
IBM Corp
3405 W. Dr. Martin Luther King, Jr. Blvd.
Tampa, FL 33607
800-727-2222

Infonet
Infonet Services Corp.
2100 East Grand Ave.
El Segundo, CA 90245
800-342-5272

Mark*Net
GE Corp.
Information Services Div.
401 N. Washington St.
Rockville, MD 20850
800-433-3683

SprintNet Data Network
US Sprint
12490 Sunrise Valley Dr.
Reston, VA 22096
800-736-1130

Tymnet Global Network
BT North America Inc.
2560 N. 1st St., Box 49019
San Jose, CA 94161
800-872-7654

Vendors of Data Switches, PBXs, and Related Products

AISwitch Series XXX
Applied Innovation, Inc.
651-C Lakeview Plaza Blvd.
Columbus, OH 43085
800-247-9482

MDX
Equinox Systems, Inc.
1 Equinox Way
Sunrise, FL 33351
800-275-3500 FAX: 305-746-9101

Instanet6000
MICOM Communications Corp.
Box 8100
4100 Los Angeles Ave.
Simi Valley, CA 93062-8100
800-642-6687 FAX: 800-343-0329

Data PBX Series
Rose Electronics
10850 Wilcrest, Suite 900
Houston, TX 77099
800-333-9343 FAX: 713-933-0044

Gateway Data Switch
SKP Electronics
1232-E S. Village Way
Santa Ana, CA 92705
714-972-1727

INCS-64
Western Telematic, Inc.
5 Sterling
Irvine, CA 92178
800-854-7226 FAX: 714-586-9514

Slimline Data Switches
Belkin Components
14550 S. Main St.
Gardena, CA 90248
800-223-5546

MetroLAN
Datacom Technologies, Inc.
11001 31st Place, West
Everett, WA 98204
800-468-5557 FAX: 206-290-1600

Intelligent Printer Buffer
Primax Electronics Inc.
2531 West 237th St., Suite 102
Torrance, CA 90505
213-326-8018

Data Switches
Rose Electronics
10850 Wilcrest, Suite 900
Houston, TX 77099
800-333-9343 FAX: 713-933-0044

ShareNet 5110
McComb Research
Box 3984
Minneapolis, MN 55405
612-527-8082

Aura 1000
Intran Systems, Inc.
7493 N. Oracle Rd., Suite 207
Tucson, AZ 85704
602-797-2797

Logical Connection
Fifth Generation Systems, Inc.
10049 N. Reiger Rd.
Baton Rouge, LA 70809
800-873-4384

Vendors of Network Remote Access Software and Related Products

Distribute Console Access Facility
IBM Corp.
11100 Metric Blvd.
Austin, TX 78758
800-426-2255 FAX: 800-426-4329

PolyMod2
Memsoft Corp.
1 Park Pl.
621 NW 53rd St., #240
Boca Raton, FL 33487
407-997-6655

Remote-OS
The Software Lifeline Inc.
Fountain Square, 2600 Military Trail, #290
Boca Raton, FL 33531
407-994-4466

APPENDIX C

Vendors of TCP/IP Hardware and Related Products

Isolink PC/TCP
BICC Data Networks
1800 W. Park Dr., Suite 150
Westborough, MA 01581
800-447-6526

PC/TCP Plus
FTP Software, Inc.
100 Brickstone Sq., 5th Floor
Andover, MA 01810
800-282-4387 FAX: 508-794-4488

TCP/IP for OS/2 EE
IBM
Old Orchard Rd.
Armonk, NY 10504
800-426-2468
10Net TCP

Digital Comm. Assoc.
10NET Comm. Div.
7887 Washington Village Dr.
Dayton, OH 45459
800-358-1010

WIN/TCP for DOS
Wollongong Group, Inc.
Box 51860
1129 San Antonio Rd.
Palo Alto, CA 94303
800-872-8649 FAX: 415-969-5547

PC/TCP Thernet Comm.
UniPress Software, Inc.
2025 Lincoln Hwy.
Edison, NJ 08817
800-222-0550 FAX: 908-287-4929

Vendors of Zero Slot LANs, Media Transfer Hardware and Software, and Related Products

LANtastic Z
Artisoft, Inc.
2202 N. Forbes Blvd.
Tucson, AZ 85745
800-233-5564 FAX: 520-670-7101

PC-Hookup
Brown Bag Software
2155 S. Bascom, Suite 114
Campbell, CA 95008
800-523-0764

Brooklyn Bridge
Fifth Generation Systems
10049 N. Reiger Rd.
Baton Rouge, LA 70809

LapLink
Traveling Software, Inc.
18702 N. Creek Pkwy.
Bothell, WA 98011
800-343-8080 FAX: 206-487-1284

FastLynx
Rupp Corp.
7285 Franklin Ave.
Los Angeles, CA 90046
800-852-7877

MasterLink
U.S. Marketing, Inc.
1402 South St.
Nashville, TN 37212
615-242-8800

Glossary

Account Boot Disk. A disk used to load DOS into the computer when it is turned on.

ASCII. The acronym for American Standard Code for Information Interchange. This is a standard code for the transmission of data within the US. It is composed of 128 characters in a 7-bit format.

Asynchronous. A communication that places data in discrete blocks that are surrounded by framing bits. These bits show the beginning and ending of a block of data.

Bandwidth. This is the capacity of a cable to carry data on different channels or frequencies.

Baseband. A network cable that has only one channel for carrying data signals.

Baud. The rate of data transmission.

Bit. An abbreviation for binary digit. A bit is the smallest unit of data.

BOOTCONF.SYS. A file on the file server used to indicate which boot image file each workstation will use.

Bridge. A device that connects different LANs so a node on one LAN can communicate with a node on another LAN.

Broadband. A network cable with several channels of communication.

Bus Topology. A physical layout of a LAN where all nodes are connected to a single cable.

Byte. Normally a combination of 8 bits.

CAPTURE. A NetWare utility program used to redirect output from a printer port on the workstation to a network printer.

Coaxial Cable. A cable consisting of a single metal wire surrounded by insulation, which is itself surrounded by a braided or foil outer conductor.

Computer. An electronic system that can store and process information under program control.

CONSOLE. The file server.

Control Code. Special nonprinting codes that cause electronic equipment to perform specific actions.

CPU. Central processing unit. The "brains" of the computer; that section where the logic and control functions are performed.

Glossary

Device Driver. A software program that enables a network operating system and the DOS operating system to work with NICs, disk controllers, and other hardware.

Directory Rights. Access attached to directories on a NetWare file server.

Driver. A memory resident program usually used to control a hardware device.

FCONSOLE. A NetWare utility program used to monitor file server and workstation activity.

Fiber-Optic Cable. A data transmitting cable that consists of plastic or glass fibers.

File Attributes. Access rights attached to each file.

File Server. A computer running a network operating system that enables other computers to access its files.

Full Duplex. In full duplex communication, the terminal transmits and receives data simultaneously.

Gateway. A device that acts as a translator between networks that use different protocols.

Group. A collection of users.

Group Rights. Rights given to a collection of users.

Half Duplex. In half duplex communication, the terminal transmits and receives data in separate, consecutive operations.

Handshaking. A set of commands recognized by the sending and receiving stations that control the flow of data transmission.

Interface. A communication channel that is used to connect a computer to an external device.

Internetwork Packet Exchange (IPX). One of the data transmission protocols used by NetWare.

LAN. Local area network. A network that encompasses a small geographical area.

LOGIN. A NetWare utility program that allows users to identify themselves to the network.

Login Script. A series of statements executed each time a user logs into a NetWare network.

MAP. Association of a logical NetWare drive letter with a directory.

Modem. An electronic device that converts digital data (modulates) from a computer into analog signals that the phone equipment can understand. Additionally, the modem converts analog (demodulates) data into digital data.

NetBIOS. A network communication protocol that NetWare can emulate.

NETGEN. A NetWare utility program used to configure and load NetWare onto a file server.

NetWare. A network operating system produced by Novell Incorporated.

Network Address. A hexadecimal number used to identify a network cabling system.

NIC. The network interface card is a circuit board that is installed in the file server and workstations that make up the network. It allows the hardware in the network to send and receive data.

Node. A workstation, file server, bridge, or other device that has an address on a network.

Novell. A company based in Provo, Utah, that produces the NetWare network operating system.

NPRINT. A NetWare utility program used to send a file directly to a network printer. Its name stands for Network PRINT.

Packet. A discrete unit of data bits transmitted over a network.

Password. A secret word used to identify a user.

PCONSOLE. A NetWare utility program used to configure and operate print servers. Its name stands for Print server CONSOLE.

PRINTCON. A NetWare utility program used to create print job configurations.

PRINTDEF. A NetWare utility program used to create and edit print device files.

Print Devices. Definition files for different type of printers to be used on a print server.

Print Forms. Definitions of different types of paper size to be used on a print server.

Print Job Configurations. Complete descriptions of how a file is to be printed on the network.

Print Queues. Definitions of the order and location in which a file is to be printed on the network.

Print Server. A computer running the PSERVER program that allows it to accept files to be printed from other workstations.

Protocol. The conventions that must be observed in order for two electronic devices to communicate with each other.

PSERVER. The NetWare Print SERVER program.

RAM. Random access memory.

Remote Print Server. A computer running the RPRINTER program, enabling it to print output from other network workstations and operate as a normal workstation.

Remote Reset. The process of loading DOS and the network drivers from the file server.

Ring Topology. A network configuration that connects all nodes in a logical ring-like structure.

ROM. Read only memory

RPRINTER. The program that allows other workstations to print to a workstation's printer.

Shell. Under NetWare, the network drivers.

SHELL.CFG. A file used on a workstation to configure the network drivers as they are loaded into memory.

Star Topology. A network configuration where each node is connected by a single cable link to a central location, called the hub.

Synchronous. A method of communication using a time interval to distinguish between transmitted blocks of data.

SYSCON. A NetWare utility program used to establish users and their rights on the file server. Its name stands for SYStem CONfiguration.

Token. The data packet used to carry information on LANs using the ring topology.

Topology. The manner in which nodes are connected on a LAN.

Trustee Rights. Rights given to users to access directories on the file server.

Uninterruptible Power Supply. A device that keeps computers running after a power failure, providing power from batteries for a short period of time.

User. Under NetWare, the definition of a set of access rights for an individual.

VAP. A value-added process to the NetWare operating system provided by a third party vendor.

Wide Area Network. A network that encompasses a large geographical area.

Workstation. A computer attached to the network.

X.25. A communication protocol used on public data networks.

Index

Account Balance 53
Account Restrictions 53
Accounting 49
Application Software 212
ATTACH 60

Batch Files 11, 193
BOOTCONF 148
BREAK 61, 63
Broadcast Console Message 103

CAPTURE 175
Client Software 26
COMSPEC 62

Directories 6
Directory Rights 114
DISPLAY 63
DOS Requester 3, 137
DOSGEN 147
Down File Server 105
Drive Mappings 8

Effective Rights 118
ENDCAP 175
EXIT 64

FCONSOLE 102
File Assignments 57
File Attributes 95, 117
FIRE PHASERS 65

Group Information 50
Group Rights 218
Groups 97

IF Statement 65
Inherited Rights Mask 94
Internetwork Packet eXchange 4

Intruder Lockout 54
IPX 4
IPXODI 28, 137

Job Configurations 168

Link Support Layer 4
Login Scripts 11, 54, 58
LSL 4, 28, 137

MACHINE 68
Managers 55
Mappings 8
Menu Commands 195
Microsoft Windows 220
MLID 4
MONITOR 106
Multiple Link Interface Driver 4

NET.CFG 138
NetWare
  Customizing 136, 192
  Installing 27
NetWare Rights 217
Network Drivers 136
Network drivers 4
Network Drives 6
Network Interface Card 137
Network Management 102
Network Volumes 6
NETX 28
NIC 3
NIC driver 28
Novell
  Menus 193
NPRINT 175

ODI 4
OS/2 3

Index

Password 53
Passwords 90
Paths 8
PAUSE 70
PCCOMPATIBLE 70
PCONSOLE 174, 175
Print Devices 164
Print Forms 163
Print Job Configurations 168
Print Queues 166
Printing
   CAPTURE 175
   File Server 162
   NPRINT 175
   PCONSOLE 174
   Print Server 162
   Remote 163
PSERVER 182

REMARK 70
Remote Reset 141

Search Drives 8
Security Equivalences 56
Security Levels 90
SET 63
Shared Programs 216
Station Restrictions 56
Supervisor Options 50
SYSCON 48

Time Restrictions 57
Trustee Directory 57
Trustee Rights 10, 92, 112

User Environment 6
User Information 51

VLM 28
Volume/Disk Restrictions 58